P9-DMU-744

WITHDRAWN

A Nation of
Wimps

Also by Hara Estroff Marano

Style Is Not a Size
Why Doesn't Anybody Like Me?

Hara Estroff Marano

A Nation of
Wimps

The High Cost of
Invasive Parenting

Broadway Books   New York

URBANDALE PUBLIC LIBRARY
3520 86TH STREET
URBANDALE, IA 50322-4058

PUBLISHED BY BROADWAY BOOKS

Copyright © 2008 by Hara Estroff Marano

All Rights Reserved

Published in the United States by Broadway Books, an imprint of The Doubleday Broadway
Publishing Group, a division of Random House, Inc., New York.
www.broadwaybooks.com

BROADWAY BOOKS and its logo, a letter B bisected on the diagonal, are trademarks of
Random House, Inc.

Portions of this book originally appeared in *Psychology Today*.

Library of Congress Cataloging-in-Publication Data

Marano, Hara Estroff.
A nation of wimps : the high cost of invasive parenting / Hara Estroff Marano.—1st. ed.
p. cm.
1. Parenting—United States. 2. Child rearing—United States. 3. Parent and child—United States.
I. Title.

HQ755.8.M355 2007
306.874—dc22
2007034231

ISBN 978-0-7679-2403-0

PRINTED IN THE UNITED STATES OF AMERICA

1 3 5 7 9 10 8 6 4 2

First Edition

In memory of Diane

*Not a day of work on this book went by when you weren't
with me, tister*

Contents

A Nation of
Wimps

Introduction

Maybe it was the cyclist in the park, trim under his sleek metallic blue helmet, cruising along the dirt path . . . at three miles an hour. On his tricycle. Wedged between Mommy and Daddy.

Or perhaps it was the playground, all rubber-cushioned surface now where kids used to skin their knees. But . . . wait a minute . . . those weren't little kids playing. Their mommies—and especially their daddies—were right in there with them, co-playing or play-by-play coaching. Few were taking it half-easy on the perimeter benches, as parents used to do, letting the kids figure things out for themselves.

How about the recent survey that found that over a third of parents are sending their kids to school with sanitizing gels, tucking the stuff in their backpacks. Parents worry that school bathrooms are no longer good enough for their children.

Then there was the teacher new to the upscale suburban Westchester town. Shuffling through the sheaf of reports certifying the educational "accommodations" he was required to make for many of his history students, he was struck by the exhaustive, well-written—and obviously costly—one on behalf of a girl who was already distinguishing herself as among the most competent of his ninth graders. "She's somewhat neurotic," he confided, "but she is bright, organized, and conscientious—the type who'd get to school to turn in a paper on time even if she were dying of stomach flu." Searching for mention of the disability he was to make allowances for, he finally found it: difficulty with Gestalt thinking.

The thirteen-year-old "couldn't see the big picture." That cleverly devised defect—what thirteen-year-old can construct the big picture?—would allow her to take all her tests untimed, especially the big one at the end of the rainbow, the college-worthy SAT.

Something seemed radically different in the world of parenting.

Behold the wholly sanitized childhood, without skinned knees or the occasional C in history! Kids need to learn that you need to feel bad sometimes. We learn through experience, and we learn especially through bad experiences. Through disappointment and failure we learn how to cope. We learn what we can cope with. It motivates us to change or do better. And we seem to learn more about things through failure than by any other way.

Messing up, however, even on the playground, is wildly out of style these days. Although error and experimentation are the true mothers of success, parents are taking pains to remove failure from the equation. They are vigilant about positioning their kids directly for success, which is now deemed to run on the straight-and-narrow path of academic achievement, from the earliest age, without what seems like dilatory downtime.

"Life is planned out for us," says a Cornell University student. "There's parental pressure for a life plan. But we don't know what to want. We don't know what success is." Parents and schools are no longer attuned to child development; they're geared exclusively to academic achievement. And parenting has become a joyless management exercise.

No one doubts that there are significant economic forces pushing parents to invest heavily in their children's outcome from an early age. But taking all the discomfort, the disappointment, and even the play out of development, especially while increasing the pressure for success, turns out to be misguided by just about 180 degrees. Overprotected and overmanaged by their parents, and with few challenges all their own through which to sharpen their instincts and identities, kids are unable to forge their own unique adaptations to the normal vicissitudes of life. That not only makes them extraordinarily risk-averse; it makes them psychologically fragile. In the process, they're robbed of identity, meaning, and a sense of mastery, which underlies real happiness. Forget, too, about perseverance, not simply a moral virtue but a necessary life skill. These features have turned out to be the spreading psychic fault lines of twenty-first-century youth. Whether we're aware of it or not, we're on our way to creating a nation of wimps.

College, it seems, is where the fragility of young people is making its greatest mark. It's where the intellectual and the developmental converge as the emotional training wheels come off. By all accounts, psychological distress is now rampant on college campuses. Colleges are experiencing record demand for counseling and intensive support services from students with serious psychological problems. The epidemic of mental health problems on campus is new, and it is prime evidence that this generation is breaking down in ways that previous generations did not. Their troubles take a variety of forms: anxiety and depression—two faces of the same coin—binge drinking and substance abuse, eating disorders, self-mutilation and other manifestations of self-disconnection.

The mental state of students is now so precarious for so many that, says Steven Hyman, provost of Harvard University and former director of the National Institute of Mental Health, "it now threatens the core mission of the university." Of course: it's impossible to learn when your brain has been hijacked by anxiety or alcohol. Because the burgeoning crisis disrupts not only the educational but the communal tenor of campus life, universities are also struggling to fulfill their other intrinsic function—to socialize the young and shape the next generation of society.

Parental efforts to protect offspring now extend well into adulthood. Parents' desire to protect their children is undoubtedly well-intentioned, but it is likely the single largest factor contributing to the sharp rise in mental health problems among the young and the propensity of today's kids to stay stuck in endless adolescence. Extended dependency does not bode well for a democracy. And because it ultimately produces a failure of nerve and unwillingness to take risks, it also ultimately threatens American leadership in the global marketplace.

Consider these facts:

- In response to parental anxieties, success has been redefined in increasingly narrow terms in the past decade as academic achievement—so narrow that skyrocketing numbers of kids now must be medicated just to get through childhood. More than twenty-one million prescriptions are written each year for stimulant drugs to enhance attention, primarily in kids ages six to fourteen, a 400 percent increase over a decade ago. Antidepressant use in children has risen 333 percent over the same time.
- The overscheduling and overmonitoring of kids keep them off the

street—but by depriving kids of opportunities to discover themselves, they also keep them from eventually having their own shot
at happiness.

- A great deal of play has been taken out of childhood. Over forty
thousand U.S. schools no longer even have recess. But play is actually critical to healthy development, a biological imperative for higher
animals. It sharpens and limbers intelligence. It is the only activity
that directly prepares people for dealing with life's unpredictability.
Delay play and you delay adulthood.

- Dramatically fewer young people are meeting the classic benchmarks of adulthood by age thirty and even thirty-six.

- Tremendous performance pressures are being put on kids, often the
brightest kids—but in fact the really brightest kids underperform
when under pressure, studies show. Stress impairs the kind of memory at which they excel. To the degree that high stakes are placed on
children's performance on SATs, the resulting stress dooms some of
the most gifted and creative minds to test as merely average.

- The widespread use of cell phones may help parents keep track of
their kids—but it may have negative neurodevelopmental effects on
adolescents, interfering with the maturation of brain circuitry underlying mood and decision making.

- The generation of young people now coming of age is extraordinarily endowed in material terms—but unusually experience deprived.
Their lack of challenging and life-defining experiences all their own
impairs their ability to develop vital coping skills and build the inner resources necessary to adapt to life in all its unpredictability.

- The huge rise in self-harm and self-mutilation among the young in
part reflects the shrinking sphere in which they are free to act out
their anxieties.

- Overparenting isn't just bad for kids—it has terrible effects on
adults. The disproportionate investment of parental emotions, finances, and time in one's children erodes marital bonds and contributes to a continuing high divorce rate. It also gives rise to a
destructive culture of parenting that reaches into many societal institutions. The privatization of parental concern and fear distorts
public discourse and diverts attention from the need for institutional
change that could benefit all.

These facts form the backdrop of *A Nation of Wimps*. The book began as an article in the November/December 2004 issue of *Psychology Today* magazine. The reaction to it clearly indicated it hit a nerve. But I didn't at first see it as the beginning of a book. I wrote the article to answer the question why—why were America's top kids now breaking down in record numbers? I had been on the front lines of that story for over two years, and I wanted to know what was so different about this generation. With the breakdown of college students at the vortex, I began looking upstream at what might be causing the epidemic of distress, and downstream at what the consequences might be, not just for them but for the society that they will one day be called on to lead.

I have spoken to parents, educators at all levels, and of course young people. I've talked to kids who are not yet in college and those who are already out. I've looked at research bearing on many different issues and talked to researchers all over the world. I've given invited talks across the country and always spent time listening to the concerns of those who asked me to come—parents, teachers, college administrators, deans, even athletic directors and coaches.

Through my research I've assembled a nuanced picture of what is going on with our youth today. What is happening, of course, is not just about college. It's about child raising and adulthood and the value we place on each. It's about our dreams and hopes for our children's future. It's about our understanding of human development and trust—or, especially, lack of it—in human nature. About creativity and how we define success. It's about the culture and what it values, sometimes in contrast to what it says it holds dear. It's about mental health and how you get it, especially against a backdrop of rapid cultural and technological change. That makes it also about the limits of adaptability. It's about stress and distress—and the ways that experience keeps the former from becoming the latter. And it's about that most American of desires, the pursuit of happiness.

This book makes the case that the pressure put on middle-class (and above) kids to get in to college is making them sick. It is also clear that through the same processes, the failure to engage less affluent kids is keeping them poor. Both are jeopardizing the country's future.

Parents, like lovers, must always negotiate a fine line between nurturing and controlling. In recent years, responding to their own fears, many have stepped way over the line into controlling, so that there are few boundaries between parent and child. Fear always makes people grip tight what is closest to them. But hyperinvolvement is almost always counterproductive; through the very fact of their invasiveness parents co-opt developmental pathways and transmit anxiety to their children, undermining a sense of self-efficacy while promoting self-preoccupation.

Even after I wrote the article, I was certain that the fragility among the young that I was describing was strictly an American phenomenon. But I'm now persuaded it is far more widespread. As soon as the article was published, I was besieged by media in Australia, Brazil, Sweden, and elsewhere. And I've traveled to other parts of the world where I've been told stories about invasive parents that rival anything I've heard at home.

The response to the article, my own travels, and conversations with reporters, parents, and researchers around the world have convinced me that the issues I am describing are seen to some degree in most affluent, developed cultures responding to the pressures of globalization. But they may have their most intense expression in the United States, thanks to the highly publicized status ordering of our universities—and the extremely individualistic, and thus competitive, nature of our society. The status ordering of schools is a reflection of the need for guarantees of success, which heightens interest in brand-name education. It's not beyond the realm of possibility that the wimpification of the young is becoming one of our sturdiest if most ignominious exports.

There is no question that the vast majority of parents mean well. They want to see that their children are well prepared—better than they themselves felt prepared—for the dynamic world they will inherit. How is it, then, that those who want only the best for their children wind up bringing out the worst in them?

As I explain in the pages ahead, it starts with the hothouse conditions in which so many middle-class and upper-middle-class children are now being raised and the obsessiveness with which parents engineer their children's lives. That's because social standing, once something kids inherited from their parents, has become something parents now take from the achievements of their children. But the cost of turning tots into trophies is high: the developmental needs of the young are subordinated to the psychological needs of adults; perfectionism is born from the pressure and emerges as an ultimately self-defeating standard.

The attachment bond that normally develops between parent and child naturally equips children to explore the world on their own terms—but adults are hallucinating hazards to keep kids from exercising the separation that nature has prepared them for. The highest cost of the pressures now placed on kids may be the loss of play, the very thing that facilitates their creative adaptation to the fast and flat world we find ourselves in. The extraordinary value of play is almost entirely counterintuitive—play looks like such a waste of time—but kids can't grow up without it.

All-consuming parental anxiety has completely disconnected parents from the fact that kids have their own built-in drive for competence. To a considerable degree, the need for vigilance has arisen in large part because schools are generally less engaging for all children today. But instead of overhauling educational institutions, parents have chosen to intensify control over their children in an effort to smooth their path to success. Their efforts, however, weaken children from within, creating fragility by directly transmitting anxiety and then compounding the problem by depriving kids of coping skills and a sense of self-efficacy.

There is abundant evidence that once they leave the protective cocoon of home for college, once they must begin functioning on their own, young people today are breaking down psychologically in record numbers and acting out against themselves. They are also staying stuck in endless adolescence, tied to their parents long past the age at which they need to exercise autonomy. Part of the problem lies in the desire of parents to make their kids happy; it may be well-intentioned, but it backfires because it violates the brain's need for meaningful challenge.

The meanness and competitiveness that parents impute to their children's world to justify their intervention more likely reflect their own experiences of dislocation in the switched-on, sped-up, hyperlinked, globalized economy of the twenty-first century. Modern kids are not fundamentally more flawed than those of previous generations.

Hothouse parenting has culture-wide consequences. It's bad for the children, bad for the parents, and bad for the future of democracy and the economy.

Parents suspect that the pressures they are putting on kids are not healthy, but they fear that if they let up, their child will singularly be "left behind." The solution, therefore, must be community-wide. Nevertheless, there are many ways parents can help prepare their kids for the modern world without sacrificing anyone's sanity.

ONE

Welcome to the Hothouse

I've just been in the emergency room for two and a half hours," Sarah announced, pushing on as we passed on the street, "and I've *got* to see my daughter." I had seen Sarah, the daughter of a neighbor, grow up, a few years ahead of my two children, and nowadays run into her only when she comes to visit her parents with her own family. Her right foot was freshly cradled in the clunky contraption doctors call a walking boot but is more accurately a limping boot.

"How old is your daughter now?" I asked.

"Almost four," she said. "And," she added, her voice suddenly shaky with panic, "I've never been separated from her this long before. And she's never been away from me."

There was a time when two and a half hours away from one's four-year-old would not have been seen as a separation. It would have been sought after and thought of as a respite, a reprieve, a welcome break for both mother and child. It would have been seen as a small but necessary step on the long march toward independence, toward a child's adaptation to a world composed of people who are not biologically devoted to satisfying her every wish and making her happy. And it would have been seen as a chance for a parent to reconnect, however briefly, with interests in the world at large.

But this is 2008 and the children—or at least many of them—are never safe enough, never happy enough, unless they are directly in the laser sights of Mommy, and sometimes Daddy. The perpetual presence of

Mom is supported by a burgeoning belief that only she is competent enough, that no one can provide care for the children or meet their needs as well as she can, that depriving the child of her direct attention in the first few years could, in fact, cause psychological damage for life. For this, a growing number of successful women are giving up significant careers to stay at home with the little ones, demographers report. It seems that to justify such application of their skills and education, they have to elevate child rearing to a challenge worthy of their time.

Parental hyperconcern about safety and well-being turns a two-and-a-half-hour interlude of what once, in calmer days, may have been looked on as a break from the kids into a window of intense worry. Hyper-attendance to children falsely breeds a sense of control and erroneously endows every action of the child with an importance it does not have. It also violates a cardinal rule of development: attentive and responsive care to an infant is absolutely necessary, but there comes a point when it is oppressive, robbing children of the very thing they need for continued growth. In small doses at first, and larger ones later, separation is essential to activate the system the infant will call on for exploring the world and mastering inner and outer life. Buried in overattachment and overinvolvement is an assumption of fragility, the belief that by not having some nuance of need met, the child will be irrevocably harmed. The paradox of parenting is that the pressure to make it perfect can undermine the outcome.

Parents, nevertheless, will not have to relinquish scrutiny of their children to others, even trained professionals, when the kids enter school. Many live in a school district that maintains a Web site just for parents and runs a computer program that allows them to keep an obsessive eye on their kids throughout the school day, from the minute they enter kindergarten to the day they graduate from twelfth grade. Zangle is one such program favored by a number of midwestern school districts. Parents in affluent areas like Bloomfield Hills and Birmingham, Michigan, where up to 70 percent of the highly educated mothers may be stay-at-home moms, are so tickled by the remote control it provides them that they spend hours "zangling" their kids—and comparing the results with other parents passing their days the same way. With a secret password, they log on and check whether their kids have turned in their homework assignments, review the grades they are getting on tests and reports and daily homework assignments, discover whether there have been any "behavioral incidents," and even find out whether their kids chose chocolate milk or Pepsi with their burger and fries in the school cafeteria.

Programs like Zangle are "feeding parental obsessiveness," insists a parent of two young girls in Birmingham, Michigan, who "forced myself to pull back and not do what everyone else does—because I'm not the one who has to prepare for college. The parents spend all day checking in on their kids. They demand to see all their kid's assignments. Sometimes the teachers are forced to say, 'It's your son's homework, not yours.' "

"Do We Need a Speech Therapist?"

Parental pushiness and protectionism gain momentum as children move from preschool to primary school to high school. Not long ago, parents might have thought their function was, say, to provide good nutrition at home, recognize that direct parental control extends only so far, and, on a sliding scale from begrudgingly to confidently, grant their kids increments of freedom along with allowance money to make choices on their own outside the house, even if the choices were sometimes less than perfect. Zangle and other monitoring programs beginning with kindergarten train parents in intrusiveness and normalize it, even celebrate it, without accommodating so much as a whimper of protest—all the while disrupting the fragile flow of trust that development toward independence has always required and still does.

"I noticed it immediately with my then-one-year-old when we moved to suburban Connecticut from a more alternative community in the Southwest," reports the mother of a four-year-old boy and a seventeen-month-old daughter. "How many words was my child saying? Did he know his alphabet? When could he write his name? Do we need a speech therapist? I know parents of a three-year-old who monitor their child so obsessively they send him to an occupational therapist two times a week to work on scissor skills—for no discernible reason." The mother of two confesses that she herself "took my son in to the occupational therapist to be evaluated after his preschool teacher said something about his fine motor skills. Now, mind you, he is highly verbal, he can read, he is a fine artist. But I took him in for an evaluation. I'm not proud of it. It forced me to do some soul-searching, and we never went back."

The push for achievement in all quantifiable realms, especially the academic, begins so early that preschools all around the country are focusing less and less on the development of social skills and self-regulation and more and more on academics. However, children of that age are so unready for curricular focus that preschools report a rising tide of behavioral problems—and wind up expelling six out of every thousand students. Imagine: expelled from preschool! With so much expected of them when they have not yet mastered socialization and self-regulation—two skills that are intricately interconnected and both of which foster academic excellence—more of them are acting out. Expectations for children have gone completely haywire, untethered from any reference to children's developmental needs, referenced only to deep adult anxieties. "The great effect of Head Start was to convince the upper middle class that their children need a head start and they could do it better," says the historian Steven Mintz, professor at the University of Houston and author of *Huck's Raft: A History of American Childhood*.

Inside the Hothouse

Childhood under the constant gaze of adults is a new and growing phenomenon. The idea that a life—anyone's life—is on some precise schedule amenable to control is a by-product of the syllogisms of success that parents today are frenetically writing for their children.

The giant Citigroup company was rocked by scandal in 2002 when one of its superstar stock analysts, Jack Grubman, bragged in an e-mail that he had upgraded the rating of then-flagging AT&T stock to curry favor with Citigroup's then chairman, Sanford Weill. Grubman's overarching goal was to get Weill, a prominent New York figure, to exert his influence to get Grubman's twin toddlers into one of New York's prestigious preschools. (AT&T's chairman sat on the board of Citigroup and was a client of Citigroup, and Weill sat on the AT&T board.) What made the preschool so essential, apparently, was its track record in sending its graduates to the elite private grammar schools that in turn feed the prestigious prep schools which in turn dump their graduates into the Ivy League. It was the first logical step in the syllogism of academic success that parents construct for their children: if this is the right kindergarten for Harvard and Elijah gets into it, then he will be on track for Harvard. In the hothouse that child raising has become, nothing is left to chance. (Weill made the call, and the Grubman twins were admitted, once Citigroup pledged a million dollars to the school's umbrella organization.)

In the hothouse, parents plan out the lives of their children and propel them into a variety of programmed activities that are intended to have Ivy League appeal; they then ferry the kids around to classes and activities. The critical element in this setup is not that it leaves the kids with little unstructured time but that there is no way of opting out. Someone is always there to see that they get to the next stop in the circuit of activities. Playing hooky, daydreaming, or just kicking back is out of the question, and the programming starts early in order to carve the groove as deeply as possible. "My neighbor's boy goes to karate, soccer, swimming, and baseball after going to school four days a week from 8:30 to 2:30," says one mother in suburban Connecticut. "He's five years old. And he has no free time." Neither does his mother.

The Hottest of Hothouses

The ultimate in hothouse parenting is undoubtedly homeschooling, a phenomenon so appealing to today's parents that it is growing at the rate of 7 to 15 percent a year. To the best that anyone knows, well more than 1.1 million children in the United States are now schooled at home by their parents, perhaps 2.1 million, with or without additional tutors. Homeschooling is now legal in every state in the United States, but it is not uniformly regulated, and in some states it is not regulated at all; whatever parents choose to do, they can. The adults often provide many rationales for homeschooling, from the inculcation of religious or political values to inferior public school instruction to the avoidance of educational regimentation that does not keep pace with their child's needs. Their children may even excel academically.

That is not its danger. Whatever else it does, homeschooling deprives children of any chance to breathe, of opportunities to discover themselves on their own and to escape from parental vigilance, parental bias, or parental ignorance. It gives parents license to micromanage every detail of their children's lives. It gives children a false sense of their own preciousness; many parents, in fact, choose to homeschool their children because they feel their kids are "special," surveys show. There is a deeper, more subtle issue: the nonstop scrutiny that comes with making the home a school disables in children the mental mechanism that is activated only by separation from parents, the mechanism that will endow children with the eventual ability to navigate securely on their own in the world.

"I'm My Parents' Hobby"

If you're searching for someone to blame, consider Dr. Seuss. "Parents have told their kids from day one that there's no end to what they are capable of doing," says John Portmann, an assistant professor who teaches in the religious studies department at the University of Virginia. "They read them the Dr. Seuss book *Oh, the Places You'll Go!* and create bumper stickers telling the world their child is an honor student. American parents today expect their children to be perfect—the smartest, fastest, most charming people in the universe. And if they can't get a child to prove it on their own, they'll turn to doctors to make their kids into the people that parents want to believe their kids are." What they're really doing, he stresses, is "showing kids how to work the system for their own benefit."

And subjecting them to intense scrutiny. "I wish my parents had some other hobby than me," one young patient told David Anderegg, a child psychologist in Lenox, Massachusetts, and professor of psychology at Bennington College. The author of *Worried All the Time,* Anderegg finds parents are anxious and hyperattentive to their kids, reactive to every blip of their child's day, eager to solve every problem for their child—and believe that's good parenting. "If you have an infant and the baby has gas, burping the baby is being a good parent. But when you have a ten-year-old who has metaphorical gas, you don't have to burp them. You have to let them sit with it, try to figure out what to do about it. They then learn to tolerate moderate amounts of difficulty, and it's not the end of the world."

And "best" now means only one thing. "I have found, both as a [former] student and in working with students, that young adults are pushed by parents and society to be 'the best,'" says Alison Malmon, founder of Active Minds, an organization devoted to improving campus mental health. "But 'the best' means only: get into the best college, excel once there, and get a high-paying job right after graduation."

Invasion of the Mind Snatchers

Talk to a college president and you're almost certainly bound to hear tales of the parents who call at 2:00 a.m. to protest Johnny's C in economics because it's going to damage his life. The thinking is, "If my son doesn't get this course, then he's not going to get the internship he wants, he's not going to get into the grad school he wants, and he's not going to get to become a judge." Too often, say administrators, that's how detailed the parents have gotten in their thinking about collecting "the right combination of stuff," foreclosing the possibility their child might by serendipity discover something that interests him.

Not long ago, Judith Shapiro, president of Barnard College, wrote an article in the *New York Times* urging parents to back off their desire to manage all aspects of their children's college lives. "One mother," she recounted, "accompanied her daughter to a meeting with her dean to discuss a supposedly independent research project." Then there was the father who called his daughter's career counselor so he could contact her prospective employers to extol her qualifications. And the one who took a year off to supervise the preparation of his daughter's admissions portfolio.

Shortly after the California psychologist Robert Epstein announced to his university students that he expected them to work hard and would hold them to high standards, he heard from a parent—on official judicial stationery—asking how he could dare mistreat the young. Epstein eventually filed a complaint with the California commission on judicial misconduct, and the judge was censured for abusing his office—but not before he created havoc in the psychology department.

Enter: grade inflation. When he took over as president of Harvard, Lawrence Summers publicly ridiculed the value of honors after discovering that 94 percent of the college's seniors were graduating with them. Safer to lower the bar than to raise the discomfort level. In 1968, 17.6 percent of students received As in high school, and 23.1 percent got Cs. In 2004, 47.5 percent of students had an A average, and only 5 percent had a C average. Educators view the current generation as brighter only on paper; in the aggregate, they are less prepared to take on the challenges of college. In 1987, 47 percent of high school students studied six or more hours a week; in 2004, 33.3 percent did; six-plus hours is the time most college professors expect to be devoted to *each* course.

It is a mark of the devaluation of education at every level that a C serves as the impetus not for the hard work of self-improvement but for parental intercession. The institutional response to parental anxiety about school demands on children, grade inflation is a pure index of emotional overinvestment in their children's success, contends the social historian Peter Stearns of George Mason University. And it rests on a notion of

children's frailty—"the assumption that children are easily bruised and
need explicit uplift," he says.

Through the syllogisms of success that parents establish, the grades
their children receive from preschool through college become markers
not merely of the children's academic achievement but of adult success
at parenting. That transaction, however, commodifies their children and
their children's efforts; even learning, insofar as it is pursued to be translated into a transcript with Ivy potential, is a commodity with exchange
value. Learning isn't the joy of finding things out, as the physicist Richard
Feynman once described it, or even excelling at finding things out. It is
an instrument with no intrinsic value. All it has is commercial utility in
wowing the gatekeepers at Harvard. And so parents are poised to put
pressure on schools to change their children's grades when they don't
score well. These are the same parents who are transforming schooling
into a consumer experience.

Parents who pay forty thousand dollars a year, says Arthur Levine, former president of Columbia University's Teachers College and an expert
on grading, expect nothing less than As in return. "If the teacher gives you
a B, that's not acceptable, because the teacher works for you . . . If I'm
getting Bs, I'm not getting my money's worth." True grades are critical, he
argues, because they provide invaluable feedback. They let you know
what you are good at and what you are not. You can use that information
to direct your efforts in learning. But instead, teachers are more like service employees, and parents call professors and administrators to complain. When he surveyed his faculty on the phenomenon, one college
administrator was told of an overwrought mother who called a professor
directly to voice her discontent. She introduced herself by saying that she
and her husband were both attorneys. The professor understood that was
meant to intimidate him.

At a small eastern liberal arts college, a father recently yanked his
freshman daughter out of school before the end of the first week because
she was unable to get a specific course. "This is her first semester," says
a top administrator, incredulous that anyone would not welcome college
as a time and place for exploration and exposure to new ideas. "Of course,
the reason they sent her to a small college—I guess the rest of the sentence is, so they can have everything that they wanted. They say lots of
different things, but that's what they mean. This father had planned out
his daughter's college career for four years, and he knew what courses she

needed to take every semester for the four years she was going to be here. And if she could not get this course and we could not make that possible for her, she had to go home. We had to say bye." The administrator sighs and says: "We now have a generation of students who believe that you can make one mistake and ruin everything, as if their entire future rests on every single step. That makes it so hard for them to explore. That doesn't give them permission to fail. It doesn't give them permission to test—because the stakes are so high."

The vice president for student affairs at a well-known East Coast university insists that students whose parents are pathologically overinvolved still make up a minority of the campus population—but they hog administrative resources. They make a disproportionate amount of "noise"; they make incessant demands and want frequent reports and constant feedback from the deans. In addition, they're constantly on the cell phone with their kids—"living and breathing for their kids." It's not unheard of for a kid to be facing a standard decision point, such as choice of a major, and to have a parent book a hotel room on or near campus for a month, the easier to oversee the child and the school administration. "I want to tell them to let the kid handle it," the administrator says, "to remind them that the goal of education is to have kids develop their own judgment, their own decision-making ability, their self-confidence."

Officials at one well-known university thought they had heard everything when they received a call from a father complaining that his daughter was stressed out over a roommate problem. It seems the roommate didn't do her laundry often enough, and there was a smell. The daughter felt she couldn't study in the room with a smell, so she picked up her cell phone and dialed her father, over a thousand miles away. The father didn't tell her to talk to the roommate. He didn't coach her on how to do it or what she might say. He didn't even *expect* his daughter to have the social skills to talk to her roommate. He called the vice president for student affairs.

One or two of these parents "is equal to a thousand others." That, says the East Coast vice president, may make them seem more numerous than they actually are. What's more, as the affluent educated elite, they have the time, the resources, and the knowledge to manipulate the system to their benefit. And because they are the culture shapers and standard-bearers, they set the style for all parents and children.

Let schools at any level try to raise the bar for students and parents protest forcefully. Tiny Duvall, Washington, is a town of fifty-five hundred near Seattle. In 1993, the town's Cedarcrest High School instituted a senior project as a requirement for graduation. Students had to write an eight-page paper, make an oral presentation lasting eight to twelve minutes, and create some kind of related product. Things seemed to be working just fine until recently, when one senior failed his project. His parents got furious—but not at him. They hired a lawyer to protest his grade. So many parents disliked the project and the weight the grade carried that the school was forced to halve the requirement to a paper of four pages. Moreover, it pared down the weight of the grade, too, making it just part of an overall grade for civics.

"We get painted as nitpicking asses out to ruin students' lives," said the program's coordinator. "It's been a constant battle." All he wanted was for students to be prepared for the job market or college classes.

Astonishingly, parental protectionism does not even end in college. Graduates are surprising prospective bosses by bringing their parents with them on job interviews. Or dialing them in to hiring calls that turn into conference calls so the parents can negotiate salary and benefits packages on behalf of their offspring. The manager of staffing services at General Electric made an offer to one recruit last fall. The next day he got a call from the recruit's mother seeking to negotiate an increase in salary. The manager held firm.

"It's unbelievable to me that a parent of a 22-year-old is calling on their behalf," said the director of college relations for St. Paul Travelers, who was on the receiving end of calls from parents "telling us how great their children are, how great they'd be for a specific job." She views this generation of adults as "kamikaze parents," the ones who "already mowed· down the guidance and admissions offices" and are now encroaching on the workplace. Sometimes parents call the recruiters wanting to know why their child was turned down for a job. Says a veteran staffing director, "That's something I haven't faced in 15 years" in the field.

Machinery of Heavy Lifting

There are names for the parents who do all the heavy lifting for their children. In the beginning—say, four or five years ago—school officials, among the first to feel their effects, would gather at meetings, roll their eyeballs, compare notes on the onslaught, and call them helicopter parents, because they hover and make a lot of noise, rescuing their children whenever difficulty arises. They might protest what they deem an unfair grade or demand to know what is being said in college-counseling sessions. At the very least, they want to know what the school is doing to help their child thrive. And if something occurs that they, or their child, don't like, they're apt to dial the headmaster or president directly.

"We started referring to helicopter parents in the 1970s," says James Fay, then a school principal in upscale Evergreen, Colorado, now head of the Love and Logic Institute he founded to educate parents about parenting. "The first day I was there, half the kids went to the phone in the office to whine to their parents that they forgot a field trip permission slip or something. I really clamped down on their getting rescued." But, he contends, as willing as parents were even then to solve problems that the children needed to solve for themselves, he is astonished at how helicopter parents have evolved. About five years ago, Fay surveyed seventeen hundred teachers in the United States about the most difficult aspect of teaching today. "I expected them to cite school violence; this was not long after the Columbine incident. But the number-one thing they cited was parents who would not allow the kids to learn about the world in real ways. They want discipline in schools, but they don't want their kids to be held accountable for anything. These parents are constantly running interference and intimidating teachers to give kids better than they deserve. They're doing the homework for the kids, even lying for them. Today they are a jet-powered turbo attack model." So ferocious have parents become, Fay notes, that principals have told him they prefer working in an inner-city school "because they don't have to put up with so much of the entitlement stuff from parents."

Other educators see them as "snowplow parents": they work hard to clear the path for their kids, push obstacles out of the way, and make the traveling as smooth and safe as possible. They pasteurize parenting. From helicopters to snowplows, more than equipment has changed. There is a growing sense that a deleterious process is in operation and probably augurs trouble ahead. Accumulating snowbanks, after all, keep those on the road from seeing anything that is not positioned directly in front of them. Whether snowplows or helicopters, parents exert great force so that children do not have to solve problems, make decisions for themselves, or take responsibility for their course. The children also have no personal investment in or responsibility for the road down which they are guided.

"Parents are our worst enemy when their child isn't getting what they want. They'll whisper in the bleachers and send letters to administrators," says a soccer coach at an NCAA Division I university on the East Coast. For the first time ever, the team held a preseason meeting in the fall of 2006—for parents. "Our parent situation reached all-new levels last year. Some of our parents—of college athletes!—became a cancer which spread quickly to their children and quickly throughout our team. The goal of the meeting was to set PARENTAL STANDARDS OF BEHAV-IOR, not player standards! We felt it was necessary to let the parents know how dangerous and destructive their behaviors can be to team chemistry and performance. So far, so good and they seem to be behaving themselves. One of the main themes of the meeting was that it is a *privilege* for their children to play NCAA Division I athletics, not their *right*."

Helicopters, snowplows . . . the names for pushy parents are proliferating. But they all do the same thing: remove from their children opportunities for learning how to problem-solve. And so far there seems to be only one name for the children—teacup kids. Because, as we will see, without opportunities to experience themselves, to develop and call on their own inner resources, to test their own limits, to develop confidence in themselves as problem solvers, they are fragile and shatter easily.

"All Sorts of Crazy Stuff"

"It's not something you think is going to happen to you in your freshman year of college," says Marissa. "You think it's going to be this amazing party, with friends and all sorts of crazy stuff. I certainly had plenty of the crazy stuff. It just came in a different form."

In Marissa's freshman year at Yale, the girl who was best, who was cast from a very early age as The Achiever, slipped into suicidal depression. She lost interest in eating and gradually withdrew from her friends. She was constantly cold. Because her grades stayed high, no one thought anything was amiss. But when her five-foot-nine-inch frame withered to a mere hundred pounds, a dormmate finally noticed something was wrong and called Marissa's father, a physician. A nearby doctor was located who took one cursory look and "slapped on the label of anorexic" without bothering to find out what might be troubling her. She was weighed every morning "like I was a piece of produce." Her weight slipped further, and sterner measures were required. Marissa spent a chunk of her spring semester locked in the fluorescent haze of the Yale Psychiatric Institute. Day and night she was forced into "the fishbowl," a centralized glass enclosure, so the staff could assure themselves that she was swallowing her meds and drinking her calorie-dense cocktails. She wandered the wards with "a mind-blowing mix of local crazies and suicidal Yalies."

It was the best thing that ever happened to her.

Before she became a Yale honors graduate, before she became a Fulbright scholar with three years of self-guided travel, study, and anthropological work in South America, Marissa had to come back from emotional desolation and despair. Bred to be the quintessential upper-middle-class success machine, running a little too obediently on the expectations of others, Marissa had to find her own purpose, her own meaning, her own identity, her own voice, her own nerve. It took a taste of lockdown for her to stumble upon what so many in her generation are missing—a basic sense of self.

Psychological breakdowns are nothing new to adolescence or young adulthood. But what Marissa and so many peers are experiencing is not the breakdown characteristic of previous generations. What's significant about these kids, observers say, is that they commonly lack a fierce internal struggle toward a deeper state of authenticity. When they have a breakdown, it is not the product of introspection in which people seek to be aware of their own inner workings. It is not Kierkegaard's angst, a crisis of neurotic hyperawareness in an indifferent universe. No, it is more "the gray drizzle of horror," to borrow William Styron's stunning description of depression, a steady stream of performance pressure against an inner landscape of desolation.

Disconnected from themselves, they suffer unfocused anxiety and panic because they can't even identify their fears. Stricken students can be so robotic in their ability to perform, totally disengaged from themselves, that, like Marissa, nothing comes between them and their grades, not even a bout of hospitalization. They don't have a strong sense of self, because they have not been allowed to build one, not allowed to struggle, not encouraged to take the necessary time for reflection and introspection, for making experience their own and forging their own meaning.

This, it must be stressed, is not due to any fault of their doing; it is the nature of the world they have inherited. It appears to be the logical end product of a culture that insists on engineering all the serendipity and spontaneity out of human experience and of parents who intrude on their every minute and motive. An order of curly fries in the school lunch line is such a taste of dietary disaster that these parents microplan every detail of their children's lives. Their concern has given rise to the belief that they—and only they—know what's good for their children, and can secure their safety, that the children will be harmed in the absence of eternal, exhausting, intrusive—but, unfortunately, ultimately crippling— vigilance.

Rich Dad . . . Poor Kids!

The hothouse is most intense among the most affluent. Their experience in building and maintaining the hothouse is instructive for everyone, however, as affluence and prosperity forge the dominant tone of American culture today.

Once upon a time, the most privileged youngsters often followed a time-honored tradition and went off to boarding school to acquire a good college-prep education, pick up some social skills, and get in some substantial rehearsal for independence. The adults had time to play. But somewhere in the 1990s, priorities shifted dramatically, children were given starring roles in the family drama, and preparation for adulthood lost ground to parental need for emotional closeness and control. Adults with means began *following* their kids to boarding school. They literally uproot themselves and the rest of the family and relocate near the campus. When one fourteen-year-old girl was accepted at a top boarding school in California, the family sold their house in the suburbs of New York City and moved to a ranch two miles from the new school. "We couldn't cope with the idea of her being here without us," the mother explained.

The hothouse approach to child rearing is becoming most intense among the most affluent in part because the affluent can afford to live on one salary. Indeed, demographers report, increasing numbers of women are dropping out of the workforce to become stay-at-home moms (SAHMs, they call themselves). For some, the impetus to stay at home comes from their partners. There are men who see it as a visible badge of their earning power to have a wife who doesn't need to work. The well-equipped nursery, the Bugaboo stroller (or a fleet of them), the nanny, the stay-at-home wife—according to the women who prowl and growl in the rarefied precincts of UrbanBaby.com, all are accoutrements of high-earning men whose competitive drive not only lands them a variety of lux-uries but persuades them to make a public statement of them. Today's stay-at-home moms tend to be highly educated; their affluence enables them to be free all day every day to devote their formidable talents and know-how to their children. The new breed of hothouse mother, says one, "spends all day talking about parenting. There's a little bit of nostalgia thrown in for the pre-child-raising days." Often, they become volunteers for school activities—where not only do they get to apply their scrutiny but their influence serves to intensify the pressures on kids.

As one informed me: "The stereotypical mother in this town is college educated, married, upper-class or upper-middle-class, and taking time off from a successful career to raise and nurture her children." Suddenly stranded with no visible means of achievement, "she also measures her success through her children's successes." That encourages her to turn the school activities for which she volunteers into competitive events. Take the medieval fair held annually at an elementary school in her middle-size midwestern city.

Medieval Fest is a regular adjunct to the history curriculum when the second grade studies the Middle Ages. All three classes—representing about a hundred kids—participate in it. Instructions to parents outlining the event suggest they provide simple foods, such as raisins and nuts, and simple costumes, such as an inverted heavy-duty trash bag with strategi-cally cut holes as a suit of armor for a knight.

Two years ago, when one mother got to the school gymnasium, "I dis-covered that the other mothers had spent weeks sewing elaborate gowns and costumes. My daughter was dressed as a simple jester. She felt left out by comparison." But it got worse. Last year, the fest grew too sump-tuous to be held in the humble precincts of a public school. "The parents made elaborate medieval meat dishes, when I'm sure that the kids would have preferred chicken McNuggets. These kids are seven and eight years old." The costumes got even more elaborate. The fair was moved to the Tudor-style clubhouse of a country club owned by one of the parents. It was fifteen minutes away, and the parents had to carpool to get the kids there. "It was ridiculous. The parent volunteers made everything more important and more elaborate than it needs to be. They compete as vol-unteers, making it a full-time career." Volunteering is supposed to be a support function, but in the hothouse of modern parenting it overtakes the event it was supposed to be helping. The history lesson is lost. The contributions of the kids themselves are overshadowed. And life in the Middle Ages becomes a competitive pageant of prosperity. Somewhere along the way, the educational value of the fair was sacrificed to the needs of high-powered parents to make the event worthy of their input.

Affluence Affords the High Price of Pressure

If she wants to slack off between runs, she can tune in to a TV channel dedicated just to her, to validate her approach to child raising and urge her on. Lest anyone think these women bear any resemblance to the stay-at-home mothers of previous generations, they call themselves, without any trace of irony, Alpha Moms, or Moms to the Max. They have won whatever the competition is to get to the top of the heap. They have top drive. They have top expectations. They can do it all, and they do it all for themselves and their kids. Not for all kids—just for their own kids. The very concept of Alpha Mom—and if your job is to be a mom, who wouldn't want to be alpha?—implies that there is such a thing as successful motherhood and that it is possible to perform the role with perfection; in fact perfection becomes absolutely necessary to be worthy of the title. "Maybe," the *New York Times* columnist Maureen Dowd lamented not long ago, "there would be more alpha women in the working world if so many of them didn't marry alpha men and become alpha moms armed with alpha SUVs, alpha muscles from daily workouts and alpha tempers from getting in teachers' faces to propel their precious alpha kids."

The hothouse is hottest among the most affluent because they can literally afford to put the most pressure on kids. They hire specialists with the aim of perfecting their children. Tutors, at five or six hundred dollars an hour, are brought on board even when the child is in preschool, and even in the summer; the affluent import tutors to their summer communities as performance enhancers who function as academic steroids. If the child is a little further along, they can shell out fifteen thousand dollars for what some tutoring and college-counseling services tout as their Ivy guaranteed admission program, or IGAP. Of course, it's best to start such "application management and strategies" programs early, preferably in ninth grade, so the kid can be steered right through to success in the college admission process. In the Ford-like assembly line production of successful college candidates, a child's own goals and interests are subordinated to the counselor's guarantee. And when the children finally settle into the dorm, their affluent parents are available to call them every morning to wake them up.

Population dynamics play a role. In New York City, where the number of parents with children is growing and wealth is concentrated, there are said to be fifteen applicants for every coveted slot in the top-tier nursery schools. As a result, parents hire educational consultants for their three-year-olds. They also enroll them in Japanese classes, swim classes, and art classes. Actually, said one observer of urban patterns, "the search for distinction starts in the womb."

The most affluent parents have the means, the power, and the know-how of the system's workings to influence it on behalf of their children. Unlike parents at lower income levels, they are not afraid to challenge the system and make it serve their interests, actions fed by their sense of entitlement as "full payers." They have the confidence and skills to tangle with high-ranking officials. Or to use their income to influence outcomes directly.

"Birmingham and Bloomfield Hills are tops in the state in the MEAP [Michigan Educational Assessment Program] testing," a Birmingham parent told me. All public school students, from elementary school through high school, are tested annually. "Of course we're number one," she observed. "A large number of the students are being tutored. The parents are spending on private tutors. Many are tutored because their parents want them in an Ivy League school." "Ivy League" has become the top educational brand, the closest parents believe they can get to a guarantee of success.

The aggressiveness that affluent parents display on behalf of their children may also have its roots, at least in part, in the social philosophy affluence often bestows. The well-to-do tend to be politically and economically attuned to search for individual solutions to social problems. As a result, they may seek advantage for their own kids over general improvements that would help all kids, including their own. We are all prone to make errors of attribution regarding our successes and failures. We tend to internalize success, erroneously ascribing it to our own superior innate characteristics—often overlooking the powerful hand of luck or special opportunity—while attributing failure to general conditions or adverse circumstances. The affluent are at greatest risk of such self-serving biases—

in fact, affluence may be the necessary condition for the attribution bias. It may intensify their motivation for acting on their own individualistic interests for their kids.

At colleges and universities across the United States, admissions and financial-aid administrators say it has become fairly common for parents with substantial six-figure incomes to seek financial assistance. "I have never seen so many families with incomes of $200,000 to $300,000 applying for need-based aid," one such administrator told the *Chronicle of Higher Education*. "They look at their financial outlays and think they have need. But it's really about lifestyle choices they have made." The dean of enrollment at Kalamazoo College in Michigan received a three-page, single-spaced letter from a cardiologist explaining that his take-home pay of $17,000 a month might seem like a lot, but really wasn't.

Then, too, affluence has a way of expanding people's expectations about their life and their happiness. They want it all and often believe they deserve it all. Their rising expectations are applied to their kids as well as to the institutions that serve them. Ever-rising tuition costs fuel their expansive expectations. In making parents more consumer oriented, they drive a kind of demandingness that independent schools in particular are struggling to handle. Rising tuition costs, say administrators, make parents "harder to manage." As the cost of education necessities increases, children are viewed as prized possessions—and thus more precious, more worthy of monitoring and protection.

Globalization, says the Swarthmore College psychologist Barry Schwartz, has done two things that conspire to make people miserable. It has changed their pool of competitors, and it has changed people's aspirations, especially among the affluent. "There was a time before instant universal telecommunications when you were operating in your own little pond. You weren't competing with everybody. Those days are gone for the educated elite. You're competing against everyone, and increasingly that means everyone in the world, because there really are no natural boundaries to contain the set of people who might take your spot. There has always been competition, but it wasn't competition without bounds, the way it is now."

Aspirations have been ratcheted up enormously because "any magazine you open is giving you evidence of what your life could be like if only you tried a little harder. You no longer want a house that's a little bigger than your neighbor's house; you want it bigger than Bill Gates's house.

You get to see everybody's house everywhere. Since we know our evaluation of how good things are is almost always in comparison with our expectations, the surest recipe for misery is high expectations. No experience can actually meet them."

What's more, "once you get told you can be anything you want to be, you want a job that pays you well, that's respected, that's fun, where you have good colleagues. You don't inherit the job your father had. Multiply that by romantic partners. You don't have to marry in your religion. You don't have to marry someone who lives in your town. A blond and blue-eyed movie star is possible." When experiences fail to live up to expectations, which is a certainty, "it is almost impossible to avoid concluding that it was your fault. You end up making a causal account of your failure that blames you rather than circumstance. So you have a significant contributor to the epidemic of depression. The competition for the goods and the escalation of expectations is really doing us in."

One thing money does is provide a sense of control. It matters little how much of that sense is an illusion. The ratcheting up of expectations has also inflated the sense of control the affluent believe they should enjoy. But against perpetual technological change, twenty-four-hour markets, economic volatility, and constant competition, it takes strong and sometimes desperate measures to impose a sense of control. What is a hothouse except an attempt to control the growing conditions of the young?

Reversal of Fortunes

Hey, wait a minute. This isn't the way life is supposed to be. Affluence traditionally insulated families from paying too much attention to their children and certainly relieved them of the necessity of putting pressure on them to succeed academically. As long as the kids didn't wrap themselves around a tree in an alcoholic haze, affluence itself would protect them. Sooner or later they would inherit the farm or the family business, or at least the stock portfolio. It's the upwardly mobile middle class that traditionally set its hungry sights on academic achievement as the route to general success in life, and it is the middle class that often gives their kids a healthy push down that path. But those are the old rules. Over the past two decades, the world has been turned upside down, or at least it feels that way to the adults. No one even knows what the new rules are, because they are constantly changing.

Behind this reversal of fortune stand two very important new developments: the radical transformation of everyday life by technological change and the emergence of the highly dynamic new economy via the globalization of markets. In the United States, these changes are set against a widening gap between the rich and the rest of us.

The speed and volatility of the marketplace leave no room for complacency; today's haves could be tomorrow's have-nots. The rich have the most incentive to push the hardest because they, potentially, have the most to lose.

In many corners of the culture, the upper class now works harder than the middle class, the historic source of America's drive and strength. What is moving upper-class people to work longer hours than the working class is their realization that, given the dynamic uncertainties of a very fast and fluid economy, a relatively new development, they have the most to lose from a day at the beach and the most to protect, and even gain, by rolling up their sleeves.

Just as the affluent now work the hardest, they are the most worried about their kids—because they realize their children will have to work even *harder* to be where their parents are. They want their children to at least maintain the socioeconomic status they grew up in, but understand that it is getting increasingly difficult to do so while living in a precarious world. With formidable resources to push their kids, they often muster all that they've got. In trickle-down fashion, it becomes the new standard of parenting.

Here's only one irony: what they are pushing the children toward may not be worth the effort. It could be argued that the lifestyle that parents are struggling to launch their children into is a source more of stress than of freedom—a kind of Astroturf affluence, quite slippery, something that very much resembles the real thing but functions quite differently. According to the New York psychiatrist Maurice Preter, the affluence that has overtaken America does not deliver many of the traditional benefits of real affluence.

Working harder than ever just to maintain their socioeconomic status, the affluent, despite all the accoutrements of the good life, live in a state of near-chronic stress. They have few of the deep rewards affluence is supposed to bring: happiness, a sense of security, time to relax, time to spend with friends. "What's missing," Preter stresses, "is a social code unrelated to exchange of commodities." Studies persuasively show that

Americans' circle of friends is dramatically shrinking. Families conduct almost all their socializing within the family unit, minimizing the exposure of children to adults other than their parents and thus limiting their knowledge of other perspectives. Activities intended to be restorative may be enjoyable in some ways, but they also wind up intensifying nuclear pressures and scrutiny. Preter calls it "ideological affluence," because it is no more than symbolic of true affluence and lacks its substantial social and emotional rewards. Ideological affluence is a lot like eating a gorgeous-looking cream pie made with artificial flavors and ersatz whipped cream. You keep devouring more in search of true flavor, but instead of being satisfied through intensity and authenticity of flavor, you wind up bloated, still unsatisfied, and unhappy.

It's not difficult to understand why all parents today are so on edge. The world shifted on our watch. We're the ones who've been blown sideways by the new technologies and ever more rapid speed of cultural change. There are real changed conditions of our lives. The technology changed completely; it didn't require just a retooling of the imagination—it continues to change at such a rapid pace it takes ongoing effort to keep up. The globalization of markets generates deep job insecurities and an endless supply of competitors; there are now no geographical limits to who can enter. The effects are still rippling through—and promise to ripple through continuously from here on in.

Nervousness about globalization has made parents so concerned about competitiveness they believe that they must do everything in their power to not let their kids fall behind. But they make the assumption that their kids have been hit, too. And meaning the best for their kids, they try to protect them.

The new insecurities of affluence and the growing economic divide for all create fertile terrain for hothouse parenting. Benefiting from affluence is no buffer against the sense that some pernicious new form of economic volatility will play out in the children's lifetimes, if not ours. This fact, tucked away in the psyche of those most aware of current events, powers anxiety about the children and drives overwrought attempts to see that they are as well equipped as possible for success in whatever the future brings. "Because the adult workplace is so competitive today, we therefore think we have to equip our children with a competitive edge," one parent told me. "This couldn't be more true than about the metro Detroit area. My husband has worked as an executive for Ford Motor Company for twenty years, yet he comes home every night filled with anxiety about losing his job! It seems everyone around us is losing their jobs—maybe another reason we are so crazy!"

"It's easy to get sucked in," adds a parent in an affluent Connecticut town. "The parents are living vicariously through their children. And they want their children to eventually have the same lifestyle as they do. At some point you have to stand back and ask, 'But at what price?' If my child grows up and wants of his own accord to be a forest ranger, I could live with that. The parents around here would not, even if it reflected his own goals and his own interests." Parents elsewhere are saying the same thing. In talking to parent groups around the country, I found that the wealthier the community, the pushier the parents were—and the more anxiety they exhibited about their children's future socioeconomic status. Even when they suspected they were harming their kids by overinvolvement in their lives, they couldn't loosen their grip—"because then my kid will be at a competitive disadvantage to all the other kids and I'm terrified he'll be left behind."

The Age of Uncertainty

At bottom, hothouse parenting is the response of adults, fathers as well as mothers, to tremendous uncertainty and anxiety about what the next generation will need to thrive in the new economy. They know the rules have changed. Having been knocked for a loop themselves by new technologies and often the need to retrofit themselves to the economy, they assume their children are facing the same prospects. Their solution is to intensify parenting, to start at or near birth with classes and programs to equip their child with as many skills as they can cram in, in the hope that at least some of them will provide a ticket to success. Because landing on the right side of the yawning economic divide is so critical, they judge the stakes so great that each child is essentially in competition with all the others. The sense of competition encourages parents to do all in their power to create an advantage for their own child. Affluent parents hover and clear the path for their kids, making demands of teachers, administrators, and coaches. The less affluent might vie to have their child singled out as special by being designated a genius, or an "indigo" child. Or they might seek neuropsychological testing to have their child declared "differently abled" and accorded academic accommodations that typically come down to taking their tests without time constraints, most importantly the SATs.

It is almost touching that in times of such anxiety and uncertainty, middle-class and affluent parents still see education as America's salvation. But their approaches reflect the desire, whatever way they can, to seek individual advantage, rather than to strengthen a system of public education for all. The almost exclusive focus on achievements that can be measured—such as reading skills—comes at the expense of more subtle abilities that can't be readily measured—creativity, willingness to experiment, social skills—but have a broad influence on development, on eventual success, and on quality of life. "The emphasis on performance is not developmentally meaningful and fails to furnish a philosophy of life," says Edward Spencer, associate vice president for student affairs at Virginia Tech. "College is treated as a credentialing factory rather than a place for developing the whole mind and the whole person."

Hothouse parents do exactly what everyone does when anxious. They tighten their grip. Anxiety narrows and shortens their range of focus, as it does for everyone. They exert pressure on their kids and hang on tight, overcontrolling them. It is the nature of anxiety to exaggerate dangers and apply hypervigilance.

Parental anxiety, however, is badly matched to the needs of children. In just the most obvious of instances, the children, unlike their parents, are digital natives, virtually born masters of the new technology that adults are still struggling with. Parental anxiety is also nonproductive. If there's one thing people need in a fast-changing world, it's the freedom to experiment and even fail, so that they can figure out what it takes to succeed, match that knowledge to their own interests, and find a way to make their own creative adaptations to the conditions of contemporary life.

Moreover, the ordinary obstacles and challenges that are swept from children's paths keep them from developing the skills they need to cope with life's uncertainties and vicissitudes. This might be fodder for stand-up routines were the consequences not so sad.

Intrusive parenting undermines children in the most fundamental ways. It spawns anxious attachment to the children. In doing so, it sets them up for lifelong fragility.

Despite all the parental pushing and overinvolvement, despite the six-hundred-dollar-an-hour top-of-the-line tutors, despite the accommodations and untimed SATs, despite constant surveillance down to the last curly fry, the kids who have virtually sacrificed their childhoods for a shot at the Ivy League are poorly prepared for changing a major or handling romantic rejection, or for the real world when they get there. "I see the interactions between parents and students," says a high school history teacher in New York's affluent Westchester County. "I wonder how much anxiety this parent is creating for the student by laying out, when they're in the sixth or seventh grade, that they need to get into Harvard. And then that parent seeks to relieve anxiety not by addressing the issue at hand, not by dealing with the anxiety and giving the child tools to cope with it, but by seeking out an accommodation. The child never learns to get past the anxiety."

Child Abuse by Any Other Name

There's abundant evidence that parental obsessiveness has reached the point of abuse. It's most obvious in children pushed to achieve their best in athletics; their pain typically declares itself in a frank, physical way that can prevent them from functioning at all and can even derail future development. Across the country, orthopedic surgeons and sports doctors report skyrocketing rates of overuse injuries in kids as young as eight— the kind that until a few years ago were seen only in adult athletes after years of playing professionally. More kids today are being urged to specialize in one sport at an early age and train year-round so they can engage in high-stakes competitions. Forget neighborhood pickup games; there's nothing casual or recreational about sports anymore; if you play, you play to win. That's how kids and their parents define success at sports.

And for such kids, summers are increasingly for suffering. It's an epidemic, say sports physicians. Dr. Sally Harris is one of them. Based in Palo Alto, California, she found that the number of overuse injuries virtually doubled from the summer and school year of 2005–6 to the summer of 2006. In 2003, the latest year for which national data are available, more than 3.5 million such injuries in children under age fifteen were treated in the United States, out of approximately 35 million children from six to twenty-one who participate in team sports. Parents not only push their kids to practice and encourage them to join traveling teams, especially if they are teens, but send the kids to highly specialized sports camps where the training can be superintensive. Many kids from affluent families fill their summer vacation by going to a succession of such high-powered programs and even squeeze in a few during holidays and breaks in the school-year schedule. "It's not enough that they play on a school team, two travel teams, and go to four camps for their sport in the summer," said one family sports medicine expert. "They have private instructors for that one sport that they see twice a week. Then their parents get them out to practice in the backyard at night."

Dr. James Andrews, a prominent sports orthopedist in Birmingham, Alabama, makes no secret of his astonishment. "You get a kid on the operating table and you say to yourself, 'It's impossible for a 13-year-old to have this kind of wear and tear.'" Like others, he regards it as "a new childhood disease." Concerned observers believe that coaches and parents are pushing bodies that are not ready for such stress. Muscles, bones, tendons, and ligaments get painfully inflamed or break down faster than young bodies can repair when pushed beyond their physical limits by the repetitive motions that incessant practice demands. Cortisone shots can relieve the pain but not heal the damage. When an orthopedic surgeon explained the nature of her child's injury to one mother, she broke down crying—not because her son was suffering but because the baseball-playing boy wouldn't be able to pitch for a whole year. "Sports are everything to *us*—that's the pronoun she used," the surgeon relayed.

Those who treat the pediatric injuries point the finger at an overaggressive culture of organized youth sports in league with overinvolved parents. The adults tend to push their kids back into competitive play before they've fully healed. For the kids, the gain is often more than pain. Around the country, in affluent communities, parents are now paying their children if they achieve in sports. "It's amazing how many parents are doing this," a suburban Michigan mother told me. "In my community, the going rate is fifty dollars every time the child competes and gets first place or the team wins. It's easy to get caught up in this. My daughter is a swimmer, and she came right out and asked me why she doesn't get paid." The mother thinks "it's causing kids to rot from within, while parents are living their glory days through their kids."

Commerce is complicit in the pushing of children to the point of abuse. The highly competitive athletic shoe companies openly reward superspecialization in youngsters with cases of free merchandise and invitations to select sports camps that they run. They are hoping to discover and groom the next face of the sport. Adidas has its Jr. Phenom Camp for basketball players in middle school. If they are good enough, they might graduate to the Phenom 150 Camp when they enter high school. National scouting services the shoe companies hire leave no child unscrutinized and unevaluated; they comb the country looking for promising talent. Invitations can come with guarantees of media exposure and attention from college recruiters. As Reebok's senior director of grassroots basketball says, "We're going to find them, expose them and get them used to the grind at an earlier age. I believe in that theory." Not content to let Adidas and Reebok run away with all the middle schoolers, Nike recently made its own bid to put competitive pressure on ever-younger children by launching a new national tournament for sixth, seventh, and eighth graders. One scout said that he never hears parents complain when their kids show up on the lists of prospective talent. Instead, he hears from parents who think their kids should be ranked higher.

Before child rearing became a hothouse, sports-minded kids might have played baseball, basketball, and football all in one day. According to Dr. Lyle Micheli, head of sports medicine at Children's Hospital Boston, that was actually good for their bodies. Because the different sports make different demands on differing body parts, the bodies of those who played them developed in balance. Now, he says, "young athletes play sports supervised by adults who have them doing the same techniques, the same drills, over and over and over. There is no rest and recovery for the overused parts of their body. Parents think they are maximizing their child's chances by concentrating on one sport. The results are often not what they expected."

A Philadelphia orthopedist tells the story of a mother who recently asked her if there wasn't "some kind of shot or fix-it procedure I could do for her 11-year-old daughter's ankle so she could be ready for an upcoming regional competition. I told her that if it were the Olympic Games coming up, perhaps we could treat this situation differently. But as far as I understood, her upcoming competition wasn't the Olympics. At this point, the daughter is giggling—but the parent is in the corner crying. I said: 'This isn't Curt Schilling in the World Series. It's not worth not being able to run anymore for a plastic gold-plated medal.' "

TWO

Rocking the Cradle of Class

A sluggish traffic light brought three acquaintances together on the neighborhood street corner with plenty of time to catch up on one another. "My daughter is still in the public school system," said one woman; this is, after all, New York, and one can't take such things for granted, even in the outer boroughs. "My son is, too, and it's going really well," said the one dad. And after an expectant pause, "*We* go to [insert name of highly selective, outrageously competitive private school here]," announced the other mother.

How's that again? This wasn't the plural *"we"*; the woman had arrived solo. Nor was it the royal *"we"*; no footmen were in sight. No, Ladies and Gents, say hello to the fused-identity "we," in which fully grown adults openly appropriate the accomplishments of their wee ones, flash them like Olympic medals for parenting, and take much of their own measure from them.

It used to be that infants slid down the birth canal into the class and social ranking of their parents and spent the rest of their lives basking in its embrace. Social class used to be something you were born into. But now that the world is flat and fast and fluid, parents are seeking status in the achievements of their children. Not only is class status far more up for grabs; it is also far more flaunted than it has been in decades.

Of course, parents have always taken pride in their children's accomplishments. But children's accomplishments have become a marker of how the *parents* are doing in the increasingly prominent job of parenting—and, by extension, how the whole family is doing. In a novel twist of the age-old status dynamic, parents now rely on children's competitive performance in athletics and especially academics for their own inner sense of security and social approval.

As the engines of status shift into reverse—with kids fuel-injecting parental egos with every A they get—they create a new kind of child labor. Kids no longer have to till fields from dawn to dusk or toil in sooty factories, but more and more they are handed the burden of power-lifting their parents' sense of self. The trouble with turning tots into trophies is that the developmental needs of the young are sacrificed to the psychological needs of adults. It's hard for children to wend their way down their own developmental paths when they must advance someone else's.

In sharp contrast to eras past, parents have shifted their primary concern from the child's long-range health and welfare to their own narcissistic fulfillment through the child's current achievements. And the pride parents once felt in their children's accomplishments is no longer a private matter but a public one, to be paraded: hence the rise of the bumper sticker announcing that your child is an honors student.

Adults today seek so much of their sense of self in their children that prospective parents no longer just *buy* a stroller. They *invest* emotionally in it. And that, astute manufacturers recognize, translates into a willingness to invest financially as well. Describing the advent of buggies that cost upwards of eight hundred dollars and "parents who pore over product options" in the hopes "that their research will help their children get a better start in life," the *New York Times* recently declared that "strollers can come to mean much more than just transportation." A spokesperson for the baby-product manufacturers' association explained why some people buy and dispose of dozens of different models before settling on a wardrobe of, say, three models. "A stroller is part of the parents' image and a reflection of themselves—personal style, parenting style, their lifestyle."

In the same way, the schools to which parents send their kids have come to symbolize much more than education. No one knows this better than the students at a certain Ivy League university, admission to which is sometimes considered prima facie evidence of success in child raising. The announcement that one's kid goes to Harvard may win the conversation among hypercompetitive parents, but students' feelings are more mixed. For them, it can create performance expectations that are paralyzing, especially on the first job or two. They call it the "H-Bomb." As one alum blogs, "It is what inspires Harvard graduates to say things like, 'I came to the East Coast for college,' or 'Yeah, I went to school in Boston,' instead of giving their school by name, because once the inevitable question pushes the issue, the H-Bomb explodes."

The child psychologist David Anderegg sees proof of the accessorization of children in the way decals of prestigious colleges are placed on car windows—even before the kids go off to school. "It's a competitive display and it's not about the kids. It's about the parents." A professor at Bennington College in Vermont and consultant to area schools as well as a clinical practitioner, Anderegg insists that kids do best when they go to a school that makes sense for them. "It's about what they need, not about what you need. It's not like their life is going to be ruined if they don't go to a prestigious school." Unfortunately, he notes, "college entrance has become your final exam as a parent."

Jim Conroy, chairman of college counseling at New Trier High School in Winnetka, Illinois, tells the story of a father who came into the counselor's office with his son and asked whether the young man had a chance of being admitted to MIT. When Conroy said it was unlikely, the father replied, "My dream is shattered." In this case, the child had more sense than the parent. The son turned to his father and said, "Dad, it's your dream, not mine. There are plenty of good schools I can go to." Conroy says more and more parents act as if they, and not their children, are the ones applying to college.

My Child, My Self

Childhood is being radically transformed right before our very eyes. Children are now extensions of parents' sense of self in a way that is new and unprecedented. "More than in the past, children are viewed as a project by perfectionist parents," contends Steven Mintz. "Today's parents are imposing on their kids a violence of expectations. They are using kids for their own needs. We've decreased the threat of physical violence but increased the psychological violence."

While attending a professional meeting, a brilliant psychologist I know received a call from her daughter at an Ivy League college. Immediately, over her cell phone, she began dictating the opening paragraphs for a term paper the girl was charged with writing. "This is my second chance in life," the mother volunteered when she finished.

It all started in the 1970s, when postwar optimism came to a crashing halt against stagflation and the oil crisis. The American economy shifted dramatically. Parents translated that into a fear of not passing on their class status to their kids, says Mintz. Their solution: give the kids whatever advantages possible and introduce into childhood the totally alien idea of specialization. "Nervousness about globalization made parents so concerned about competitiveness they began believing they must do *everything* in their power to not let their kid lose."

The economy of the 1970s also attuned people to social class—a radical shift from the 1960s. "Even the food people consumed became class-connected," says Mintz. "The type of lettuce you ate said something about your social class. But increasingly it meant your kids. The nice suburban school just wasn't good enough any more." Today 13 percent of white children attend private schools. Many more live in exclusive suburbs whose public schools function like private ones. "Parents aren't worried about all kids," says Mintz. "They are focused on 'our kids.' "

In the new calculus of caring, competitiveness and class concerns result in obsessiveness over their own children.

The good side of the new approach to parenting is that fathers are more involved, although they are typically inducted into child care by their wives, on their wives' terms. And parents try to cultivate their children's potential. But then there's obsessiveness, increasing class stratification, and competitiveness that focus so exclusively on academic achievement that kids see no other path to success. Historically, it was very different; children raised themselves or were raised by older siblings, Mintz points out. "Our society seems to have the view that our kids can't raise themselves, that parents need to do it, but kids have been quite good at this in the past." In contrast, parental control is at an unprecedented level today—making it difficult for kids to separate and individuate.

Kids are so much driving the status engines for families that just having them is on its way to becoming a status symbol, the human equivalent of a limited-edition Hermès satchel. In a consumer culture, where parenting a child is a very costly enterprise, kids are the ultimate acquisition. One new mini trend identifies the very wealthiest (income above $250,000) as having more children (2.3) than middle-class families (1.8)—slightly more, even, than lower-class families. And the very wealthiest families have the most children by far—averaging 2.9 kids.

The cult of the kid is so strong that tabloids that were once preoccupied with the sex lives of the stars now blare headlines about Britney's babies. With many top designers creating luxury fashions for infants and toddlers, children provide vastly expanded opportunities for the signaling of status. When baby outgrows the cashmere throw on the Bugaboo, she can graduate into the unmistakable patterns of Baby Burberry or Sonia Rykiel fashions for toddlers. The market for costly kiddie couture fashion and accessories is booming—an estimated forty-five billion dollars a year in the United States. It has grown 10 percent annually over the last decade. Even the Disney Company, creator of Mickey Mouse and sprawling theme parks for the masses, has contracted with a manufacturer of premium infant clothing to make ninety-dollar cashmere rompers. Kiddie couture, much of which will be marketed to children themselves, gives kids another source of status by promoting them to full economic partnership as consumers.

Rapid technological change has done its share to elevate the status value of children. It has turned expertise upside down so that children serve as the household gurus on new gadgetry. They are the prime possessors of digital capital, a valuable resource in the digital era. They're the digital natives, born into the technology; for them it is second nature. They don't have to unlearn anything and are unafraid to explore it; they become easy and early adopters of it and are often the ones who teach parents—"digital immigrants" lacking the kids' familiarity, commitment, and comfort with the new tools—how to use cell phones and various computer features. This shift alone accords children high status in a technologically advanced culture.

A growing intensity of family life virtually forces adults to take more of their meaning from their home and especially their children. Everyone knows parents are working more hours and feeling very stressed. (And loaded with guilt, too.) The shrinkage of free time to play—parents are going to the movies less, for example—and to socialize with other adults puts the burden on kids for meeting parents' emotional needs. Kids have very little intergenerational contact with adults other than their own parents or teachers—and fewer models for success than in the past. Approximately 20 percent of American families have only one child. About one in five children under the age of eighteen is an only child. In the climate of hyperintensification, parents overpersonalize everything in their relationship with their children. The fragility of marriage in an era of continuing high divorce rates encourages adults to invest emotionally even more in their children than in their spouse. Some studies show that marital dissatisfaction especially encourages parents to exert psychological control over their children.

Take the case of children's summer camps and programs, which serve the important function of physically extricating kids from family pressures. For decades, well-off families have sent adolescents abroad for summers of professionally monitored study, exploration, and some independence. But responding to adults' requests to get in on their kids' fun, some teen tours now allow parents to join their offspring for part of the trip. When I mention this to my own children, now grown, or their peers, they find it unimaginable. Only a few years separate them from close relatives who had no such escape hatch and didn't even seek one; they actually assented to parents joining up with them and their already well-chaperoned peers on travels abroad.

Laundry, Not Hegel

Because it is the new "critical turning point in American society," the sociologist Lynda Lytle Holmstrom and her Boston College colleagues David A. Karp and Paul S. Gray have conducted an in-depth study of the college application process among upper-middle-class families. One question they pondered is why parents pay for college. After all, it's extremely expensive—private colleges now cost over forty thousand dollars a year just for tuition, room, and board—and money spent on the kids can't be spent on themselves or socked away for retirement. But, the researchers found, spending money on the kids isn't really diverting funds from themselves—not if the children are seen as extensions of the parents. To a surprising degree, the researchers found, the parents' "identities and aspirations are wrapped up in the achievements of their children."

In agricultural societies, parents provide food and shelter to kids, who contribute labor and the promise of care in old age. But in modern societies, Holmstrom explains, there's no economic payoff or reciprocity in having children. Kids don't take on the burden of care for aging parents. Parents shell out lots of money for education, iPods, and other gear. What do the children do in return? Why even have them? Because, increasingly, what they supply are strictly psychological rewards. "More and more, parents have come to be identified with their kids," says Holmstrom. "They are emotionally attached and involved in their children's lives. They enjoy their successes. Parents today reap an emotional benefit from having and raising kids."

Further, paying for college is the way the social class system replicates itself. "It's clear to upper-middle-class parents that education is the way for kids to maintain their social class. The parents are increasingly aware of the fact of competition; there is the perception that the stakes are high." It's not necessarily this way throughout the class structure. For other classes, it's the ticket to upward mobility, and there is a great deal more ambivalence about their children attending college, to say nothing of leaving home for a residential college.

When the upper-middle-class kids do go off to college—and most go to residential colleges, although they often stick close enough to home to still be taken care of—they're worried about how they will fare. But it's not Hegel or Heisenberg that concerns them. They're terrified of doing laundry—and operating solo, without the scheduling and timekeeping their parents have provided. "They've never had to manage everyday affairs on their own," reports Holmstrom. Their doting parents structured and ran everything for them, providing total "backstage support." The definition of a good parent today, she says, is one who helps the child with education, who facilitates the child's education.

The researchers were "struck by how spontaneously, frequently, and uniformly the high school seniors spoke about their uncertainty, fear, and anxiety." The word "scary" appeared with alarming frequency in their conversations with the sociologists. But "although these high school seniors certainly spoke about academic challenges of college, they appear far more worried about how they will handle the logistics of everyday life." The researchers contend that among the economically comfortable, "the relative paucity of independent life experience explains students' focus on nonacademic everyday matters as they anticipate the transition to college." As one student explained her reasons for choosing a nearby college: "When I'm sick I'd rather be home with my mother cooking for me than like having to stay in the health center or in my own dorm room. And if there ever was a problem like too much noise and I had a big test, I could get home."

The Value of Identity

In subsidizing a college education, parents are also buying for their kids another resource for maintaining class status. Increasingly, sociologists recognize, class consists of not only financial and cultural capital but "identity capital" as well: your investment in "who you are." It includes such psychological factors as ego strength and cognitive flexibility and complexity, critical thinking abilities—capacities that help people negotiate the obstacles and opportunities in modern life. College, of course, has traditionally been the prime proving ground of identity, a safe enough place to experiment and discover what one is capable of, to develop the confidence that one is strong enough to survive outside the doting embrace and surveillance of parents. A residential college education allows the young and the well-off the maximum luxury in expanding their identity capital.

So parents come to see as one of their primary jobs helping their kids succeed in school. "Upper-middle-class family life is centrally organized around the singular pursuit of children's education," Holmstrom and her colleagues report in the journal *Symbolic Interaction*. "Parents see it as their job to provide all the infrastructural support to guarantee their offspring's educational success." And that enlarges *their own* identity playground (at the same time that it makes children the emotional glue of the family). Parents have so assumed the right to take every step of college orientation with their kids that colleges are being forced to devise ways to keep the adults from sessions in which their offspring consult with academic advisers or discuss sex with peers.

As the emotionally involved adults push and micromanage their kids, they get to feed off and celebrate the signs of their children's academic and athletic progress. Annexing their children's achievements gives them a way to amplify their own class position; it also heralds a new and more elusive form of reciprocity—identity reciprocity.

The Professionalization of Parenthood

It isn't that parents have never had unreasonable expectations for their children before, and some have even attempted to live vicariously through them. But that was pretty much regarded as a parenting flaw—not a practice to be openly promoted. During the 1980s, there was a tectonic shift in the world of child rearing: parenting became virtually akin to a profession. We went from *having* and *raising* kids to *parenting*. With that change, we left behind a laissez-faire approach to raising children, abandoned any trust in the natural course of events, and began *managing* the tasks of child development.

In this new profession, the performance of the parents not only became materially quantifiable, and thus subject to competition and anxiety, but superseded the long-range goals of the enterprise—raising independent people. Children are now reeling from this change. Because the outcome of parenting is now managed and measured down to the last detail, you could say that we're on our way to precision-producing designer children.

In the 1980s an unabashed emphasis on making money and material success became a central part of the culture. Further, an emerging generation of professionally educated women didn't leave their new career and management skills and values in the office. They brought them home and began applying them to child rearing. For many of them, parenting has become not just an occupation but a preoccupation, a mark not just of what they do but of who they are.

Parents have come to believe there is much they can do to design their children. They start before birth, feeding a diet of Mozart to the fetus, in the expectation that this will result in superior intelligence. After birth come Mommy and Me classes, Baby Einstein books and programs, the alphabet in letter shapes. Add soccer, ballet, art classes, French lessons. The goal—the new American dream—is to raise a child that will make it to Princeton and go to a fancy law school. "Seeing children as a well-designed product, like a highly efficient Mercedes-Benz, and figuring out how to make your child a well-oiled machine, is really a bad idea," says David Anderegg. "There are a tremendous number of parents who do that."

With so much at stake, parents no longer leave any aspect of their children's lives to chance. Call it the art of micromanaging at home. And in this, both the mothers and the fathers are complicit. Such a management style leaves nothing for their children to discover for themselves or call their own, except, perhaps, their Nikes and iPods. The problem is that normal human development is a little more discursive.

It may be that people insert professional values in parenting because they are so rewarded for them at work. Indeed, mothers are more highly educated than ever and wait longer to have their babies. Many are well entrenched in careers before starting a family. It's understandable that they would want to bring home what they know and are rewarded for in the office—setting long-range goals, keeping complex schedules, managing projects, controlling outcomes, and running things efficiently. Anderegg cites a mom who, clipboard in hand, stood at the door of the kindergarten as her child entered. She was taking notes, she said, because she wanted her child to get into an Ivy League school and she needed to make suggestions to the teachers on how to improve her child's education.

Mothering is a difficult job today, and it is not widely acknowledged, insists Suniya Luthar, a developmental psychologist, researcher, and, yes, mother. Since 2000—reversing a forty-year trend—women of peak working age, twenty-five to fifty-four, have been dropping out of the workforce, increasingly to concentrate on raising children.

Based at Columbia University's Teachers College, Luthar has conducted pioneering studies of childhood today among the suburban and urban affluent and among poor inner-city youth. She has both personal and professional perspectives on the inner and outer lives of mothers. "Parents are generally aware of the shallow subculture in which children today are growing up," she says. "They are worried about whether their kid will make it. The economic split between rich and poor is widening. They know that the stakes are higher. They want more for their kids." Since their own sense of self and sense of efficacy rest on their accomplishments, they buy into the same proposition for their children: you're only as good as you achieve. "So," she adds, "they do what they know how to do, which is to exert control." Parents are "oblivious to the damage to kids" precisely because "we grow up thinking accomplishments are important to self-worth."

Women in the higher socioeconomic classes set very high standards for themselves both professionally and as parents. "They are successful, smart, high-achieving, accomplished," says Luthar. "They have a professional attitude of wanting to do parenting well. It is, however, a dangerous combination." It underwrites perfectionistic strivings. And kids become the projects of professional moms, especially those who have dropped out of the workforce and have all their energy to focus on the kids.

THREE

Parenting to Perfection

The idea of parenting to perfection may reflect some uniquely American strivings. "My sister in the U.S. has two kids," says an American mother now living in Germany. "She wants to give her children everything. She sends them to a private Montessori school even though she can't really afford it. She doesn't want to say No to the kids; she never even wants to use the word. She has stopped working altogether. She will buy only super brands, because she wants only things of high quality for her kids. She buys only organic food. She's trying so hard to give her kids the perfect childhood. But she won't correct them if they fail to say please or thank you. She must avoid discomfort and maintain a high standard of living because the perfect childhood is about pleasure. Children are supposed to be happy."

Leaving nothing to chance, anxious parents are rewriting child development as a business plan. Doing so provides the illusion of control over a process that is more like sleep and sexual arousal: it can only be allowed, not willed; it unfolds on its own timetable. However, scheduling and time management, basic elements of professionalism, constitute one way a generalized sense of pressure slips surreptitiously into the lives of children. "I find parents less willing to indulge their children's sense of time than they used to," reports the social historian Peter Stearns. "This represents a change particularly for mothers. You're busy. You don't have the time it takes to let kids do things at their own pace in their own way. So you either force-feed them or you do it for them."

"Parents treat children as projects, as things to be helped and shaped and pushed and prodded," says Steven Mintz. "It's the sense that I am going to create a resume on two legs." Parents have always dreamed of perfection, but it used to be a very surface thing—posture, strict feeding schedules. Now, he says, perfection is defined so exclusively in terms of achievement that no other path to adulthood exists. As he laments in *Huck's Raft,* there's no room for "odysseys of self-discovery outside the goal-driven, overstructured realities of contemporary childhood."

Parenthood in the grip of professional values is detrimental to children, but the incredible shrinking family almost demands the encroachment of professional values on parenting. "The fewer kids you have, the more precious they become and the more risk-averse you get," explains David Anderegg, who chronicles the rise of parental anxiety in *Worried All the Time.* The more kids you have, the more you understand that each has his own temperament—and that your contribution is not the only thing influencing developmental outcomes.

Parenting has been so colonized by professional values that even toddlers have business cards. Not long ago I was introduced to a writer I knew only by byline. When she got up to leave, we vowed to be in touch, and I asked for her card. "I don't have one," she lamented. "But I do have my daughter's." Her daughter, she told me only moments before, had just turned seven. "Your daughter has business cards?" I blurted, before I had time to rein in my surprise. "We used them more when she was younger," she explained. "They are especially handy for making playdates."

The intentions of parents in arranging things for their kids are actually noble. In reality, says Stearns, parents are spending more time with their kids today than parents did twenty years ago. "All of this is with the best motives." But in getting such "well-organized, regimented childhoods, kids just don't have much of their own breathing room in which they can say, 'Well, you know, I've thought about this and I actually don't like it very much,' or, 'I'd like to try that, I'm not very good at it, but I'd still like to try it for a while.'" Parental guidance today has as its "main goal the turning in of the kinds of performances that will get you into the best possible college." There isn't much room for a child to build his or her own identity.

The goal orientation that inspires early Princeton dreams hinges on an outsize sense of control, a belief that outcomes are thoroughly predictable, that high-achieving children can be simply, predictably engineered by parents—if they are conscientious enough and dedicated to the task. "Not only do people expect perfection in all things, but they expect to produce this perfection themselves," says Barry Schwartz, professor of psychology at Swarthmore College. They will fail—*inevitably*—because while people do indeed exert far more control over their lives than previous generations dared hope, the amount of control they *expect* to exert keeps ratcheting upward. The goalposts keep moving. "The more we are allowed to be the masters of our fates in one domain of life after another, the more we expect to be." So despite the increased control, there will be occasions that people will, by their own reckoning, count as failure. Sometimes they will lose a game. Because we live in a culture whose "officially acceptable style of causal explanation focuses on the individual," people will blame themselves rather than circumstances, leading to a widespread sense of stress and the ubiquity of clinical depression and anxiety. If the amount of control that you expect to exert keeps going up, then the fact that you have more control is of dubious psychological benefit, Schwartz explains. "Control, like everything else, is evaluated against expectations." Whether or not it brings psychic payoffs for parents, that doesn't stop parents from desperately trying to exert ever-increasing amounts of control.

The Endless Report Card

"I don't understand it," said one bewildered student, speaking for the five others seated around the dining table with me during lunch at a small residential college in the Northeast. "My parents were perfectly happy to get Bs and Cs when they were in college. But they expect me to get As." The others were nodding in agreement and offering their own particular versions. Hothouse parents are not only overinvolved in their children's lives; they demand perfection from them in school. Because parents now gain their status from the performance of their children, they attempt to engineer perfection in their kids. Parental pressure plus an excess of expectations creates perfectionist parents, who in turn create perfectionist kids. If ever there was a blueprint for breeding psychological distress—crippling rigidity, intense self-involvement, perpetual self-evaluation, relentless frustration—that's it.

No one knows this better than the psychologist Randy O. Frost, a professor at Smith College. His research over the past two decades has helped define the dimensions of perfectionism, examine its antecedents, and establish its effects.

"If someone does a task at work/school better than me, then I feel like I failed the whole task."

"Other people seem to accept lower standards from themselves than I do."

"My parents want me to be the best at everything."

"As a child, I was punished for doing things less than perfectly."

"I tend to get behind in my work because I repeat things over and over."

"Neatness is very important to me."

Each one of these statements captures a facet of perfectionism:

Concern over mistakes, reflecting negative reactions to mistakes, a tendency to interpret mistakes as equivalent to a failure and to believe that one will lose the respect of others following failure.

Personal standards, reflecting the setting of very high standards and the excessive importance placed on these high standards for self-evaluation.

Parent expectations, the tendency to believe one's parents set very high goals.

Parental criticism, the perception that one's parents are (or were) overly critical.

Doubting of actions, reflecting the extent to which people doubt their ability to accomplish tasks.

Organization, reflecting the tendency to emphasize order and orderliness.

By itself, having high standards (or being orderly) does not impale a person on perfectionism; it is necessary, but not sufficient. "Most people who are successful set very high standards for themselves," observes Frost. "They tend to be happy." What turns life into the punishing pursuit of perfection is the extent to which people are worried about mistakes.

Concern with mistakes and doubts about actions are absolute prerequisites for perfectionism. Perfectionists fear that a mistake will lead others to think badly of them; the performance aspect is intrinsic. They are haunted by uncertainty whenever they complete a task, which makes them reluctant to consider something finished. "People may not necessarily believe they made a mistake," explains Frost, "they're just not quite sure; they doubt the quality of their actions. This intolerance for uncertainty is a very big variable in obsessive compulsive disorder and generalized anxiety disorder, too."

But it's only paralyzing in the presence of parental criticism and demanding expectations. It's one thing to strive for perfection, another to demand it. "Overly demanding and critical parents put a lot of pressure on kids to achieve," says Frost. "And our studies show that is associated with perfectionism." It's transmitted in subtle ways. There's a modeling effect, so that parents who are obsessively concerned with mistakes have children who are. And there's an interpersonal effect, transmitted by an authority figure in your life who is overly critical and demanding. Demanding and harsh parents, particularly fathers, produce perfectionistic daughters who constantly evaluate themselves critically; as they approach adolescence, girls become especially sensitive to the judgments of others.

Concern with mistakes is a reflection of what Frost calls the core issue in perfectionism, the unspoken belief or doubt that arises in a child's mind: "I'm incompetent or unworthy." It leads to hypercriticalness and the rigid adherence to strict standards of performance under all conditions. It is the element of perfectionism most associated with psychopathology. And it comes about because a child has been made to feel that approval is contingent on performance. The conditionality of love doesn't have to be stated and can be communicated in "the way the whole environment is structured," says Frost. "If the parent is enthusiastic only when the child accomplishes something or spends a lot of time working at something, then it's unspoken yet demonstrated by the environment. The child feels she has to pursue perfection in order to feel like a true, worthwhile person."

Pushing for perfection seriously clashes with children's developmental needs. If a child's sense of self comes to rest on her accomplishments, she buys into the idea that she's only as good as she achieves. Driven from within to achieve that impossible ideal, perfection, she becomes compliant and self-focused.

"There's a difference between excellence and perfection," explains Miriam Adderholdt, a psychology instructor at Davidson County Community College in Lexington, North Carolina, and author of *Perfection-*

ism: What's Bad About Being Too Good? Excellence involves enjoying what you're doing, feeling good about what you've learned, and developing confidence. Perfection involves feeling bad about a 98 and always finding mistakes no matter how well you're doing. It leads directly to obsessiveness, negativity, and depression. Perfectionism is transmitted from parents to kids. "A child makes all As and one B," says Adderholdt. "All it takes is the raising of an eyebrow for the child to get the message."

Once perfectionism seeps into the psyche and creates a pervasive personality style, it lowers the ability to take risks and reduces creativity and innovation—exactly what's *not* adaptive in the global marketplace. It keeps kids from engaging in challenging experiences and testing their own limits; they don't get to discover what they truly like or to create their own identity. Further, perfectionism reduces playfulness and the assimilation of knowledge. If you're always focused on your own performance and on defending yourself, you can't focus on a learning task. Perfectionism, well recognized as a basic feature of anorexia, destroys self-esteem. It is a steady source of negative emotions because, rather than reaching toward something positive, those in its grip are focused on the very thing they most want to avoid—negative evaluation. They are hyper-attuned to signs of possible failure.

You could say that perfectionism is a crime against humanity. Adaptability is the characteristic that enables the species to survive, and the one thing that perfectionism does is rigidify behavior—just when the world requires flexibility and comfort with complexity and ambiguity. It reflects all-or-nothing thinking, and it turns kids into success junkies, needing steady fixes of achievement, even accolades. It is the academic analogue of celebrity.

The truly subversive aspect of perfectionism is that it leads people to conceal their mistakes. Unfortunately, that very self-protective strategy prevents a person from getting crucial feedback, feedback that confirms the value of mistakes and feedback that affirms self-worth. Thus there is no way of countering the belief that worth hinges on performing perfectly. The desire to conceal mistakes eventually forces people to avoid situations in which they are mistake-prone—an outcome Frost sees in athletes who reach a certain level of performance that gets too much for them, and then abandon the sport altogether.

Frost also looked at writing ability and perfectionism in college students. "We found that those who were high in concern over mistakes and doubts about actions did poorly on a writing test. The way people learn to write well is by sitting down and writing something, showing their work to others, and having it critiqued. Those who are perfectionistic avoid having anyone else look at their writing. They avoid courses that require them to give writing samples for someone else to read. They don't have the opportunity to develop their writing skills because they don't put themselves in that environment." So it is that the pressures of perfectionism keep people from developing the very skills—including social skills and emotion-regulation skills—that would help them cope with many of the challenges they will encounter in life.

Perfectionism is self-defeating in still other ways. The incessant worry about mistakes actually undermines performance. The Canadian psychologists Gordon L. Flett and Paul L. Hewitt, who have observed the elements of perfectionism in children as young as four, studied the debilitating effects of anxiety over perfect performance on athletes. They uncovered what they call "the perfection paradox." "Even though certain sports require athletes to achieve perfect performance outcomes, the tendency to be cognitively preoccupied with the attainment of perfection often undermines performance." Overconcern about mistakes gives them a failure orientation.

Performance pressures don't harm only athletes. They undermine performance in cognitively based academic skills such as math—especially in those students who would otherwise be likely to succeed because of superior working-memory capacity. Such students are most apt to choke under pressure, which selectively erodes their memory capacity—and they wind up performing only as well as average students.

Perfection, once understood and admired as an abstract ideal, is now imposed on the reality of children, whom it harms not least because it makes them bear an excess of parental expectations. To consign children to the pursuit of perfection is to trap them in an illusion. Like the anorexic literally dying to be thin, perfectionism consumes more and more of the self. Among its many paradoxes, there's yet one more: it is ultimately self-destructive to devote all one's psychic resources to oneself.

Because parental actions are more powerful in children's lives than adults may realize and criticism conveyed the wrong way is a sine qua non of perfectionism, parents desperately need to know how to criticize kids. Criticism that communicates that affection or approval is conditional on good performance is lethal. It can lead to perfectionism and to enormous self-doubt. It wrecks self-esteem. What's toxic to kids is the actual or threatened withdrawal of affection or the parental expression of anger when they get something wrong. Adults who are disappointed in a child's performance would be better off using their dissatisfaction constructively, not as an occasion to lash out. Best is to ask the child to evaluate his or her own performance: "Are you happy with it?" "What did you get out of it?" "What would you do differently next time?"

How to praise kids is critical, too, because the wrong messages can also reinforce the need to be perfect. It's more effective to single out effort rather than praise talent, intelligence, or achievement. Instead of telling a kid he's brilliant or smart when he gets a great grade on a paper, a parent should say, "You're a really good thinker," and specify what is good about the thinking: "It's great that you connected this to that." Better still to ask a question that focuses a child on the thinking: "What did you learn?" or "What got you interested in this?" If kids are praised for intelligence and then they do poorly at something, they think they're not smart anymore, and they lose interest in work. But kids praised for effort get energized in the face of difficulty. Praising effort shifts focus to the process rather than the product, and that illuminates the pathway to maintaining excellence without enslavement to perfectionism. It highlights the means of mastery that will generalize to success in many different areas. Trophy kids turn out to be commodities, tied up in what they produce, not how they handle things. When parents say "How did you make that happen?"—not "Wow, you did that well"—they help kids discover what they are good at and why. Even seemingly innocuous praise that says "I'm proud of you" when a child does well can put the kid in a bind. It can make a child feel responsible for a parent's emotional state.

Emote Control

Seen from the macro level, perfectionism is a truly intrusive form of parenting that attempts to control the psychological world of the child. The behaviors and attitudes of parents are imposed on children irrespective of the child's own needs and point of view—there is a fundamental lack of regard for the individual child—and those attitudes have a stranglehold on children's personal thoughts and feelings. The destructive power of perfectionism comes from manipulative parenting techniques that make love totally conditional; withdrawal of affection is waiting in the wings should performance slip.

But where does the psychological control come from? The developmental psychologist Luc Goossens, who heads the Adolescent Research Group at the Catholic University of Leuven in Belgium, has been parsing perfectionism. He and his colleagues have identified two distinct sources of psychological control. One is the parents' own perfectionism, an excessive concern with mistakes, which he terms "maladaptive perfectionism" (to distinguish it from the "adaptive perfectionism" of high standards). The parents, in turn, are strongly achievement oriented and approving of their children *only* when high standards are being met. Using covert, indirect techniques communicated in a subtle, implicit way—a sigh, a strategic silence, a raised eyebrow—perfectionistic parents apply their psychological control to the children, who become self-critical and suffer depression and anxiety as a result. Psychological control is how perfectionism and fear of failure are transmitted from one generation to the next.

But not all parents who exert psychological control of their children are themselves perfectionists, as the students at my table knew. A second major source of psychological control, Goossens's group has found, is parents' separation anxiety. The adults are overly attached to their kids and display anxiety about the growing autonomy of their children because a child's continued development poses the threat of emotional loss and abandonment to the parent. Goossens can see it at work in adults' response to such statements as "I am sad because my teenager doesn't share as much as he or she used to with me." In contrast, parents who are comfortable sitting back a bit say: "I am happy when my teenager relies on me for advice about decisions."

In this type of psychological control, which he dubs "separation-anxious control," parents also use conditional approval, albeit in different circumstances. Parents who have trouble with the increasing autonomy of their children guilt-trip the kids, approving of their children's behavior only when the children remain close to them and dependent on them. Goossens's group found that parents who enjoy their children's increasing autonomy, "and who are ready to serve as a source of security to their children's expanding social world, refrain from autonomy-inhibiting parenting tactics and, hence, show less psychological control." Parents are most apt to resort to keeping their children dependent when their own adult relationships are less than fulfilling.

Whether stirred by fear of loss or need for status markers, both types of psychological control are created by parents who are focused primarily on their *own* personal needs. They "lack an appropriate sense of empathy for their children's perspective and goals." Both types intrude on children's self-direction and sense of self and self-worth, creating kids riddled with depression and anxiety. The difference is that one type of control gives rise to dependency in the kids, the other to self-criticism in them.

In an invited address to the Society for Research on Adolescence in the spring of 2006, Goossens summed up the group's findings. Because a controlling parenting style pressures children to comply with standards that ignore their personal needs and values, it inhibits and constrains children's autonomy. It undermines the development of a mature identity, something all children need to see them through life.

Identity formation is an ongoing dynamic process of constructing and revising a sense of self that may be most intense during the college years. For young people, the university setting is especially conducive to exploring a variety of identity alternatives, making an informed decision or commitment to a single identity, investigating the option in depth, and further identifying with that commitment. There comes a time for choice—say, of career—and once a commitment is made, a focused search for information is likely to only strengthen identity. But the more psychological control students had experienced, Goossens found, the more they were stuck in identity limbo—perpetually exploring a broad array of identity options and forever keeping their options open.

It's hard to know who you are if you can't commit yourself to a path. That lack of a solid identity may help explain a vague sense of inauthenticity that haunts so many young people today. For invasive parents, a child's identity is too insubstantial up against something as quantifiable as achievement and an acceptance letter from Princeton.

The Landscaped Lane to Maladjustment

Suniya Luthar was not at all prepared for the discovery she made about the pressures on kids today. "Children of upper-class, highly educated parents are generally assumed to be at low-risk" of mental health problems, she explains in a highly influential 2005 article, "Children of the

Affluent." But she found that they experience just as many problems as inner-city kids—and in some cases more.

In scouring the "pathways to maladjustment in affluent suburbia," Luthar pinpointed its antecedents. First and foremost are achievement pressures. "Statistical analyses showed, in fact, that children with very high perfectionist strivings—those who saw achievement failures as personal failures—had relatively high depression, anxiety, and substance use, as did those who indicated that their parents overemphasized their accomplishments, valuing them disproportionately more than their personal character." Here is the key point: *among the young, high pressure for achievement is ipso facto experienced as parental criticism.* Children come to feel that their failures to accomplish will seriously diminish the affection, regard, and esteem with which their parents view them as individuals.

The second antecedent was "isolation from adults, both literal and emotional." What that boiled down to was "the surprising unique significance of children's eating dinner with at least one parent on most nights." Dining together was linked not only to kids' self-reported adjustment but also to their performance at school. Resilience, she finds, rests on healthy relationships. It is, after all, an element of relationships—parental attitudes toward achievement, namely excessive pressure for achievement—that is "the big one," the most powerful risk factor for problems.

Incidentally, Luthar found that overscheduling by itself was not harmful to children. Yes, it's a common characteristic of hothouse parenting. But Luthar's data suggest that it's dangerous only when it is combined with criticism, real or implied. She believes that excessive involvement in extracurricular activities has been unfairly scapegoated as a source of distress—when the truly toxic element of children's lives is the perceived parental criticism that comes bundled with adults' high achievement expectations. This is especially true for adolescent girls, sensitive as they are to perceived criticism from those they are close to.

Whatever else, perfectionism is a chronic source of stress. It makes people rigid and fearful. "It takes away our old notion of childhood as a moratorium," says Mintz. "It inflicts adult achievement norms on kids. This is something new. The achievements are defined in adult terms. I suspect that they aren't very meaningful to the kids themselves."

The Tufts University child psychologist David Elkind, long an observer of "hurried children," sees "a lot of underlying worries" among kids today.

Divorce is one. The environment is another. So is the war. Students cite their deep indebtedness by the time graduation rolls around. But the big pressure on kids is achievement. What transforms pressure into disturbance, he says, is that "the notion of progress is all but gone today. We don't see the world getting better; if anything, we see it getting worse. There is a lot of stress, and kids don't have that rosy picture of the future. Plus it is no longer the case that you could always do better than your parents did. That's got to be depressing. There are some few who are able to manage everything. But fewer kids are able to manage all the pressures without becoming depressed and unhappy."

Engineering Versus Endurance

The pursuit of perfection in kids stems from a fundamental misunderstanding of the task of parenting, Anderegg believes. "Parenting is not an engineering task, it's an endurance task. It requires patience and a high tolerance for boredom. Engineering is based on the gathering of knowledge so that if you do something right the first time, you don't have to do it over and over again."

Efficiency, however, is inimical to child rearing. "Parenting is a problem to be solved every day. It's a repetitive quotidian task." That's what maximizes parent-child interaction and persuades children that they are loved. "Seeing kids as a well-designed product is a disease of really smart people," he notes. "They feel they have to make it a task worthy of their time."

Parental perfectionism, unfortunately, is "more and more of a problem." As Exhibit A of the increasing misunderstanding of childhood, Anderegg cites a discussion with a Philadelphia couple about childproofing their home:

> There are childproofing consultants who for $5,000 will go over your home when you have a baby. They put rubber padding on the bathtub tap so your child doesn't bump his head. That attempts to do the job in an engineering way so that you don't have to do it the old-fashioned way of supervising your kids—but the old-fashioned way is better for kids. You don't have to worry about them bumping their head in the bathtub because you're there when they're having a bath. The whole point of parenting is you do it over and over and

over again. The idea that you resolve a parenting problem once and for all, then you don't have to do it again, reflects an impatience with normal, mundane daily life that is a kind of perfectionism. The parents who were paying for all of the childproofing were actually saying "we want to engineer the house so we don't have to watch the kids." But you're supposed to keep an eye on toddlers. It's like running a marathon or being a farmer; you can't just figure out the best way to milk your cows so they stay milked once and for all. You have to milk your cows every day.

It's bad enough that parenting has now become a profession for many people. But for some it has gone further and become a religion—their only source of transcendent meaning. The resulting expansion of parenting into all available psychic space—spiritual meaning as well as professional identity—directly fuels attachment fever, the near-hysterical exaggeration of dangers awaiting kids, overinvolvement in their affairs, and the gross magnification of competition for resources. If your only meaning is through your children, then you have no other explanation of the causality of events—say, whether or not your son gets into Princeton—other than your own efforts.

"If being a parent is all that you do, then of course you're not going to separate," says Anderegg. "Separation isn't even on the table. The child is not only a person but also your work. Even if you can experience your child as a separate being, it's not a separate job. I deal with parents all the time who feel that parenting is such a difficult and time-consuming job that they have to quit their job to be a full-time mom. It is the sole source of their self-esteem. People misunderstand what parenting is all about. In truth, you don't have to be really smart to be a good parent. You have to be imperfect and you have to be reliable. It requires empathy and a fair amount of self-knowledge on the part of the parents. But you don't have to be brilliant."

Parental perfectionism inhibits creativity, curiosity, and innovation; it creates a classroom where only results matter. It makes children unwilling to experiment, explore the unknown, or take even the slightest risk. "Everything students do is calculated to produce better credentials—high grades, great SAT scores, impressive extracurricular activities. They choose classes that play to their strengths, rather than those that might correct their weaknesses or nurture new interests," observes Barry Schwartz. "Even though applicants look better than ever, they may actually be entering college with less learning."

Having watched a whole generation of kids grow up, Anderegg observes that the push for perfection makes kids highly effective—but eventually miserable. "They become adults who can accomplish a lot, but lead terrible home lives. You don't get a sense that you can contribute anything meaningful to your family. If a child has chores and gets to hang out and go for walks with a parent or make stuff together in the kitchen, he gets a sense he can contribute to the family in all kinds of ways. But if you're treated like a little prince or princess where you don't have to do anything except achieve, then it puts a tremendous amount of weight on your achievements."

In short, the push for perfection *undermines* the identity capital of kids. Never allowed to experiment, they can't develop an identity, because they are not allowed to discover, let alone exercise, their own interests. "When in the pursuit of perfection a parent writes a college essay for a child, or pays a professional to 'revise' it, the adult is not protecting the child," says Anderegg. "The adult is corroding the child's sense of self. The adult is robbing a child of a sense of efficacy. The child winds up feeling completely inauthentic."

Masking the Secret of Success

Using children as adult status markers comes at a high cost to children. But the biggest problem with pushing perfection may be that it masks the real secret of success in life. Any innovator will tell you that success hinges less on getting everything right than on how you handle getting things wrong. In real life, you can't call the teacher and demand that a C be changed to an A. This is where creativity, passion, and perseverance come into play. The ultimate irony is that in a flat world, you make kids competitive not by pushing them to be perfect but by allowing them to become passionate about something that compels their interest.

Americans commonly think that talent is the key to success. But a series of provocative new studies suggests that what counts even more is a fusion of passion and perseverance. In a world of instant everything, grit may yield the biggest payoff of all.

Researchers at the University of Pennsylvania have found that those with grit are more likely to achieve success in school, work, and other pursuits—perhaps because their passion and commitment help them endure the inevitable setbacks that occur in any long-term undertaking. Their studies show that intelligence accounts for only a fraction of success—25 percent of the differences between individuals in job performance and a third of the difference in grade point average. A grit questionnaire administered to all 1,223 cadets entering the Class of 2008 at West Point showed that grit is the single best yardstick for predicting who will survive the punishing first weeks at the U.S. Military Academy. It was more telling than high school class rank, SAT scores, athletic experience, and faculty appraisal scores. Character counts.

What fuels grit is probably passion, a mix of emotional and intellectual connection to a goal. Helping children find their passion, by exposing them to an array of academic and artistic pursuits, may be one of the most important things parents can do for their kids. Grit thrives in the face of moderate challenges, those that are attainable but require considerable effort. Optimism supports grit; it enables people to see the value of working hard to overcome obstacles and solve problems.

The need for grit is generally hidden from young people—until they start college or enter the workforce. That's when they first get to chart their own course and set their own goals. Before then, achievement hinges largely on doing homework—something chosen by others and assigned to you. Grit may be the real secret of success among students of Asian background, who tend to be praised more for effort than ability. Their parents generally have high expectations for their success, but those expectations may be detoxified by lit-from-within passion.

The Shifted Burden

Although parenting has moved to center stage in American culture, it's a very difficult time to be a parent. "Even a quarter century ago there was much social support for healthy parenting," contends Elkind. "The schools were more progressive and child oriented. There was no academic pressure on kids." Media censorship protected kids. Toy makers looked to parents for direction; toys had to reflect parental values. The rights movements of the 1960s and 1970s, he says, were "well-meant and well-needed," but they were falsely extended to children. Society felt it no longer had to protect children—which shifted the burden to parents. And parents are stuck. "Society has changed so rapidly parents can't look to their own childhood for guidance, or their own parents. They look to experts, but they often disagree with one another. So they look to other parents, and that creates a great deal of parent peer pressure."

The biggest issue parents contend with, he believes, is what the future will bring. "It's hard to know what the world is going to look like even 10 years from now. How do you best prepare kids for that? Parents are well-intentioned and they think that somehow earlier is better. But children are still biological beings that develop at certain rates, and that can't be hurried. Sometimes by introducing things too early you do more harm than good." Elkind, among many others, is concerned about the dramatic increase in cheating and plagiarism that he sees resulting from the pressure to get good grades—breaking the rules in an all-out attempt to gain an advantage. He also observes "too many of my students who are too interested in the grade and not at all interested in what they are learning." The pressures are forcing students to take more time to get through college, and they are a major contributor to bad decisions about alcohol and sexuality.

Luthar and Anderegg are troubled by yet another finding each of them has made independently. Although parents who want their children to be perfect are inflicting considerable damage on their kids, they shun psychological help for their children. "They wouldn't ever dream of bringing their kid to see a therapist," says Anderegg, "because that would mean that the kid isn't perfect. More and more in my clinical practice, I see adults who think that their child might need to see me, but they don't want their child to feel stigmatized by coming to see a shrink, so they try to get what I would have to offer to the child without me actually seeing the child." This is yet another example of how perfectionism foils a child's best interests.

Ironically, it could be that the children of working-class immigrants to the United States—one out of five children in 2006—are really in the most privileged position today. With parents who speak little English and lack the knowledge and ability to manipulate the system on their behalf, they have no one to run interference for them, no one to clear the path before them or to clean up a mess in their wake. They are forced to learn to bring in their homework and to handle life on their own. They often have a strong social support system at home, but it operates in another language. Perhaps because of language differences, they are apt to use science and math as their paths to upward mobility. That puts them in prime position to make valuable contributions to the new economy.

According to a recent study of over eight hundred college students published in the journal *Child Development* by the developmental psychologist Vivian Tseng, children of immigrants—whether Latino, Afro-American, European, or Asian—are more likely to pursue math and science in college than students from the same ethnic groups whose families have been in the United States for at least one generation. "In interviews, immigrant parents, especially those working in low-wage, low-status jobs, channel their greatest hopes for upward mobility in this new country to their children," says Tseng. "They tell their children that they must do well in school so they can have better lives and more satisfying, better paying, and higher status jobs than their parents. At a time when the U.S. economy is facing demands for highly educated workers in technology and science, children of immigrants may well contribute to our nation's changing workforce needs." Telling a kid to do well is one thing; pressurizing an entire childhood, manipulating a child's environment, and infantilizing a child in the service of success are another.

On a recent cross-country airline flight, I was seated next to a woman who is a vice president of a major investment group. She herself isn't a parent, but she comes in regular contact with young people. She confided that she now makes it a point *not* to hire any but the children of first-generation immigrants. Why? I asked. Because, she said, she has found that the kids of immigrant parents are resourceful, hardworking, and good at figuring things out and at problem solving. The "fancy kids," she said, are not persevering, not willing to work hard, not clever at problem solving, not resourceful. The kids she hires who did well in school but whose parents didn't speak English all that well had to figure out things for themselves; they couldn't rely on their parents. Their "disadvantage" wound up making them stronger.

FOUR

We're All Jewish Mothers Now

There was a woman born in a small East European village in the late eighteenth century, a time when the Jewish population there faced real dangers of persecution. Buxom, benevolent, a natural nurturer, she started her career as mother with unremitting solicitude about every aspect of her child's welfare. Worry—especially that her child might not have enough to eat—was both her expression of affection and her duty. Without her protection, the family might not survive. Excluded (by gender) from the communal prayers and rituals revered by her religion and through which commitment to it was expressed, and lacking political or religious authority of her own, she could seek fulfillment and power—validation—only by living vicariously through her children, especially her sons, and by obsessing over her daughters' marriage prospects.

Eventually she came to America, where she was both transformed and assimilated, perhaps beyond her wildest dreams. She still wielded emotional and psychological power, specializing in guilt and anxiety, but, like the landscape itself, her expectations expanded enormously. The traditional Jewish worship of education now had free expression—her son must be a doctor, and her daughter must marry one. (Question: According to Jewish law, when is a fetus considered viable? Answer: When it graduates from medical school.) She would take pleasure and pride in their achievements, so she applied pressure on them to be perfect or, failing that, excellent. (Question: What is a genius? Answer: An average student with a Jewish mother.) Freed from constant household chores by modern technology, she focused even more intensely on mothering. (Question: What's the difference between a Rottweiler and a Jewish mother? Answer: Eventually the Rottweiler lets go.)

She became Molly Goldberg, *The Nanny*'s Sylvia Fine, and reached her apotheosis as the suffocating Sophie Portnoy in Philip Roth's *Portnoy's Complaint*. "Alex, I don't want you to flush the toilet," Sophie yells to her son. "I want to see what you've done in there . . . Don't lie to me. Do you or do you not stuff yourself with French fries and ketchup on Hawthorne Avenue after school?" Guilt, manipulation, fear, demandingness, overprotection, aggressive overinvolvement, invasiveness, and supreme infantilization in one brief outburst.

"The mother-child relationship is so intense, because it is fulfilling lots of needs of the mother," says Myrna Hant, a scholar at the UCLA Center for the Study of Women who has tracked the evolution of Jewish mothers as portrayed on television. "It provides her full Jewish citizenship. She lives through her children because, originally, she had no other options." Psychotherapists—to say nothing of novelists and comedians—have for nearly two full generations earned their livelihood off the psychic violence she did, especially to her anxious, angry, or impotent sons.

Although women today have their own means of esteem and validation, the Jewish mother has triumphed as a cultural archetype of anxiety and aspirations, an icon of invasiveness. In the ultimate rags-to-riches saga, she transported herself from the confines of the shtetl to the sprawl of America's suburbs with the remarkable effect of recasting parenthood in her image while shedding ethnic specificity. We are all Jewish mothers now—even the fathers, because a whole generation of men who felt their own dads hadn't done the job right came along just as women needed them to pitch in. In teaching their husbands how to parent, modern women have been instructing them in the concerns and expectations of Jewish mothers. They, too, see the world as a hostile place. They, too, wring reassurance from baby monitors and obsess over educational toys. They, too, panic about sexual predators, stranger abductions, even germs lurking in shopping carts. They, too, hover and demand perfection. The difference is that there once was a genuine historical context for "intense and insatiable" Jewish mothering, and there was far more reality to the fears the Jewish mother faced in the shtetls of Europe, punctuated as they were by pogroms. Today's parents, on the other hand, are highly entrepreneurial; they thrive on worries mostly of their own manufacture.

Overinvolved parents do more than create havoc for school officials and coaches. They infantilize their children, creating dependent children who are stuck developmentally and are psychologically fragile. Their children are unable to manage everyday affairs. If they hit a minor speed bump—getting laid off from a job, as the economy almost continually shifts—they often fall apart. They are frequently thrown by minor setbacks, and they seem to come unglued over serious challenges. They can't master the tasks of adulthood—and seem to have little inclination even to try. They are overly attached to their parents and their parents to them. Think of their upbringing as death-grip parenting. It's a case of emotional attachment gone badly awry.

Attachment: Nature's Contribution to Parenting

The emotional attachment of parent to child and child to parent is absolutely necessary for an infant's safety and survival. It is also crucial for the development of his brain, both in its physical architecture and in its function. Attachment is the means by which an infant gets his primary needs met, and it becomes the engine of subsequent social, emotional, and cognitive development. The early social experience of the infant stimulates growth of the brain and shapes the emerging mental processes, including perception, motor activity, the generation and regulation of emotion, memory, even a sense of self. Moreover, attachment sets up nature's first coping system, the one that is the foundation for all the others. In doing so, it carves out in the infant's brain the neural pathways that will sculpt what are likely to be lifelong patterns of response to almost everything, from later tolerance to solitude, to reaction to stress, to behavior with romantic partners. Through influence on the neuroendocrine system, it also establishes the sensitivity of the infant's inborn alarm system and level of reactivity to fear. Attachment contains in it the platform for the child's ultimate separation, development of an independent identity, and ability to survive autonomously—individuation, as it's known in the psych biz.

In their death-grip parenting, today's adults are setting their children up for fragility and failure by overriding and overwhelming the necessary conditions for attachment. For all its importance, attachment has its share of subtlety.

Nature puts mothers in the leading position to be the primary attachment figure to their infants, but because the process is so critical to survival, they are not an infant's only option. Anyone who becomes the steady, responsive caregiver—it could be a mother, a nanny, a father, or a grandparent—can come to serve as the primary attachment figure for an infant. The attachment figure is the person the infant is most likely to turn to under stress, and attachment is the means through which the infant learns to regulate distress. The attachment figure is the infant's primary solution to experiences of fear.

While the bond of mother to child normally gets off to a quick start—propelled internally by hormones as well as externally by holding and feeding and eye contact with an irresistibly adorable creature—the attachment of child to parent forms over the first year of life. Researchers report that first attachments are generally formed by seven months of age, and that attachments develop to only one or a few persons. First in physical reality, gradually in an internalized replica or image, the attachment figure becomes for the infant a source of security, a bona fide source of comfort in times of stress, and a resource of stability and support enabling him to gradually move out into a wider world and explore the environment. A secure attachment confers enduring resilience in the face of difficulty and affects eagerness to explore and comfort level in novel surroundings.

If there is magic to attachment, it is that this most powerful of engines of development swings into gear completely on its own, without much fanfare. It doesn't require custom-made nursery furniture or cashmere swaddling blankets. It doesn't take flash cards, Baby Einstein, or Mommy and Me classes. It *does* require social interaction. It grows unceremoniously, spontaneously, and naturally while other things—the most mundane of experiences—are going on. It develops in the ordinary course of events, the outgrowth of a million quotidian interactions, a parent being near and responding with regularity and sensitivity day in and day out to an infant's signals, his needs for care and contact and comfort—a warm hand placed comfortingly on a baby's belly as her diaper is changed, a gaze of affection during feeding, a smile or an expression of surprise elicited and returned. It's the regularity, the *reliability* of response that counts. Infants turn out to be little wizards at some things, and they are good at detecting inconsistencies and setting up expectations based on prior experience. The reliability of care gets engraved into their nervous system and becomes the cornerstone of their sense of security in life.

The Seeds of Self-Regulation

Although the primary goal of attachment is to ensure the survival of the infant, it does much more than that. As with all development, early experience organizes later behavior. It does this by literally shaping the growing brain, stimulating its structure and paving the pathways that will underlie subsequent mental functioning. As the infant's experience in the world activates neurons, it establishes patterns of nerve connections throughout the brain; each neuron forges connections to many other neurons, so that experience elaborates and strengthens specific circuits in the brain through which all nerve impulses travel. The intricate networks of interconnected neurons that flourish in response to experience give rise to all our mental processes. It is one of the most fundamental facts of modern neuroscience: the attachment relationships of the infant shape the developing brain. In short, social experience is the cradle of emotional and intellectual development.

"Human connections create the neural connections from which the mind emerges," says Daniel J. Siegel, a neuroscientist at UCLA. What is especially important about the first years, he points out, is that "the brain structures that mediate social and emotional functioning begin to develop during this time, in a manner that appears to be dependent upon interpersonal experience." There is, he stresses, "no need to bombard infants or young children (or possibly anyone) with excessive sensory stimulation in hopes of building better brains. This is an unfortunate misinterpretation of the neurobiological literature—that somehow more is better. It just is not so . . . More important than excessive stimulation in the early years of development, however, are the patterns of interaction between child and caregiver. Attachment research suggests that collaborative interpersonal interaction, not excessive sensory stimulation, can be seen as the key to healthy development."

Underlying the infant's capacity for attachment are basic neural circuits that are already in place at birth to drive the infant to form a strong social bond with his caregiver; this is the hard-wiring of the attachment system. That attachments emerge in response to interactions with maltreating persons is testimony to the built-in motivation for attachment infants come equipped with from the start. Through myriad synaptic connections that will arise in the brain as the process unfolds and experience accumulates, attachment comes to influence many other functions of the brain. One of the most important is emotion regulation, the ability to manage and cope with emotional arousal, particularly the negative emotions—anxiety, sadness, anger—but also including such positive emotions as excitement. It matters little whether the emotions are generated externally by life events or internally by memories of such events. Emotion regulation is a requirement for paying attention and for learning. Attachment also powerfully influences cognition itself, social adjustment, and overall mental health. Although we may never recall explicitly what happened to us as infants, the experiences we have with our caregivers insinuate themselves into our emotions, our behavior, our perception, and our mental models of the world of others and of ourselves. Nurture, scientists now know, becomes nature.

What is important about the interaction between caregiver and child is that a parent's responses are directly contingent upon the signals given off by the infant. There is attunement between the two, a deep mutuality of experience—a collaborative dance of emotional engagement, through which their states of mind become closely aligned. The parenting isn't overbearing; it isn't intrusive. It is subtle, applied with sensitivity for recognizing the signals sent by the child and a willingness to make sense of them. "The signals sent by each member of an attuned dyad are directly responsive in quality and timing with each other," explains Siegel in *Infant Mental Health Journal*. "These attuned communications often have their foundation in the nonverbal signals that are shared between two individuals. Eye contact, facial expression, tone of voice, bodily gestures and timing and intensity of response are all fundamental aspects of nonverbal signals. The sharing of nonverbal signals creates a joining of two minds at a basic level of 'primary' emotions."

Through the subtleties of attuned communication, the adult—much like an experienced dancer leading his partner in a waltz—comes to regulate the infant's emotional states, both positive and negative. The interactive dyadic process is really a form of mutual co-regulation. The infant thus comes to use the connection to the parent to regulate her own states of mind (it is never the parent's prerogative to use the infant to regulate her own states of mind). Ultimately, in a secure attachment, that ability is gradually taken on wholly by the child herself, and she develops a more autonomous form of self-regulation, one that is always available to her as she moves into the wider world. It is what actually enables her to move into the wider world without being crippled by fear.

All the while, through the aligned states of mind, the contingent communications, and the responsive connections with others, the infant builds a coherent sense of self. It is rooted in the direct experience of the brain as the infant interacts with the external world, his own body, his mind, and especially those closest to him. The sense of self emerges as a result of healthy connections with others.

By staying connected to the infant through negative emotional states and sharing them with her, the adult helps reduce the negativity and soothes the distress. The infant comes to know that she will not be abandoned during such moments and that painful emotional states can be calmed.

The primary caregiver who becomes the agent of attachment functions as a "safe haven" and a "secure base," the person the infant turns to at times of stress or emotional upset and the person who, through the accumulated experience of availability when needed, also allows movement into a widening world. When scared or upset, the infant goes searching for his attachment figure for comfort and reassurance. The availability, the presence of the attachment figure by itself, has a calming influence; that enables the child to pay attention to the world around him and explore his environment, deploying curiosity, gaining information and understanding, developing interests, learning about and expanding his own abilities, and, over time, gaining confidence in his ability to manage on his own. Willingness to explore is crucial, because exploration is the key to resourceful thinking. The attachment figure is also a source of connection and joy, as well as of soothing.

Coping by Contact

Attachment is usually so well established by the end of an infant's first year that it is possible to test the nature and quality of the bond at that time. By one year, clear patterns of individual differences in attachment emerge. Traditionally, attachment is tested by gauging how a child responds to a series of short separations from and reunions with his caregiver in an unfamiliar playroom. Will the child feel secure enough to explore the room and its toys or interact with a stranger who briefly takes the place of his mother when she leaves the room? And when Mom returns minutes later, how will he react to her? Will he chillingly ignore her? Or will he cling to her for a dose of comfort before he toddles off her lap to try out some tempting new toy in the corner? In short, it's a test of coping strategies, how the infant uses the mother when he is stressed by a brief separation from her.

Observers discern three basic patterns of attachment. An attachment is said to be *secure* when an infant, who may or may not cry on separation, welcomes his mother back by looking at her or hugging her, possibly asking to be picked up or climbing onto her lap; is reasonably quickly comforted by her presence; and then quickly scampers off to turn his attention to other things around him. Because he has learned that his mother's response is reliable and predictable, he can relax and play in her presence. His attention is flexible—he is capable of playing when his mother is around and crying and calling to her when she is absent. Never having been rejected, such infants grow up with the ability to spontaneously express distress and other emotions. Attention can then be freely devoted to the full development of abilities. Studies show that securely attached infants grow up to have enhanced emotional flexibility, social functioning, and cognitive abilities. They appear to have resilience in the face of adversity.

There are at least two kinds of *insecure* attachment. Some infants become *anxious-avoidant*. Outwardly, they are indifferent to separation from their caregiver and do not run to her for comfort when she returns; they actively ignore her. Inwardly, however, the biological picture is quite different. Their systems show that they are experiencing internal distress, and on reunion they are exerting energy to look away from and avoid the caretaker, diverting their attention to exploration, and often preferring a stranger to Mommy. These infants learn to inhibit expression of their emotions, especially the negative ones of anxiety and anger.

Other infants display *anxious-ambivalent* or *anxious-resistant* attachment. They get extremely distressed when the mother or caregiver leaves the room *and* when she returns, sometimes even more so, and they refuse to settle down. They are too petulant, irritated, and distressed to take comfort in her return. They are preoccupied with her when she is present, unwilling to leave her side to play or explore. They both cling to her and express dissatisfaction with her, pushing her away.

Securely attached children can run to their mother for comfort one minute, then dash off on independent explorations the next; they have no trouble transitioning between the two. And they are comforted by physical contact with their mother. Insecurely attached infants, on the other hand, have trouble switching from closeness seeking to exploring, and physical contact with Mommy often brings out negative feelings. Children with insecure attachment, whatever the form, are likely to become emotionally rigid. Their attention is inflexible; in one case the infants maintain themselves under stress by suppressing reactions, in the other by becoming preoccupied with the mother's whereabouts. They have difficulty in social relationships, experience attention problems, have trouble understanding the minds of others, and are at risk in the face of stressful situations. Studies suggest that their psychological vulnerability is enduring, because it is built on fundamental misconstruction in the brain's neuroendocrine response to stress. Both types of infants are adopting strategies to modulate their emotional arousal—one over-regulates it, one under-regulates it—because they are uncertain in their expectation that their caregiver will do her part.

In classic tests of attachment around the world, about 65 percent of children display secure attachment, regardless of the culture. The nature of insecure attachments varies by culture. In Western Europe and the United States more babies develop an avoidant attachment than a resistant attachment. In some countries, namely Israel, more babies develop a resistant attachment than an avoidant one. But that assortment may be changing, at least in the United States. It may be that more American infants are developing a resistant attachment.

How the patterns of attachment are set has something to do with the inborn temperament of the child but even more to do with the behavior of the caregiver toward the little one. From extensive observations of parents and children at home and in the laboratory, researchers have found that mothers of infants who become securely attached respond consistently and appropriately to their infant's signals, such as crying. They are sensitive, responsive, accepting, and affectionate when holding and taking care of their babies. They are prompt and comforting in responding to distress. By contrast, the mothers of anxious-avoidant infants are consistently rejecting of their infants. Their responsiveness is simply limited. They display an aversion to close physical contact with their babies and are not emotionally expressive toward them. The mothers of the anxious-resistant or anxious-ambivalent infants are different in other ways. Although they are generally insensitive to their infant's signals, they are not highly rejecting. They have no aversion to close physical contact; they are just inept, both in holding their infants and in answering to their needs. They tend to be intrusive, and their actions are not related to the infant's signals of need. Their responses are not contingent upon their babies in the pacing of face-to-face interactions. As a result, they are inconsistently responsive to their infants, and their responsiveness is, from the child's perspective, unpredictable. As the children get a little older, they often exhibit exaggerated expressions of affection on reunion with parents. The mothers also tend to discourage autonomy.

Study upon study of attachment shows that the strategies the insecurely attached infants employ when stressed or needy are not random behaviors; they are adaptations to the less-than-optimal care they receive and learn to expect.

Mental Representation: The Genius of Attachment

There is yet another, even more magical aspect of attachment. Attachment is manifested through patterns of behavior, but the behaviors themselves do not constitute attachment. Attachment is completely internal. Attachment starts as a physical process, in proximity of a real parent to an infant and responsiveness to the infant's needs. Yet it sows the seeds of its transcendence, its evolution into a nonphysical system in which the physical presence of the parent is not required.

The parent or other attachment figure undergoes a radical transformation in the infant's brain. Over the course of the first year of development, the parental figure, which is a flesh-and-blood reality, is reproduced in the baby's brain as an enduring image, an iconic representation of the caregiver, what psychologists call an internal working model. The importance of this transformation can't be overstated. It, too, happens as a result of regular care from an actual person. The internal figure also soothes the child, relieves distress, and enables self-regulation. But the internal representation of the caregiver has powers that a real parent could not possibly have. It is portable, and therefore it is potentially always present. It is flexible, applicable to all kinds of uncomfortable situations. And it can be conjured on demand. In fact, it *must* be, for development to proceed. Eventually, the internal representation is even more important than the actual parent. It is the secret agent of resilience in the face of future adversity. It also takes on an increasing load of the work of child development.

But for it to be engaged, for this ever-present parent-within to do the critical work that needs to be done, separation is absolutely necessary. It helps to remember that independence and autonomy are the eventual goals of child rearing.

An infant who cries after his mother leaves the room and embraces her on reunion is proof of a very good thing: that the mother exists in reality, but also some image, or representation, of her has taken up permanent residence in the child's brain. This representation was stimulated by the actual presence of the caretaker in early life. Through the contingent, collaborative interactions with the caregiver, through the repeated firing of nerve cells in coherent patterns, experience becomes generalized in the infant's brain and gives rise to internal maps of these encounters with the external world. As the baby's mind comes into being, he develops a mental map or schema of his interactions with his caretaker that incorporates expectations about the future behavior of the adult toward him. Based on his growing experiences, the child will also form a mental representation of himself as a distinct self. Like the brain's sensory mechanisms interpreting and responding to sights and sounds, the process of building trust in others involves constructing models of other people and using those models as foundations for making decisions.

Internal representation is the operating system of emotional attachment. It is an ingenious way of continuing the parental relationship while according the child freedom to move about the world with a sense of security. It is the long leash of development. The image of the caretaker that takes shape in the mind is portable, protean, and adaptable to any situation. It may sing arias of encouragement, supply advice, or just provide a benign sense of presence. It is the instrument of autonomy and self-regulation. It is also the template for all those we will come to love. They, too, will have a double life, the one in reality and the one inside our heads, and the representations of them will serve us the same way.

The image of the caretaker will be the stimulus of much further growth. It will shape the child's actions and reactions, perhaps for a lifetime. It becomes an agent of psychological resilience and emotional flexibility. Where attachment is secure, internal working models of the caretaker function as infinite care packages bundled into our neurons, a thou-art-with-me sense that the child can call on whenever he wants or needs to. Just as an infant issues a cry of distress to bring his mother near, which soothes him, so do we later have access to the inner idea of a loved one when we need to get through difficult times. It is almost infinitely malleable; as children grow, this representation accumulates wisdom and experience, and it is tailored to the demands put on it.

It is also the first abstraction, the first symbol to arise in the infant's developing mind, the germ of his ability to symbolize, the first shoot of his cognitive capacity. Mental representations are more than the basis for abstract mental processes; they also become a prototype for social inter-action and give the child a portal for understanding the minds of others, for figuring out their thoughts, their desires, their beliefs, their intentions—what psychologists call mentalizing, a critical milestone of development.

The mental representation of the caregiver is the psychic lever that opens the brain to later development, to the eventual ability to function as an independent person, to deploy inborn curiosity to explore the world, to pay attention, to develop higher-order mental functions, and, of course, to form our own adult attachments to others. Internal working models influence the way children process information and affect how they approach new situations. The staying power of these internal mod-els, operating largely outside the realm of conscious awareness, allows them to influence development and relationships throughout the life-span. Under some conditions—the loss of a parent, parental divorce, or other negative life events—secure attachments can evolve into insecure attachments. But generally speaking, they are very durable.

Important as it is, internalization of the attachment figure hinges on one thing—separation of parent and child. Separation activates and stim-ulates that basic system of coping with discomfort. Separation, in other words, is absolutely necessary for normal development. Separation isn't merely a test of attachment; it's the goal, the raison d'être. Without sep-aration, the child has no need to learn how to activate and use the parent-within.

It's one thing for Sarah, our friend from Chapter One, to want to be with her baby for six months. It's another to keep the baby yoked to her for four years. By definition, it is intrusive parenting. Intrusive parenting starts early, with misreadings of the child's cues. It fails to recognize the baby's need for experiences of her own, for mini tastings of independence and exposure. It puts the parent's needs for continued closeness before the child's needs for independent exploration. And it keeps the child from internalizing the attachment figure.

In the absence of separation, there can be no summoning of the internalized, mental component of attachment, and the child is deprived of the world's most portable crisis-management system. Instead of a warm and fuzzy mental abstraction that she can call on anywhere, whenever she needs it, an image that she can flex and adapt to whatever situation she finds herself in, she has the actual presence of her parent. Unable to exercise the mental imagery, she will be forever on a short psychological leash. Early interference with a very primary system for development introduces deep disturbances in the children.

"Separation is necessary for internalizing the attachment object so you can carry it around with you in your head," says the child psychologist David Anderegg. "If you never separate, it is not necessary to internalize the attachment figure. In an emergency, the only coping tool you have is to call Mom and Dad." And that impedes development both cognitively and emotionally. You have no defense against emotional distress when something goes wrong in life. And you have no ability to take risks because you don't have the inner resources to call on to calm you in situations of uncertainty. "Parents are glomming themselves on to their children on their own," notes Anderegg. "They are terrified of every aspect of the contemporary world. They are all highly educated and professional parents. To have given up their career, they have made theirs the most important child in the world."

Nurturing: An Extreme Sport

There is such a thing as intrusive attachment. For infants to develop well, there is an optimal level of caregiver sensitivity. It occurs when the intensity of response to the infant's emotional state is moderate, rather than perfect. The bond has to be porous, not airtight. The dance can't always be led and directed by the parent. There is reciprocity, or mutual regulation of parent and child emotional state. Sometimes the child leads the dance.

An overbearing parent can overcontrol a child's reactions, keeping the infant from learning what the attachment system is supposed to deliver—a way for him to regulate his own unpleasant feelings. The purpose of the system is to enable the child to exist outside the presence of the attachment figure. "Minor separations prepare children for massive ones," says Mark Solms, a neuroscientist at University College London and the University of Cape Town in South Africa. "With oppressive attachment you don't have the titrations that allow you to cope. The paradox is that children are then traumatized by the separation experience." Minor separations lead a child to understand that separation is followed by return of the parent; they teach the child to expect that the parent will return, and are not a cause for anxiety. The brain is not a set of mechanical gears. Intrusiveness at a critical developmental juncture creates a nervous system that goes haywire in response to stress.

It would be one thing if Sarah's experience were an anomaly. But such intrusive parenting seems to be taking hold among new parents. Her intense anxiety about being apart from her child becomes a form of control that breeds dependency in her daughter. Researchers have found that such parents see any expression of autonomous functioning of their child as a threat of loss, and they tend to resort to such psychologically manipulative behavior as guilt induction and conditional approval in an attempt to keep their children close and dependent.

The cost of such possessiveness is likely to be high, setting a child up to experience distress on separation. The resulting attachment panic creates widespread emotional disorganization. The child becomes flooded with negative emotion that she is unable to regulate. Parental intrusiveness breeds anxiety and depression because it carries the implicit message "You are fragile and need continuing help."

Overinvolvement creates preoccupied kids unable to detach; they are also wrapped up in their own experiences. Followed into adulthood, they seem to be unable to "let go." It could be that Sarah is dissatisfied or frankly unhappy in her own marriage. Or perhaps she is playing out an anxious attachment that she had to her own mother. It matters not. Whatever the reason, at bottom parents such as Sarah are using their children to solve their own emotional needs, rather than respecting the imperatives of child development.

Risky Business

At first glance, the Clean Shopper looks harmless enough. In fact, it's meant to protect children *from* harm. It is "mom-invented, and made of 100% cotton, quilted fabric . . . designed to fit all standard grocery carts so babies and toddlers are *not exposed to nasty germs and bacteria.*" Its first cousin, the Buggy Bagg, is also a shopping-cart liner but does double duty as a high-chair cover. It goes right to the gut issue and actually names the monsters it aims to subdue: it provides "maximum protection from illness-causing bacteria or viruses like salmonella and e. coli." It also boasts a "padded seat with detachable pillow to allow your child to feel safe and secure."

But on deeper consideration, it turns out to be an extremely cynical, even subversive product. Does anyone really need a shopping-cart liner? How did generations of children survive without them? Shopping-cart liners are invariably marketed to mothers. What mother doesn't want to provide coziness and a sense of security for her child? Forget that the hazards lurking in grocery carts are virtually nil, certainly not worthy of discussion, and any minor exposure that might result would likely be beneficial, having an immunizing effect that stimulates the immune system. Shopping carts are just not major vectors in the transmission of disease. But shopping-cart liners actually perform a sleight of mind, converting the world of experience (the child's) and attention (the parent's) into a universe of hidden dangers requiring an attitude of wariness and mistrust. In buying a grocery-cart liner, a parent is not merely accepting that grocery carts hold hidden dangers that even Jewish mothers never dreamed of. She automatically adds to the inventory of visible and hidden hazards in the world, even in familiar places, and the need for unrelenting parental—and especially maternal—vigilance. Death-grip parenting becomes desirable, necessary, even obligatory.

The desire of parents for a wholly sanitized environment for their kids, totally free from uncertainty, couldn't be clearer than in the rash of new hand-cleansing agents intended for children to take with them to school. The fear and anxiety that are increasingly a part of parenting culture are making overprotectiveness into a science. Whether it's baby monitors, nanny cams, baby-proofing devices, or sanitizing gels, nothing is left to chance. To an astonishing degree, safety concerns have eclipsed other concerns of childhood. Safety doesn't come first. It comes first, last . . . and always. It reflects a dream of total control over the child's safety and, consequently, development, a kind of parental Panopticon in which children are under the constant gaze, literally and metaphorically, of adults. Among teens, the means change, but the principle stays the same; nanny cams give way to Internet activity monitors and cell phones with GPS monitors.

The current climate of child-focused anxiety practically mandates hallucinations of hazard. But from grocery shopping to kidnapping, from sex perverts to video games, the hazards of childhood are wildly exaggerated. Fear is a great marketing prod to parents; it engages their laudable instinct for protection. Manufacturers of all the safety devices sense parental concerns—and then whip them up to a fever pitch in their marketing strategies. An advanced consumer economy such as ours requires the constant marketing of new goods and the creation of new demand. It is a core principle of marketing that one of the most effective marketing tools is anxiety. As a result, we are constantly learning of hazards we never knew existed, like shopping carts. The "cozy liner," one recent mailing to mothers informs us, "provides a cushiony, safe and familiar surface" for your bundle of joy so that "taking trips to the grocery store is a little safer and more convenient for mom." A little safer! In other words, it could be even safer. The fear that's stirred up encourages parents both to hover over their darlings to protect them, despite developmental needs for increasing independence and autonomy, and to engineer a risk-free world for them.

Pedophile Panic and Other Hallucinations of Hazard

It is only a short, frantic leap, psychologically speaking, from grocery-cart liners to pedophile panic. They are psychologically identical—responses to hazards that do not exist to the degree that warrants the kind of worry lavished on them. Sexual crimes against children are actually diminishing, not increasing, in frequency; they have fallen 50 percent in the past ten years, a time of escalating hysteria. It's an epidemic that isn't.

In their growing terror at many aspects of the contemporary world, parents of the 1980s focused their fears on substitute care, culminating in the McMartin scandals. Sensational accusations of molestation by day-care staff were later shown to be wholly without merit. Today that fear has metastasized, broken out of day-care centers, so that it is no longer contained in a specific site. It has generalized. The greatest threat is seen in the faceless predators lurking out in the community, presumed to be ogling the children from just beyond the school playground—the pedophiles.

What both embodiments of fear have in common is that they decree experiences outside the home as the most sexually threatening to children. But that is a gross distortion of risk. In fact, the greatest threat of child physical and sexual harm arises *inside* the home, presented by fam-

ily members, often stepparents, and especially stepfathers—a phenomenon known to social scientists as the Cinderella Effect. Infants and children who do not live with two biological parents face forty to one hundred
times the chance of being injured or killed within the family as those who
live with both biological parents. "Ninety percent of sexual offenses are
committed by people known to their victim, such as family members
and other trusted members of the community," observes the Columbia
University psychiatrist Richard B. Krueger in a 2007 article in the *Los
Angeles Times,* citing the "mindless laws" being passed in the hopes of
protecting communities from known sex offenders. Both embodiments of
fear put all the responsibility for danger on events happening Out There
and assume people have no other fate but to be potential victims.

Parents are more willing to point fingers Out There than to teach children how to avoid hazards that have always existed in the community—
and always will. Yet a review of studies of children taught sexual abuse
prevention strategies showed that kids readily gained the ability to dis-
criminate safe from unsafe situations. Having such knowledge in no way
burdened them with anxiety or complicated their life in any way.

Consider the recent Ohio law now being questioned even by the victims' rights groups that pushed for its passing. The legislation stipulates
that people never even charged with a sex offense could end up on a public registry of sex offenders. Legislators and prosecutors say the civil registry protects the public. It's similar to the database of convicted sex
offenders mandated by Megan's Law, which requires convicted offenders
to register their whereabouts when they are released back into the community—except for the minor detail that listees need not have been
found guilty in a court of law. In the first test of the measure in 2006, a
county prosecutor sought to list a priest accused of molesting a student
in the early 1980s. By dint of an expired statute of limitations, the priest
could no longer be prosecuted or sued. "People deserve to know if they
live near sexual offenders," the prosecutor insisted (although "recidivism
rates for sexual offenders are among the lowest of any class of criminals,"
according to Krueger). Legal observers reply that the registry is a fearmongering attempt to circumvent the law, that statutes of limitations are
necessary because the memories of participants and witnesses degrade
over time.

Fear of pedophiles is cited by many parents as a primary reason for hothouse parenting. Their pedophile panic has a long and sometimes ex-

treme reach. A board member of one of New York City's finer preschools recently reviewed its proposed new guidelines for volunteers and employees working with children. Among them are prohibitions on piggyback rides, touching of the knees or legs, or having a child older than three in your lap. "Imagine teaching preschool and being deemed a child abuser if you touch a two year old's legs!" she observed. Or being deemed an abuser if a four-year-old plops into your lap in a rush of excitement over some new discovery.

Kidnapping is a crime that provides parents with yet another reason to distrust experiences Out There in the community, and it is the most common explanation proffered by parents as to why they regiment their children's lives and manage their playtime. But fear of stranger abduction exists vastly out of proportion to its occurrence. According to the U.S. Department of Justice, kidnapping composes less than 2 percent of all crimes against juveniles, and 76 percent of the kidnappings are perpetrated by family members or acquaintances. Kidnapping collides with adult uncertainties to lead parents to keep their children under constant monitoring. Adults gild the cage with television, amusements, and comfort and see homework, other academic demands, and programmed activities as their allies in keeping kids safe.

Born to Deceive . . . Ourselves

The underlying message of all the hallucinations of hazard is that the world is a very dangerous place. And the only certainty is that home is a safe spot. The distorted view of risk paves the way for today's parents to cheat children of childhood: it creates parental and societal distrust in the natural course of development. As we will see in Chapter Ten, it's gradual exposure to risk, not its removal, that is essential for children.

It isn't that people set out to deceive themselves about risk. But by definition risk deals with uncertainty, and uncertainty gives rise to anxiety, which not only shuts down the intake of information but pitches the brain into a negative emotional state and irrational decision making. Good minds can do bad things to the perception of risk, making risky situations difficult to evaluate both cognitively and emotionally. Risk actually forces the mind to play tricks on itself so that what people think is a rational approach to decision making in the face of risk is a far cry from it.

A whole branch of psychology is devoted to delineating why and how we misperceive risk. Researchers know that the human mind seems to make certain kinds of predictable errors in evaluating risk. For one thing, we give undue attention and weight to rare events that happen to occur, something almost unavoidable if they receive widespread media attention, such as a child abduction. Second, our brains are built to be oversensitive to negative input, so unfortunate events make a bigger impact on the brain than positive events, leading us to misjudge the frequency with which they are likely to occur.

The climate of uncertainty around a specific risk makes the topic emotionally intolerable and thus subject to further distortions. Self-serving biases swing into play. We select the information we want to process, and we are highly selective in the memory search we conduct, leaving out large chunks of data. The more factors there are to consider in evaluating a risk, the more likely we are to bypass reason. By the same token, if we take any action at all to reduce or remove a risk, we are prone to ignore other possible actions that could also help and that might even be of greater benefit. Our need for a sense of control kicks in and contributes to the shutting down of rational analysis of an event's likelihood. We wind up overconfident about what is really a rush to judgment over flimsy information and analysis. The conclusion is inescapable: the perception of risk and the response to it tend to be highly subjective up against our deep desire to keep our children safe.

That could explain why there are some real risks to which we willingly, blindly expose our children and about which we do not whip ourselves into a frenzy—even though they have more of a negative impact on children with far more immediacy and far more frequency, reflecting repetitive everyday exposure. These are the very risks that are closest to us—right in our households—and about which we can do something.

Divorce has to rank high up there. At least 40 percent of all kids are exposed to parental divorce before they reach age eighteen. Every year, over one million children under the age of eighteen are exposed to a divorce in the 1.25 million divorces that occur. There need not be long-term negative effects, but only an ostrich could deny what even the most optimistic of studies show—that separation or divorce knocks kids for a loop for at least a few years, especially boys. One major reason it does so is that it distracts the adults as they contend with their own emotional and financial turmoil, so they just don't do as good a job of parenting; kids feel less cared for. But kids are not immune to direct effects of the emotional turbulence and confusion leading up to and surrounding divorce. What is virtually unmeasurable is that the breakup of their family deeply threatens children's sense of safety and well-being. They do not feel whole or protected. Very often, the feelings of dislocation run so deep that children can't even articulate them. All children undergoing divorce experience a profound sense of loss. They lose what they most love— their whole family.

How divorce will impact children and for how long will depend on many factors, including age (adolescents seem to suffer most in the long haul), the degree to which they were drawn into the conflict, other disruptions such as changes of home or school that may occur, the quality of the relationship with each parent before divorce, the degree of continuing differences and conflict after divorce. Children might display depression or defiance, they might experience more conflicts with their peers, and they often show signs of dependency. Their schoolwork usually suffers, as does their sense of self. There may be more parent-child conflict. That's just the short haul. Many researchers find that the long-term effects are truly insidious and can have a dramatic impact on how one lives one's life. These include a pervasive feeling of discontent with one's life, a floating sense of anxiety, a lingering sense of sorrow, and a heightened sensitivity to betrayal, rejection, and loss.

My point is not to present a catalog of catastrophe—the list of effects would indeed be far longer—but to suggest the rampant irrationality about risks, because it is the absurdly shaky but seldom examined foundation parents stand on for overprotecting their children and keeping them from such vital activities as playing freely. If parents were serious about attacking risks, as opposed to projecting their own fears and uncertainties, they might focus on the important events that go on every day in America's households that are of far more immediate harm to children than the possibility of kidnapping based on the report of an abduction in Colorado. If we are serious about protecting the kids from risks, we would attend to the larger and more present dangers. Adults might fight harder to repair unsatisfying marriages, for example.

Or make some effort to combat the rampant sexualization of their daughters at progressively younger ages. It has been estimated that an American child is as likely to experience the fate of JonBenet Ramsey as to be struck by lightning. Stranger abduction is exceedingly rare; most kidnappings are carried out by family members disgruntled by a custody arrangement. But parents fill their kids' closets with aggressively provocative clothing without connecting their outfits to the misfits, without recognizing how sexualizing the young might stimulate the fantasies of grown men—and without considering the effects of such product-borne precociousness on the children themselves. There's tight rhinestone-studded skinny jeans, thong underwear for six-year-olds emblazoned with the words "eat me" on the front, with an image of a cherry. There are pimp Halloween costumes for little boys. Then there are the flirtatious little Bratz dolls that, as one reporter suggested, make Barbie look like the "scrub-cheeked—albeit curvaceous—girl next door." The massive machinery used to market fashion now brings sophisticated wares conceived for an adult audience to any child old enough to sit in front of a television set. Tight jeans, deep-V tunics, and press-on fingernails are now hawked to pint-size fashionistas—long before they get the inner wardrobe for a sense of self. Parents put up little resistance to protect their children from a sex-saturated culture. They prefer to see the problem as existing totally Out There and demand that legislators solve it.

Surveys show that parents are in similarly deep denial of such real risks as drug and alcohol use among adolescents. In its latest annual survey of teenagers and parents, the National Center on Addiction and Substance Abuse (CASA), based at Columbia University, reported that 50 percent of teens find alcohol or drugs or both available at their parties. Yet 80 percent of parents insist their kids are attending substance-free parties. Only 12 percent of parents see drugs and alcohol as any kind of a problem for their kids—but for 27 percent of the teens, it's their biggest concern. A majority of parents think social pressure is their child's biggest issue. "These parents don't understand the world their children are living in," says Joseph A. Califano, CASA's chairman and president.

Because of the very nature and discomfort of uncertainty, the consideration of risk incites adults to irrationality right under their own watch. No matter how accomplished we are in other domains of life, we are not in possession of our full senses on the topic of danger—even though we think we are. Move the discussion to our children and many more elements of irrationality and emotionality enter the picture. With the generous help of tabloid newspapers and graphic television news broadcasts, the net effect is that adults misread the vague dangers around them (pedophiles living in the neighborhood) to institute laws of dubious value and to justify their own death-grip parenting.

They do it in the name of protecting the kids from predators, but it is more an expression of parental anxiety lurking inside their own heads than a reflection of actual dangers to children. The vaguer and darker the fear of what is looming out in the streets, however, the deeper the hold it can have on the parental imagination—and the more it can be manipulated and magnified to justify parental control and overprotectiveness. What is really going on when we whip up pedophile panic is adult anxiety over children's morality and sexuality, a subject wholly worthy of concern and honest discussion by parents and children and the institutions that serve them. But don't hold your breath; the topic is too uncomfortable for most adults to tolerate. Pedophile panic is much "safer" and involves a much sharper distinction between good and bad behavior.

The Biggest Risk of All: A Risk-Free World

The desire for a risk-free world for our children, a universe etched in black and white, with the discomfort of uncertainty removed, is itself very childish. Uncertainty is simply a part of life, the most challenging part of life, the part of life that encourages exploration. In responding so irrationally to the risks they misperceive, in trying to engineer the risk-free life, the adults are projecting onto the world their own anxieties. What they are really giving to their children is a sense of the world as a very dangerous place; they are instructing their children that the outside world is to be approached not with respect and preparation but with trepidation and anxiety. They are encouraging their children to define themselves not by what they can do but by what they cannot do. At the same time, they are hand-delivering to the kids a sense of fragility, a sense that the kids are not capable and will never be capable against the array of forces lurking Out There.

When parents misperceive risks, their efforts to protect their children once again wind up harming the kids. They conjure up a very negative, mistrustful, pessimistic picture of childhood and of the world, and infantilize their children by overprotecting them and assuming them incapable of handling any challenge. It may be that robbing children of a positive sense of the future is the worst form of violence that parents can do to them. It engenders hopelessness and despair. It provides no incentive to grow up and move into the wider world. It restricts the arena in which people feel they can act. As it turns out, risk is actually very necessary for stimulation and growth—not only for children but for everyone.

Remove all the risks of living and you're left with continuing irrationality on the one hand and an overwhelming sense of the preciousness of kids on the other. That, probably, explains the mother in Birmingham, Michigan, who drove eighteen hundred miles so that her precious son could go on a camping trip with his classmates while being spared the hazard and discomfort of traveling with them by airplane. The boy was instead deprived of that shared experience with his peers, which was sacrificed to his mother's irrational fear that flying is more dangerous than driving. Not once in the three days spent driving each way did she recognize that mile for mile, person for person, vehicle for vehicle, driving is far more dangerous than flying.

Preciousness, however, comes at a very high price: It recognizes only the weakest and worst sides of people. It envisions a world full of threats, where everything outside the home is a danger. The adults are negatively focused, not busy bringing about a better world for their children (and everyone's children) but preoccupied with what can go wrong in this one. Hazard-mongering makes motherhood a minefield.

It is the grip of preciousness that encourages parents to go out and buy for their tot the organic cotton T-shirt that screams "Dairy Free" so the little darling doesn't have to bear the burden of telling anyone that he is allergic to milk products. His clothing does it for him. In the same fashion, parents can buy an allergy awareness patch that declares "No Peanuts Please." Just like parents used to sew on Scout badges indicating accomplishments, they now iron on badges proclaiming vulnerabilities. (Disclaimer: even as the mother of a son deathly allergic to peanuts, I wouldn't have dreamed of turning my son into a billboard for a quirky immune system.) Aside from summing up a child by his weakness, such an approach perpetuates dependency by shifting off the child the responsibility for learning to look out for himself.

FIVE

Cheating Childhood

Play, it seems, has an image problem. The public thinks it's . . . child's play. Child's play! Do we have a more dismissive locution in the English language? The importance of play is thoroughly counterintuitive. Play looks like a waste of time—*looks like*—because it is not goal directed. That is the very essence of play, activity that's not goal directed. And we adults are goal directed. So we trivialize kids' play. It gets in the way of other things we want to do on our way to achievement, a goal we also very much want for our children and are very worried about these days—counterproductively, the evidence indicates.

Few things in life are as ambiguous as play. Suspended between reality and unreality, it both is and isn't what it appears to be. Is the act of chasing in a game of tag real or is it make-believe? Is it serious or is it antic? Is the running intended or pretend? Inhabiting a fine and fleeting line between the substantive and the simulated, play compels constant shifts of perspective along with attention to the elements of communication just for players to decipher the meaning of an action. Like art, play is an experience that is almost impossible to define—because it encompasses infinite variety—and is as elusive as an image in the Versailles Hall of Mirrors. Is it an activity or a state of mind? Spontaneous or rule-bound?

In an exhaustive examination titled *The Ambiguity of Play,* the psychologist Brian Sutton-Smith found the meaning of play playfully elusive. Like teasing, its psychological sibling, ambiguity is vastly underrated. By its very ambiguous nature it gives brains a workout. It is cognitively challenging. It requires attention, and so it sharpens senses. It both demands and inspires mental dexterity and flexibility. It thrives on complexity, uncertainty, and possibility. That makes play just about the perfect preparation for life in the twenty-first century.

The big question is why we bother to play at all. After all, play is by definition mental and physical activity not related to survival. What distinguishes it from all other activity is that it has no goal whatsoever, which is not to say that people have not tried to put play to work to serve other goals—which immediately makes it not play at all. Play is always strictly voluntary, which is the source of enjoyment and underlies the sense of freedom it generates. In a classic 1938 study, *Homo Ludens* (Man the Player), the Dutch anthropologist Johan Huizinga insisted that play is, like art, "a primary category of life," a unique state that is absorbing and involves uncertainty and often a sense of illusion or exaggeration, though it has its own rules and boundaries. And as with art, perhaps we can't define it, but we know it when we see it. But above all, play exists outside ordinary life; even though they are absorbed in play, players are always aware that the play is not "real," that its consequences do not carry over into everyday life. Play defines a place apart, a safe and protected space where the rules of normal life are suspended.

It is a basic tenet of evolutionary psychology that useless behaviors—and worse, deleterious ones, which play can seem to be since it erodes energy, wastes time that could be spent searching for food or studying for SATs, and opens players to injury—pretty quickly get drummed out of behavioral repertoires. Yet in the animal kingdom, play increases, rather than decreases, with increasing brain complexity.

If play is more prominent in advanced species, could it be that play itself plays a major role in advancing the species? "We need play to become fully human," says the groundbreaking neuroscientist Jaak Panksepp, of Washington State University, who has studied play extensively in animals and humans. Play is the signature mammalian behavior, he contends. The very essence of play, both he and Sutton-Smith propose, is to exercise and expand human variability and flexibility. We play because we can, we play because we need to, we play because it gives us a shot at keeping up with a world of unpredictably changing environments. Given the accelerating rate of cultural change, who can foretell what the world is going to be like in ten years and what information and skills will be most in demand in our information economy?

Play makes us nimble—neurobiologically, mentally, behaviorally—capable of adapting to a rapidly evolving world. Play cajoles us toward our human potential. It preserves alternatives—all the possibilities our nervous system tends to otherwise prune away as we specialize in what become our own quirks of behavior. It's no accident that all the predicaments of play—the challenges, the dares, the double dares, the chases—model the struggle for survival. Play is "a primary place for the expression of anything that is humanly imaginable," said Sutton-Smith, "a prime domain for the actualization of whatever the brain contains." Play is our free connection to pure possibility, a prime pathway to transcendence precisely because it is so mercurial. Play is the future with sneakers on.

And that is probably why it spurs creativity. In making our brain circuits more flexible, play prompts us to see the world in new ways, says Robert Root-Bernstein, a professor of life sciences at Michigan State University, MacArthur "genius award" grantee, and longtime researcher of creativity. We can make new connections. Play encourages people to synthesize knowledge across different domains. The capacity to invent is intimately wrapped up in the freedom to play. Root-Bernstein has found that genius inventors and scientists are accomplished at playing—as musicians, in the visual arts, with writing and poetry. And many had created imaginary worlds as children, engaging in the activity known in the psych biz as "world-play."

In a study he conducted of MacArthur fellows, two-thirds of the grantees cited a connection between their childhood play world and their adult work. Even among those who didn't engage in childhood world-play, half still felt that play of some kind prepared them for their adult careers. Perhaps it's the attitude and experimental freedom of play itself that stay with them and shape their working lives. Play safely allows us to take risks. As Huizinga saw it, play is by its very nature conducive to experimentation, providing an opportunity for trying on new roles and attempting tasks that might be avoided in "real" life as too difficult or unpleasant. As the highest expression of our humanity, play benefits not only individuals but society as a whole. The instinct for play is a central element in the creation of human culture. "Civilization arises and unfolds in and as play," Huizinga insisted.

Pretend play, that marvelous creation of three-year-olds acting as if a teacup is really hot, "does not just allow you to play," says the British psychologist Simon Baron-Cohen. "It allows you to 'imagine' hypothetical worlds," to "manipulate the truth in an infinite number of ways." It is, he adds, "a prerequisite for the serious enterprise of planning and engineering, as well as art or science." If play makes the most of our humanity, we are most human when we play.

The End of Play

In the hothouse that child raising has become, play is all but dead. Thanks to achievement pressures, kids' play is going the way of the hula hoop. Under pressure to create an atmosphere of achievement, schools are doing away with recess in the belief that less time for play leaves more time for study. Deemed extraneous and expendable, play, like art classes, has been sacrificed to the mistaken, mechanistic belief that the path to educational efficiency is straight and narrow and runs strictly through reading, math, and science. This is a Taliban-like approach to education, a kind of academic fundamentalism no more congruent with the richness of human nature, curiosity, and development than the religious kind.

Even in preschool, play is under assault; desks and work sheets are increasingly replacing blocks and make-believe, the play that emanates from children's free-flowing mental activity. The percentage of time that preschool kids spend in play decreased from 40 percent in 1981 to 25 percent in 1997. At the same time, a four-billion-dollar tutoring industry has sprung up—with a whopping 26 percent of it lavished on two- to six-year-olds.

What play there is has been corrupted. The organized sports many kids participate in are managed by adults according to their rules; difficulties that arise are not worked out by kids but adjudicated by adult referees. Kids' play is professionalized; team sports are fixed on building skills and on winning and losing, not on having a good time. There's nothing light-hearted about a soccer game when children are paid by their parents every time they play in a winning game.

In 1998, children were spending 50 percent more time in organized sports than in 1981. They also spent thirty minutes less time each day in unstructured play and outdoor activities. Free time decreased to 25 percent of a child's day in 1997, compared with 40 percent in 1981—and most of that time is spent watching television. Not only are children's lives more structured. More and more, play is equipment intensive and consumer oriented, a matter of pay for play.

Children's fun and games are now serious business. Americans spent $25 billion on toys in 2003, up astronomically from $6.7 billion in 1980. Truly, toys are now us. But amusement is not the same as play; the nature of the activity does not spring from children's experience or their spontaneous and ever-shifting interests, nor are the rules worked out by children themselves, through their own collaborative dialogue. As we shall see, that shortchanges play of the ability to mold attention and subdue impulsivity. The consumerization of play risks loss of two other critical elements—pretend and improvisation. It's bad enough that toys tend to be executed with such exacting and realistic detail their surface features leave little room for the exercise of imagination; the damage is compounded when toys are sold in product lines that encourage repeated purchases. The packaged products supply packaged experiences that fail to furnish the raw materials for children to learn about themselves—the real goal of all learning.

When kids do engage in their own kind of play, parents often become alarmed. The Massachusetts child psychologist David Anderegg points to kids exercising time-honored curiosity by playing doctor. "It's normal for children to have curiosity about other children's genitals," he says. And in fact, sex play is universal among the young throughout the animal kingdom, including *Homo sapiens*. Other animals mount. Human children play doctor. "But when they do, most parents I know are totally freaked out. They wonder what's wrong."

Active play often gets stopped in the belief that it is too rough for children—despite evidence that rambunctious play actually fosters maturation of the nervous system, not to mention maintenance of healthy body weight. Kids are having a hard time now even playing neighborhood pickup games because they've never done it, observes Barbara Carlson, president and co-founder of Putting Family First. "They've been told by their coaches where on the field to stand, told by their parents what color socks to wear, told by the referees who's won and what's fair. We're seeing that kids are losing leadership skills."

"Children aren't getting any benefits out of play as they once did," declares Tufts University's David Elkind, the child psychologist who first drew attention to the dangers of the high-pressure experiences in his prescient 1981 book, *The Hurried Child*. It's universally recognized by specialists that play is vital in teaching children how to control themselves and how to interact with others. When the activity itself is compromised, it can have long-term consequences for children's emotional and psychological development.

In the push to prepare kids for a radically changed world, it seems so very intuitive to remove play in favor of more time for schoolwork and testing—what educators themselves call "drill and kill." We're in an extended cultural moment where leaders think that getting tough with education is better than overhauling an educational system that is increasingly out of step with children's learning needs and informational opportunities; a system that increasingly requires clinical diagnosis and pharmaceutical support to hold kids in their seats seems more suited to the industrial age than the information age, where creative problem solving is the key to innovation. The current disdain for recess has echoes of our Puritan past, which may be something familiar enough to fall back on in the face of fear and uncertainty. Our Puritan forebears knew that work, not play, was the key to their success and saw labor as a way of glorifying God. Play, according to this view, threatens to undermine both our success and our salvation. The achievement pressures on kids reflect nothing so much as New Puritanism. But what no one has yet publicly reckoned with is that play has extraordinary intellectual and developmental value and it is almost all completely counterintuitive.

Play: Practice for Adulthood

Contrary to the widely held belief that only intellectual activities build a sharp brain, it's in play that the cognitive skills are most acutely developed. By play I'm referring not to adult-coached and adult-monitored sports but to true play: free, unstructured play, where the kids invent the activities, the activities reflect their own curiosity and interests—and they can find their own ways to be with each other. Anxious parents may regard play as trivial, but studies of children around the world demonstrate that the social engagement of play actually sharpens intellectual skills. Child's play fosters decision making, memory, thinking, and speed of mental processing. This shouldn't come as a surprise. After all, the human mind is believed to have evolved to deal with social problems.

There's no question that today's parents want the best for the kids.

They especially want them to be prepared to thrive in a fast-changing world for which they themselves did not feel at all prepared. But in removing play from childhood, they have it precisely backward. They ignore the evidence first marshaled by Huizinga but corroborated many times over—play is the true preparation for adulthood. At its heart, play is rule-bound activities in which the outcome is unknown. It's the way we learn to handle the unexpected. Play sharpens wits and makes mental processes nimble—resilient and ready for whatever life throws our way.

Play seems to be an irreducible fact of neurological development. The need for it is wired deep into our brains. The sources of play and laughter are instinctual, lying deep under the cortex. Here is what turns out to be a cosmic thigh-slapper: take away play from the front end of development and it finds its way onto the back end. On the basis of his pioneering studies of animals, Panksepp has come to the conclusion that play is one of the very fundamental motivational drives of all higher creatures. His studies show that if you deprive animals of play in early life, they spend their time playing in extended adolescence. Play, Panksepp contends, is practice for the future. He finds, for example, that the rough-and-tumble play that is so characteristic of boys the world over is critical for bonding; his studies suggest that so much bonding goes on through this activity that it may reduce aggression later in life.

Animals deprived of play in early development are hindered in their ability to eventually take on adult roles. Unless they go through a stage in which they engage in play, they become stuck in a state of perpetual adolescence.

Nature's Spitball

Play turns out to be critical neurologically. That is the great hidden secret of play. Panksepp's research reveals that play turns on hundreds of genes in the brain and it acts in specific areas. It generates the production of a nerve growth factor called BDNF (brain-derived neurotrophic factor), and it does it in the frontal cortex of the brain, the executive control center.

BDNF is well recognized as the key modulator of nerve cell development, the creation of new nerve cells, called neurogenesis, and the branching of nerve cells that literally gives us behavioral flexibility, and survival itself. It is helpful to know that other things that turn on BDNF production are learning and vigorous exercise. One thing that turns off production of BDNF is stress. Further, BDNF is what's missing in depression. All of the therapies that work in relieving depression stimulate production of BDNF. Right there is a potentially critical connection, with lack of play setting the stage for psychopathology.

What play does, by stimulating neurogenesis, is hasten the development of the frontal cortex and program it. It solidifies the executive functions of the brain. In other words, it fosters the maturation of the very centers of the brain that allow us to exert control over attention, regulate our emotions, and control our behavior. Here is the very subtle trick that nature plays: it uses something that's *not* goal directed to create the very mental machinery for people to *be* goal directed. It creates the inhibitory circuitry of self-regulation and attention.

In other words, says Panksepp, social play "helps program higher brain areas that will be required later in life." You've got to admire it—the ability of play to stimulate the maturation and transformation of the brain is concealed under the fun. The subtlety and subversiveness of the transaction probably constitute the major reason why we haven't caught on to the importance of play.

But today's parental pressure obscures the value of play and makes it seem like a waste of time, a distraction from the true goal of academic and vocational success. Such a dismissive attitude toward play leads kids themselves to view any activity that is not explicitly goal directed as worthless and dilatory. Unfortunately, human development just doesn't unfold in a beeline.

ADHD—Have We Got It Backward?

In a direct challenge to current cultural dogma, Panksepp has gathered new evidence that play, neurobiologically constructive, helps build the brain in ways that encourage kids to control themselves and learn. The "learning disorder" known as attention deficit hyperactivity disorder, or ADHD, may result not from faulty brain wiring or chemistry gone awry, as conventional medical thinking holds, but from restriction of the urge to play. Further, vigorous bouts of unstructured social play, especially in preschoolers—the kind of play that adults often put a stop to—may be the best "therapy" for reducing the impulsive behaviors that characterize the disorder, the most common childhood psychiatric problem in America.

In fact, abundant social play in animals activates genes for neural growth factors in the executive portion of the brain. The neural tendrils that sprout in the brain in the wake of vigorous play supply raw material for the development of the circuitry of self-regulation that may ultimately tame impulses such as inappropriate play urges, suggests Panksepp.

Play—could it really be the cure for ADHD? Could so many smart people have badly misinterpreted the symptoms of inattention as the disease itself and failed to see how blatantly those symptoms suggest their own remedy? Panksepp is no stranger to upending orthodoxy. His extensive studies of neural systems among mammals suggest that, like us, animals have a range of emotions. A much-talked-about 2005 article in the prestigious journal *Science* proposed that a 50-kilohertz chirp emitted by rats in response to playful tickling (by him and the graduate students in his lab) and during their own "rambunctious shenanigans" is evidence of "an ancestral form of human laughter" and joy. It's worth noting that those tickled creatures also learn tasks faster, play more, and are more socially responsive.

Panksepp's studies also furnish evidence of what Huizinga hinted—that we are wired to play, innately constituted to seek the stimulation and mental activity that play produces. Play is an activity both of intellect-driven humans and of instinct-driven animals, its universality suggesting that its roots lie deep in our brains and may well be embedded in our genes. The urge to play is a fundamental neurological "drive"—it is powerful and arises spontaneously, without any learning. Thwarted or left unfulfilled, it creates symptoms of ADHD. The 6 to 16 percent of American children diagnosed with ADHD may be normal kids who simply have a strong desire to play or who encounter greater restrictions of activity.

It may be that the way American schools and parents are pushing for academic achievement is causing the very problem that makes learning so difficult for so many. Says Panksepp: "We need to worry about the social environments we have created that do not allow enough play and that seem to be leading to a dramatic increase in the diagnosis of ADHD."

Working with newborn rats, Panksepp and colleagues have created lesions in the brain's frontal cortex that lead to ADHD-like behavior. The damaged animals are especially prone to excessive playfulness. But when they were given one hour per day of access to play during their first week of life, the extra play alleviated the impulsive symptoms. The findings imply that the fundamental disorder in ADHD is not a deficit of attention at all but the inability to control the impulse to play—a deficit of behavioral inhibition. This makes great sense in the upside-down universe of brain disorders. "Most psychiatric problems ultimately reflect difficulties individuals encounter in regulating their feelings," notes Panksepp. Not in having the feelings, but in controlling them.

Panksepp has shown that the positive social engagement of play, though it originates in lower, instinctual regions of the brain, stimulates significant cortical activity in the frontal lobes. "The more cortical activity, the more it's possible to pay attention to the outside world—you can do what teachers want," he explains. Not only does the nervous system need play to fully mature; it appears to need a sufficient amount at a specific time.

The evidence so far points to liberal amounts of rough-and-tumble play from ages three to six. Panksepp told a recent neuroscience conference in New York that he's ready "to take to the human laboratory" the evidence from his animals studies. To lay the groundwork for a play intervention program, he conducted a feasibility study of vigorous play among pre-kindergarteners in the Bowling Green, Ohio, public school system. "The kids liked it very much, even if some of the teachers did not," he reports. One of his findings: girls seem to engage in rough-and-tumble play as much as boys do; there is no gender difference in play preference at that age.

"What really needs to be done now is to identify children who are on the ADHD track and give half of them very intense and persistent natural play activity twice a day every day, like food and water, for at least half an hour each session," he says. The double dose is a direct suggestion from studies and observations of baboons in the wild, indicating that there are circadian patterns to play. Animals seem to naturally experience two periods of extended play per day, although they also enjoy shorter romps at frequent intervals.

Play's effects on the brain are not limited to the frontal lobes. During play, deep dopamine reward circuits swing into action—the same channels of motivation and attention that get hijacked by drugs of abuse and all addictive activities. Further, play stimulates the joy chemicals known as opioids; they help mediate social reward in the brain. That's what makes romping around so much fun—and so hard to stop doing just because Mom issues a call to come in from outside. "Play is a tool of nature for social learning to construct the fully social brain," Panksepp says. "It prompts the frontal lobes to mature."

Unfortunately, the drugs commonly used to treat ADHD dramatically reduce the impulse to play in animals, Panksepp has found. "Might it be that so many American children are given Ritalin partly because it reduces disorderly behaviors that arise from poorly regulated playful urges? These molecules are highly effective in the classroom—but they would be comparably effective for the kids who don't need it. They would attend and perform better, too. That's the nature of the brain."

Chemically thwarting the drive to play—particularly with potential drugs of abuse such as Ritalin and other psychostimulants—might not just undermine self-regulation. It appears to be a bad idea for other reasons as well. Studies show that especially in young animals, psychostimulants can sensitize the opioid system so that later drug use may be especially attractive. Further, the drugs can have long-lasting personality effects. "To put it bluntly," says Panksepp, "they make our animals more urgently materialistic—more eager for external rewards." Play is a natural way to induce the chemistry for euphoria, at the same time that it helps organize the brain in social ways—and boosts the motivation to learn in the social environment of school.

Parents of ADHD kids often seek Panksepp out. If the child is very young, he always asks the father whether he rough-and-tumble plays with his child. "If he says no, we recommend doing it every day, religiously, if there's time in the morning—and if the child doesn't have a playmate, again in the evening for a while, an hour or so before bedtime. We have parents who say that Johnny is better. We have anecdotal data, but no more than that—nor does anyone else." Not yet, and probably not anytime soon; the climate for a federally funded study of play is not quite favorable.

Brian Sutton-Smith suggested that play has even more of a beneficial effect on the frontal lobes of the brain. It gives those who play more practice in and more options for subduing fear responses, which otherwise have a more reflexive, automatic hold on people and interrupt information processing. Scientists know that there are direct connections to the frontal lobes from many other deeper brain structures. One in particular is the amygdala, an almond-shaped cluster of cells that specialize in fear. The amygdala acts to detect and relay alarm signals to the frontal lobes, among other parts of the brain. "What we have in play," said Sutton-Smith, "is a simulation of an anxiety attack." Fantasy may be the frame, but within the frame are real belief and real action. Think of the stylized aggression of play—a child being chased in capture the flag or any number of chase-and-escape games. "You run when you're chased and you're screaming with fear. But the anxiety attack is cosseted by its safety and its known simulation of virtuality, and therefore rendered enjoyable."

Resistance to Depression

"Play confers resistance to depression—because it develops the molecules for joy," contends Panksepp, the only scientist who has measured molecules in the brain as a function of play. Like all other mammals, we humans come naturally equipped with circuitry for play. We don't have to be taught to play; we do it spontaneously. Why? No one can say for sure, but Panksepp's work indicates that the play system is a learning system for social behavior. Through play we develop the social brain: we learn how to get along with others, and we learn to take our place in society.

In his studies, animals at play naturally sort themselves into dominant and submissive types—those whose romps end in pinning down their peers and those who wind up pinned down by their playmates. The two groups of animals are equally eager to play.

But the dominant animals develop a distinctive feature: they feel less pain. "They have their own joy molecules," Panksepp reports. In humans, that translates into decreased susceptibility to feeling depressed. "Play is the most powerful source of joy in human experience," he says. "It stimulates positive affect and insulates against depression."

When the Blocks Come Tumbling Down

If definitive biological proof has yet to roll in that play shapes the nervous system, strong behavioral evidence certainly exists. "There are no data supporting claims that recess takes away schooling time," the psychologist Anthony Pellegrini told a recent national conference on play held at Yale University. A professor of education at the University of Minnesota, he has found that play has positive short-term and long-term effects on schoolwork. It is a measure of the contempt in which child's play is generally held today that the organizers of the conference titled the conclave "Play=Learning." In order for the conference to be taken seriously among those in the educational world, the academic value of play had to be spelled out, and so much the better in mathematical terms. As the conference got under way, several experts in attendance voiced dismay at the title—indeed, they argued, play does lead to learning, but it also does so much more, and to limit the equation to learning is to actually understate the real value of play.

Its best value, and the source of all its effects, may be what success-focused anxious parents find so hard to swallow—that play has no purpose at all. It is, in the language of science, a purely autotelic activity, with no goals or rewards external from itself; participation in play is rewarding unto itself. It is, in the words of Sutton-Smith, an autonomous, intrinsically motivated activity—we do it spontaneously, just because it's fun. No single play activity is required for our survival. From this fact, perhaps, it is only a short hop to thinking that play itself is not necessary for survival, and therefore wholly dispensable.

In the short run, periodic recess breaks actually facilitate classroom learning. Tests of second, third, and fourth graders show that outdoor recess maximizes attention, especially for boys. The younger the kids are, the bigger the impact. Second graders are particularly more attentive after recess than before. Pellegrini suggests that American schools could benefit by recognizing the principle of "distributed practice"—punctuating periods of intense work with ten- to twenty-minute bursts of play, much as the Japanese do. People learn tasks better if they are broken down into discrete chunks of time rather than massed into one session.

It may be counterintuitive, but kids and adults are more attentive after breaks than before, and the longer kids are kept in, the less attentive they become. Pellegrini lays it right on the line: "Parents and teachers should be aware of the fact that classroom organization may be responsible for their sons' attention and fidgeting problems—two dimensions of ADHD—and that breaks may be a better remedy than Ritalin."

Peer play also has direct long-term effects on learning. Concealed under the fun is the fact that peer interaction on the playground is a cognitive high-wire act at the same time that it is very motivating for kids. For some it may be the only positive associations with school and may create their only feelings of efficacy in that milieu. Especially when adults aren't watching (but video cameras are), peer play stimulates sophisticated and rich language use—play seems to have its own unique grammar and distinctive use of the past tense—complex role play, and conceptual leap-frogging. The reason you might not know that is: the minute teachers or other adults step on the scene, kids constrict, turning over to the grown-ups the work of maintaining interactions.

When he measured the playground behavior of kids for two years, Pellegrini found their social behavior at recess in kindergarten predicted achievement at the end of first grade, as measured by class work and standardized tests of general knowledge, early reading, and math concepts. By a whopping 40 percent, peer play was significantly more predictive of academic success than the standardized achievement tests. Student involvement with teachers during play actually had a *negative* impact on first-grade achievement!

From observations of four-year-olds, the psychologist Laura Berk offers proof that play actively stimulates development of self-regulation—not just any old play but kid-centered, kid-controlled make-believe. At the time a distinguished professor at Illinois State University, she told the Yale conference that pretend play has such powerful effects because it is so rich in collaborative dialogue. Here's what is so important about collaborative dialogue: Of course, it boosts kids' vocabulary and their language skills. But it does much more. In pretend play, kids come up with their own rules—and then they voluntarily (*voluntarily!*) make themselves conform to the rules they have negotiated. No one has to tell them to subdue wild impulses or pay close attention; they do it simply because they want to stay in the make-believe world they have just invented together.

In other words, children are learning to use their thoughts to control and guide their impulses. Berk can't stress enough how developmentally significant such play is. "The paradox is that subordinating their actions to the rules is central to the pleasure of playing—whereas in everyday life the rules are often the source of frustration."

In one set of studies, Berk observed fifty-one middle-class kids in fantasy play in their preschool classroom, and then measured their capacity for self-regulation in the performance of two required cleanup tasks. She compared their actions at the start of the school year with their performance at the end of the year. Impartial observers rated the kids' behavior in school; parents rated their impulsivity at home. The time kids spent in fantasy play wound up correlating precisely with the time spent cleaning up. The richer their play language, the more they could get their act together for a cleanup task. The gains were greatest in the most impulsive kids. "We need to return to playful engagement in the classroom," Berk implored the Yale conferees. "The more we teach through work sheets the more we undermine self-regulation."

Like Panksepp and Pellegrini, Berk sees an urgency in the new evidence about the sometimes subtle effects of play. They all agree that kids need more time to play—preferably beyond the watchful eyes of parents or teachers. "It's important to let children interact on their own terms with peers," says Pellegrini. "Providing children with a physical education class as a substitute for recess does not serve the same purpose. They need to *play*." Panksepp makes the same argument but couches it slightly differently: "Adults tend to stop [play] engagements because they get too boisterous. Kids are continually having to break off from this kind of activity before their nervous system is eager to back off." Rough-and-tumble social play, where kids make actual physical contact, has particular value. "You must feel your partner wanting to engage," Panksepp stresses. "That's how play gets into the nervous system." Contact counts.

Not to be underestimated: the role of play in creating an environment everyone enjoys. "The big thing about play is you're happier," Sutton-Smith stressed. In a study done in Austria, children were given unlimited access to toys—provided they did their work first. Whenever their work was done, they could play with toys the rest of the day. The kids who got the chance to play performed as well academically as the kids in other classrooms—*but they wanted to go to school more*. The teachers liked the classrooms, and the parents liked the school. Similarly, a study done in the United States looked at kids coming into first grade with a reading background versus those coming in with a more old-fashioned play background, where there was talk and singing and make-believe. The kids who came in having been taught reading performed better during the first grade—but they were no better by the end of first grade. And they were much more depressed. "The opposite of play is not work," insisted Sutton-Smith. "It's depression."

That makes play essential not just for motivation but for all of mental health. Psychologists and psychiatrists have long known that emotionally disturbed children play only in very limited ways. Their play is rigid and obsessive; they enact the same scenarios over and over again. Play is often a primary therapy for children who have experienced trauma of some kind. "One of the only things that works with kids in hospitals who are anxious about surgery is play therapy," Sutton-Smith points out. Through play therapy, traumatized children get to imagine new outcomes to their dire experience. They get to exert control over their world. And in fact, if traumatized children are not given the opportunity to find a way out through play, they will enact their experience in play over and over again.

The inability to play is a sign of poor mental health. Animals deprived of play become socially inept. Mice deprived of play have a thinner cortex than other mice. Animals that do not play at mothering become incompetent mothers. And so it may be that the play deprivation of a whole generation of youth is contributing to their mental fragility.

Most American adults say they want their "children to be children." They want their children to play. But the belief in play's value doesn't translate into parental behavior. In late 2004, Shelly Glick Gryfe, director of marketing research for the Fisher-Price toy company, conducted a survey of 1,106 mothers of children under six and 106 play experts, to see how play fit into the lives of young children. Ninety-five percent of mothers said it is important to them that their children spend some time playing every day. They also felt they were not conforming to the pressures of other mothers. "But their actions tell another story," Glick Gryfe found. Sixty-six percent of them agreed that "these days, parents always have to be finding ways to help their children excel." Yet mothers believe "it's the *other* mothers who are insisting on structure and preparedness for their young children." Most mothers fear that if they don't conform, their child will be left behind. In this, their views diverge sharply from those of developmental experts.

"I think that we are all anxious that our children will fall behind, and there is no time for play among such fear," says Kathy Hirsh-Pasek, professor of psychology and director of the infant language laboratory at Temple University and an organizer of the Yale conference. "Play emerges spontaneously everywhere—even in war zones and concentration camps. And the data are incontrovertible. Thirty years of psychological research indicates that play is the crucible for learning and critical for social skills, which are critical for success in school. Playful learning increases attention, motivation, academic skill, social development, and health. Yet we are at an impasse where tutoring for two-year-olds is a reality and play is down. We can turn out robots or creative problem solvers. In a flat world, the future belongs to the problem solvers. Commerce in a flat world requires social-emotional skills as well." But instead, play is fighting for its life against the encroachment of workbooks and other forms of achievement pressure.

In the final analysis, child's play seems tethered to a pendulum that swings between two opposing beliefs about the nature of children and their development—one positive, expansive, and optimistic, one darker, mechanical, and deterministic. At one extreme, children are seen as cognitive beings that must be programmed much like computers—emphasis on the *cog* in *cog*nitive. Preschools eliminate play corners to make room for academic training in letters and numbers and color naming. It's never too soon to start cramming in information. And kids need external reinforcement to be motivated to do anything. In this scheme, play becomes the enemy of literacy activities such as reading. It's a very conservative view of children, assumes they are more or less blank slates bringing nothing to the table—and lags behind the evidence by at least half a century, in some estimates.

"In fifty years, we've witnessed great changes in understanding of human development," Edward Zigler told the play conference. Professor emeritus of psychology at Yale and longtime director of Yale's Center in Child Development and Social Policy, Zigler is the doyen of developmental psychology. Fifty years ago, in the sway of Freudian thinking, the belief was that children came into the world as essentially passive creatures and that mothers, and only mothers, influenced their development. Now it's understood that children come into the world with their own things, their own temperaments, their own dispositions, and growth occurs through a dynamic interplay of external environments and complex self-regulating internal systems. The only constant in fifty years has been the discovery that the driving force in human development in all domains—social, cognitive, physical—is child's play. It fits a more whole-child view that encompasses but is not limited to cognitive development. In this view, children learn for the same reason birds fly—they are full of innate curiosity to use all their senses and abilities to explore and master their environment. They are not in thrall to external reinforcement, as the behaviorists believed. Unless it's drummed out of them—say, by making them feel shame for trying and failing—their own internal drive for mastery motivates them to learn, and they find great satisfaction in being effective. Seen this way, says Zigler, play is the engine of human development. Mothers, for their part, are the child's first play partners.

"The movement toward early academic training is not about children," Zigler insists. "It's about parents and their anxiety to give children an advantage in the global economy." Play may be play, but it's anything but trivial.

SIX

Meet Mom and Dad, the New Hall Monitors

To some degree, parents are not to blame for their overinvolvement in their children's lives. The schools have invited them to be this way and ushered them right through the front door, asking parents to oversee basic activities, such as homework, that children should be doing on their own. Parents are asked to invest hours overseeing the work the children do at home—because in the existing educational framework, the amount of time kids are in school is insufficient to educate them for today's world. It's possible that *no* amount of time would be sufficient, given all there now is to know.

So anxious are parents for the success of their children that they don't stop to question the framework itself. It's one thing to keep children at their desks in school to drum into them the growing body of knowledge it is (mistakenly) believed they need to master to be effective adults— drill and kill, in the words of contemptuous educators. It's another to continue the desperate regimen at home. It is a measure of the impossibility of the task that parents are asked to stand over their kids' shoulders in the first place.

So it is the schools themselves that are helping reshape parenting into an intrusive activity. To the degree that they are failing in their mission in a fast-moving world, they have turned parents into hall monitors on homework and put forth a new definition of a good parent; it goes roughly like this: someone who joins us (the schools) in putting pressure on kids.

At a minimum, a parent today is asked to monitor the children's home-work and, even better, do it with them.

Casualties of the System

How badly are the schools doing?

At all levels, from kindergarten through college, schools have an inad-equate reaction to the radically changed cultural conditions of the past twenty years. The schools themselves have a sense that they are failing to produce what society needs; at every level of education and government, commissions have been chartered to study the problem. The overwhelm-ing response has been *not* to expand the capacity for innovative thinking, critical analysis, and intellectual development but to rigidify and struc-ture the curriculum, to pour as much information and as many skills as possible into children, especially math and science, and to lengthen the school day and often the school year in the hope that something in the sheer quantity will be useful in the unknowable future.

Recess has been dismissed. Play has been removed from the kinder-garten curriculum. Art is eliminated, extraneous to academic instruction. Kindergarteners get mandatory tutoring, so that the school day is ex-tended as long as an adult workday for five-year-olds. Third graders have three hours of homework, and parents are asked to make sure they do it. Start dates for the school year have been pushed forward from September to early August and even to July in some states. Students take college-level classes while in high school, although there is considerable evidence that Advanced Placement (AP) classes do not prepare them better for college or confer any advantage other than to signify—wink, wink—wor-thiness to the admissions officers of elite colleges. For some educators and politicians, a solution is to begin college preparation in the pre-schools, because, they argue, 85 percent of brain growth occurs before then.

The curriculum in place today is similar to the curriculum in place since well before 1900, when only one of every twenty seventeen-year-olds finished high school. America's schools were designed essentially for the industrial age and have not been overhauled for the information age. A hundred and fifty years ago, the goal was to subdue human nature so that people could mind the machines, not to turn creativity loose. "Do we want widgets or do we want scientific explorers, people who are creative problem solvers?" Temple University's Kathy Hirsh-Pasek asks bluntly. "Today, everyone has access to facts. How you use them determines who bosses whom." And there are a lot more facts available today than there were in 1900, as the knowledge base has expanded greatly. Whole realms of science didn't even exist then—neuroscience, genomics, molecular biology, to name a few.

In a culture of fear, people constrict; educators stick to a belief in filling children with facts. They believe that children are empty vessels and it's the teachers' job to fill them, observes Hirsh-Pasek. They think faster is better and that every moment counts. As America feels threatened about its economic hegemony, "educators think the only way to keep up is to win the fact game. Parents want to shove more stuff into their kids. This is the antithesis of child development," she notes. The irony is that "children who are allowed to explore learn things faster. How you learn is as important as what you learn." A great deal of evidence suggests not only that the fill-'er-up approach isn't working very well today but that it undermines the very viability of the information society.

Barely a third of American students now make it through the system and go on to college, although, unlike even fifty years ago, a college degree is now considered the minimum requirement for jobs that confer middle-class status. In 2002, the U.S. Bureau of the Census reported that just over 4 million young people were of age for starting college. But, according to the Department of Education, only 1.4 million students entered four-year colleges—a 35 percent rate of attendance. Most of them are white and rich—and, increasingly, female; the educational system is especially failing high school boys.

Among families making over ninety thousand dollars a year, one in two students gets a bachelor's degree by age twenty-four. But among families making less than thirty-five thousand dollars a year, only one in seventeen students gets a bachelor's degree by twenty-four. The country's most selective colleges and universities throw the discrepancies into high relief. According to a 2004 report for the Century Foundation, researchers found that in the top 146 schools in 1995, 74 percent of the students hailed from the richest socioeconomic quartile, while just 3 percent came from the lowest socioeconomic quartile. "Put differently," Richard D. Kahlenberg, a senior fellow at the foundation, observes, "wandering around one of the nation's selective campuses, you are 25 times as likely to run into a rich student as a poor one. So are rich kids 25 times as likely to be born smart as poor kids? No serious people believe that." He adds that "the research clearly shows that, controlling for ability, low-income students are much less likely to attend college than high-income students." Why would that be?

A Failure to Engage

A good part of the answer is that well-off families can afford to devote financial and human resources—time and attention, including close monitoring—to make sure that their children succeed academically in a system that increasingly fails to engage many students. According to a 2006 Harris poll, only 17 percent of American adults think elementary public education is very good or excellent; even fewer (14 percent) have faith in public secondary education. Well-off families take pains to get their children into the "right" schools to launch a successful life and see that information is poured into them from an early age.

Wherever possible, they send their kids to private schools, in the belief they will have a better shot at college. They do everything in their power to make their children attractive to admissions officers of selective colleges. They send them on exotic trips, cultivate skills in athletics and the arts, even arrange unique volunteer activities. They hire ten-thousand-dollar packages of college consulting. They turn summers into boot camps for SAT preparation or send their children to after-school weekend cram courses for SAT preparation. If that doesn't assuage their anxieties, they hire six-hundred-dollar-an-hour private tutors for the children from Princeton Review and other companies dedicated to helping parents get their children into elite colleges. If they need airtight security, the adults can pay forty thousand dollars for the guarantee of Ivy admission. At the same time, they remove every possible barrier to getting a high SAT score, often creatively recruiting the medical profession to find neurological evidence of information-processing anomalies that warrant "accommodations"—such as more time—in testing situations. They go to great lengths to assume the roles once automatically expected of public schools, because they don't want their children to fail in the dynamic world they will inherit. Parents have taken on the burden of ushering their children through the educational system because at some level they know what is growing increasingly apparent: the system as it now exists can no longer be trusted to educate children well.

Educators fight over to what degree the grade schools and high schools are failing to academically prepare most kids well enough for college, while governors hold summit meetings to improve the nation's high schools and to get more students to enroll in math and science classes. In countries like India and Singapore, where students routinely study math and science and flock to engineering and M.B.A. programs, educators are worried about the dearth of innovators their schools produce; they see a need for students willing to loosen up their brains by dipping more into the humanities. Innovators, after all, invent the technologies and the products that guarantee the future health of the economy.

America's educators also differ in the degree to which they think college is prohibitively expensive for most families; some argue that there is enough student aid to go around. But they all agree that the system needs overhauling. Schools are so out of sync with the dynamic needs of the modern world—and, it is increasingly understood, the real ways people learn—that they have come to rely on outside reinforcements to help them get their own job done.

Teaching to the Test

High schools, for their part, have descended into a thicket of tests in an attempt to demonstrate—often to legislatures that fund them—that they are doing something. The most prominent tests are those that are administered nationally and designed for college entrance—APs, SATs, ACTs—but even these are rapidly losing validity and value. So many high school students now take the SAT with specific exemptions from the time restriction, allowing them a scoring advantage, that the test is growing increasingly unfair and increasingly meaningless as an indicator of potential college performance. In 2002, the College Board, administrator of the SATs, stopped notifying colleges when scores were "obtained under special conditions." There is now no way for a college to know who was given extra time for taking the SAT and who wasn't.

In 2005, forty thousand, or 2 percent, of the two million SAT takers were granted special accommodations—double the number of 1990. However, points out Mark Franek, former dean of students at William

Penn Charter School, one of the oldest and most prestigious private schools in the United States, and currently a writing instructor at Philadelphia University, other types of accommodations—such as using tests with large type—are not increasing nearly as quickly as the time extension is. "It is clear to all of us on the inside that what is driving this phenomenon is the pressure cooker known as the SAT." SAT scores increasingly reflect some stew of the anxiety level and socioeconomic standing of families, rather than the unalloyed ability of students.

Colleges had begun dropping SATs as an entrance requirement, even before widespread testing and scoring errors in 2005 and 2006 further devalued the tests. Rather than creating a learning culture that encourages student curiosity, schools are fostering a "testing culture." Teachers know their duty is to "teach to the test," by which is meant not frequent measuring of what students have learned but tailoring the curriculum to such high-stakes exams, of which the SAT is the highest. Five years after the college stopped requiring the SAT, the president of Mount Holyoke reported in 2006 that there had been "no measurable difference" in quality of student. Colleges are finding that students do well without the tests, although most teaching in high schools is now geared to the tests, and test scores of students, not measures of student learning, have become benchmarks for how well the schools themselves are doing.

There is nothing inherently wrong with testing. In fact, testing can truly be helpful in promoting learning. But to be effective stimulants to learning, tests have to be given frequently, the information has to be generated by the student (not simply checked off on a list of multiple choices), and the student has to be given feedback about his work. But those are not the kinds of tests teachers like to give.

Where's the High in Higher Education?

It's a mistake to think that colleges have solved the educational problem. While Americans generally believe that the country has the best higher education system in the world, considerable evidence undermines any basis for complacency. Business leaders have long complained that many college graduates, even from elite institutions, lack what is so badly needed today—basic skills in writing, problem solving, and analytical thinking—what a 2006 *New York Times* editorial called "the minimum price of admission to the new global economy." For graduates to succeed

in an ever-changing economy, collaboration and the ability to work on in-
terdisciplinary projects—requiring social skills, literacy skills, and communication skills—are increasingly important.

That makes the most recent findings of the National Assessment
of Adult Literacy particularly disturbing. The test, conducted by the
National Center for Education Statistics, is designed as a comprehensive
look at English literacy. The 2003 assessment of nineteen thousand
adults, the results of which were reported in early 2006, demonstrated
declines in literacy especially among those Americans with the *most* education. The test defines literacy as "using printed and written information
to function in society, to achieve one's goals, and to develop one's knowledge and potential." Specifically, the test measures prose literacy, the ability to comprehend continuous texts, like newspaper articles and the
brochure that comes with a new microwave; document literacy, the ability to understand and use documents to perform tasks, like reading a map
or prescription labels; and quantitative literacy, the skills needed to do
things like balancing a checkbook or calculating the interest on a loan
from an advertisement.

Less than one-third of college graduates—down from 40 percent a
decade ago—were deemed proficient in the ability to read and understand ordinary text passages. A mere 25 percent of college graduates—
and only 31 percent of those with at least some graduate studies (down
from 40 percent a decade ago)—scored high enough to be deemed "proficient" from a literacy standpoint. Most could not interpret a table about
exercise and blood pressure, understand the arguments of newspaper ed-
itorials, or compare credit card offers with differing interest rates and annual fees. Nor could they summarize results of a survey about parental
involvement in school. "What's disturbing," said the center's commissioner of education statistics, "is that the assessment is not designed to
test your understanding of Proust but to test your ability to read labels."

As educational attainment rises, one would expect at a minimum a rise
in average test scores for text-based literacy. That is what education is
supposed to do. But scores actually *fell* from 1992 to 2003 for virtually
every educational level. Worse, the declines were steepest the further up
the educational ladder adults moved. "You have the possibility of people
going through schools, getting a piece of paper for sitting in class a certain amount, and we don't know whether they're getting what they need,"

said Charles Miller, head of the U.S. Department of Education's Commission on the Future of Higher Education. "This is a fair sign that there are some problems here." Or in the simple words of Ross Miller, director of programs at the Association of American Colleges and Universities, "It is hard not to be embarrassed by the data." There's a growing suspicion that colleges are doing too little to prepare students to think for themselves, and to manage complex information processing, to say nothing of manipulating information with facility enough to pull off feats of innovation.

Casualties of the System

Unless parents exercise tight control, dropout rates are high, especially among high school boys—even though the students know there is a huge financial cost to quitting school. Over the course of a lifetime, high school dropouts will earn at least a million dollars less than those who obtain a bachelor's degree, data show. In a 2006 study commissioned by the Bill and Melinda Gates Foundation of 467 high school dropouts ages sixteen to twenty-four, 68 percent said their parents were not involved in their education—until they were on the verge of dropping out. By then, it was too late; nearly half said they had missed too many days of school and could not catch up. The leading reason dropouts cite for leaving school (47 percent) is that their classes were not interesting.

Researchers have known for years that those who drop out are no less intelligent than those who go further with their education. Some may lack social skills and drop out. Kids who are excluded from activities or otherwise shunned by their peers are especially likely to withdraw from the classroom and to suffer academically. Many more students drop out of school because they discount themselves for lack of resources—parental and financial—to continue their education. They don't have parents pushing them and paving their path. Administrators at Arizona State University recently made an interesting discovery. Concerned about the large numbers of students who were falling off the educational wagon in high school, yet viewing them as a potential pool for science studies, the administrators developed a program to reach into the high schools, turn students on before they turned off, and assure them access to the university. To their surprise, they found that fully half the would-be dropouts lured to the university by the program, called Access ASU, were *more* talented academically than the students enrolled through standard paths to college.

Boys are especially likely to be casualties of the educational system as it is now set up, their motivation lost early in the process and their attention easily diverted. By every measure, they are falling behind. They are given diagnoses of learning disabilities in elementary school at twice the rate of girls and funneled into special education classes. In high school they perform worse than girls on tests of writing. The number of boys who say they don't like school rose by 71 percent between 1980 and 2001, according to a University of Michigan study. And boys are becoming an endangered species on college campuses, where they now make up 44 percent of the student body. Because admissions officers seek to maintain a gender balance among their student populations, it's far easier for a middling male student to get into a good college than it is for a talented female.

What's hurting boys, evidence suggests, is not an innate lack of talent. It is a narrowing definition of success in school. Boys find it harder to sit for the longer periods of academic instruction that now begin in kindergarten or even before; they find it harder to focus without the relief of recess, especially needed by their body makeup of larger and longer muscle masses. Once they start falling behind, it's hard to catch up, and they quickly lose interest in doing so.

Further evidence that schools today are failing to engage students is the large and growing segment of homeschooled students, at the other extreme of involvement. If homeschooling stands for anything, it is a measure of the burden middle-class parents will assume to try to position their children for success.

Drugs as Reinforcers

Perhaps the ultimate sign that schools are out of step with today's needs is the drugs increasingly required to hold children—most of them boys—in their seats so they can receive the text-based information teachers wish to instill in them, even though that is not the most efficient way to learn for large numbers of students and alternative approaches to information acquisition are readily available. Learning disabilities such as ADHD are now diagnosed in approximately 16 percent of American boys, but the array of symptoms—from inattention and defiance to hyperactivity and frequent losing of things—has always generated a great amount of skepticism. The issue is whether a discrete information-processing disorder exists or whether boredom, frustration, and/or behavioral problems destroy patience and motivation for classroom instruction. With child behavior, it's often hard to disentangle cause from effect. Nevertheless, applying a diagnosis to make sure children acquiesce in the classroom has become a popular route for increasing the effectiveness of schooling as it currently exists.

A classic test of the validity of a diagnosis is the specificity of remedies for the disorder. By that criterion, ADHD doesn't even come close to measuring up. The stimulant drugs used to treat ADHD wind up concentrating and improving attention in everyone, not just those said to have the disorder. Some scientists point out what many successful people discover on their own: we are all, to a greater or lesser extent, cognitively distinctive, even idiosyncratic. Through trial and error, and usually a great deal of experimentation, we cobble together an array of focusing techniques that work for us. Part of our own education has always been to discover and develop strategies of information gathering and processing that suit our own needs and meet the demands of the environments in which we find ourselves. An unwillingness to do such basic work propels many to pursue medication instead.

Many solidly mainstream pediatricians have long been skeptical of the rush to medicate children. One is Lawrence Diller, author of *Running on Ritalin* and *Should I Medicate My Child?* In his experience, the more appropriate solution, because it reflects the cause of the symptoms, is a change in parenting strategies or classroom management. "Just because [medication] works doesn't make it an ethical substitute for giving kids the proper attention at home and school," he argues.

Drugs, like accommodations, are increasingly prescribed to subdue kids for an antiquated model of learning. Both approaches require a medical diagnosis. Drugs are prescribed in an attempt to fix the child on the grounds that he does not fit well into the current system of education. Accommodations alter the circumstances of testing. An emerging view of ADHD recognizes that the condition does not exist as a discrete physiological disorder at all; it is almost completely created by a specific context. The "symptoms" are characteristics that constitute a disorder or disability *only* in the context of a knowledge-based society. And the symptoms disappear when the context is changed.

What might the disorder-causing contexts be? In a *New York Times* article titled "Attention Surplus? Re-examining a Disorder," the psychiatrist Paul Steinberg of Washington, D.C., pinpoints "the tedium of school" and the "drab paperwork" of many tasks. "The term attention-deficit disorder turns out to be a misnomer," he explains. "Most people who have it actually have remarkably good attention spans as long as they are doing activities that they enjoy and find stimulating. Essentially, ADHD is a problem dealing with the menial work of daily life, the tedium involved in many school situations and 9 to 5 jobs.

"In essence, attention-deficit disorder is context-driven. In many situations of hands-on activities or activities that reward spontaneity [the positive side of impulsivity, which is a hallmark of ADHD], ADHD is not a disorder." Steinberg argues that more than drugs, a fundamental societal shift would be highly beneficial—to recognize that each child and adult learns and performs better in certain contexts than in others. What students need is education that is individualized and customized. "Some children and young adults with attention disorder may need more hands-on learning. Some may perform more effectively using computers and games rather than books. Some may do better with field work and wilderness programs." What needs changing, he insists, is not the kids. It's their context—the schools. Along with the growing involvement of parents, the widespread reliance on Ritalin is one more sign that the schools are failing the kids.

Schooling Versus Education

It's bad enough that schools rely not on the curiosity of children but on the anxious arm of parents to motivate and monitor their homework. Further, the system assumes that schooling and education are the same thing. That is a fatal mistake in an era when anyone with a computer can conduct a Google search on any imaginable topic and take in and learn vast amounts of information at her own pace and on her own time day or night—that is, whenever she needs or wants to—virtually anywhere in the world. As a result of access to the Internet, many high school students today know more than their teachers in specific areas. And with every retrieval of information, they learn how irrelevant school is to their lives. For increasing numbers of kids, the most interesting part of the day begins only when they *leave* school to go home. The extracurricular has superseded the curricular in importance in their lives.

Over the past several years, the world of psychology has been filled with a great deal of new information about how people really learn. Much of it flies directly in the face of traditional educational policy and the way almost every school is currently organized. In an information-based economy, it is almost mandatory to build learning situations about this critical knowledge. For example, it is now known that students learn in a variety of ways and settings, not just the one way that schools traditionally use. The concept of "multiple intelligences" has entered the popular culture—people learn different things differently, and their learning progresses at different rates. Not everyone responds to the same type of instruction the same way. Many of the students who have the most trouble in school are bright children who get bored and tune out intellectually.

Computer programs are available that supply flexibility of learning materials. Course materials can be delivered in text-based, graphics-based, and video-based formats to supplement live classroom strategies and meet the panoply of learning needs. But they are banned in most classrooms, along with the very elements researchers know now are significant aids to learning.

Take physical movement, and specifically that bane of the classroom, fidgeting. Increasingly, researchers are finding that learning and memory are boosted by physical movement and even fidgeting. Fidgeting frees the hands for gesturing—and gesturing, it turns out, helps children think, even retrieve words and articulate concepts that are lodged in their brains. And it helps them retain information. As things now stand, kids who fidget may be an annoyance to teachers, but they learn more. Fidgeting literally lightens the mental load, energizes the memory system, and helps problem solving and speaking.

Gesturing solidifies learning, perhaps by giving learners "an alternative, embodied way of representing new ideas," observes Susan Goldin-Meadow of the University of Chicago in the journal *Cognition*. And then, as if to drive home the point that schools are currently structured around antiquated ideas of education, she adds: "We may be able to improve children's learning just by encouraging them to move their hands."

Art is another portal of learning, even though art classes are being cut in public schools. Education in the arts is now largely available only to those whose parents have expendable income. Researchers find that art is about more than just drawing. It develops analytical skills and stimulates specific parts of the brain, different from those stimulated by intentional learning activities. Art also enlarges our humanity. It awakens creativity, ingenuity, and innovation, the ingredients for success in the new global marketplace.

Conversation may be the ultimate stimulus to learning, researchers now know, but it is still banned in most educational settings. People are motivated to learn through their curiosity about other people. Language itself is a social proposition. Every word each of us knows had to be learned. How does it happen? "Infants are motivated to learn names for the same reason that adults are," report the psychologists Roberta Michnick Golinkoff and Kathy Hirsh-Pasek. "Knowing what to call something allows one to share the contents of one's mind with another person, even when the object is not present."

Perhaps the most stunning information is research that highlights the value of failure. We learn more from our mistakes than we do from getting things right. By definition, mistakes violate our own expectations. The surprise in discovering we are wrong, scientists find, is particularly conducive to learning—it galvanizes our attention, amplifies it, and speeds up learning. The need to learn from mistakes is so crucial—in our ancient past on the savanna it likely saved lives and is the reason why we are here—it is allocated priority processing in the brain. Researchers find that when we come up against things for which we earlier made incorrect predictions, a brain mechanism is stimulated that helps us avoid repeating the error. The brain sends out a signal of recognition amazingly quickly—in just one-tenth of a second—almost immediately after seeing the object that first foiled us, in an effort to prevent us from repeating the error. This happens automatically, long before there is time for conscious consideration. Learning, then, hinges on the surprise of getting things wrong. Failure, after all, is just information, a signal to try something else, another chance to learn. But failure is information—and not a fixed and frozen outcome or catastrophe—only if children are allowed to see themselves as problem solvers, little scientists learning by trial and error, and not as trophies of talent or perfection who need to look smart and always produce the right answer.

None of this new information, however, informs current educational practice. And in a culture of fear, curricular reform is not on the agenda. That takes optimism.

The Google Effect

Our culture hasn't even begun to grapple with the Google effect, the consequences of easy availability of information all the time, anywhere—the phenomenon that lets me, at 4:00 a.m. or whenever I wake up with a question on my mind, pad to my computer and access the equivalent of, say, the Bodleian. Google is my twenty-four-hour information supermarket. Information is now accessible to people all the time, especially when they need or want it—that much-celebrated teachable, or more correctly, learnable, moment. That should force us all to ask, what purpose do schools and universities serve and how should they function? Don't get me wrong. I think they're important. I want the dedicated time and space for stretching and thinking and discovering and learning. I want the critical mass of people. I want the conversations. I want professors who know things and wear their learning in interesting ways, because human contact is still a great stimulus to knowing, probably the best one. I want a great professor to pour what's in her mind into mine because I admire that person and that mind. Contact is a motivator to know what others know or at least acquire their perspective.

But how are we going to organize the schools to do this? And what should the appropriate entrance requirements and goals be? Should they be tests of rote knowledge that well-to-do kids can pay to cram for? Should they be extracurricular activities and sports programs and overseas travel that the affluent are hurtled through to fill up a résumé? The fact that by the time they get to college so many students are so depressed and anxious or cutting themselves or binge drinking into oblivion suggests that the cost of this approach is not only intellectual disengagement but emotional disconnection as well. That's not a desirable condition for learning.

In part, their disconnection is an effect of being pushed, micromanaged, and intruded on by overinvolved parents. This is not good for the parents, and it's terrible for the students. It destroys kids' motivation and tramples their best learning instrument, their own curiosity. At best, it breeds only a desire to please parents. Parents have been called in as reinforcements by the schools simply because the schools have hit a brick wall. They have followed a model of education that is now coming up against the limits of human receptivity and information overload—an approach to education that makes no sense in the information age.

Starting earlier and earlier, the schools are trying to pour as much information as possible into kids and then test them on it as a marker of how well the schools are doing. In the process, too many kids are being turned off prematurely and dropping out of the system altogether. Others need drugs to boost concentration or are turned into dutiful robots or break down from the burden of trying. But the knowledge base has expanded remarkably since this model of education was first adopted over 150 years ago, and it really only worked for an elite few even then. Now that the information base is available for people to access anytime they want or need it, no one has to memorize it; it's always at their fingertips. In the same way, it isn't necessary for everyone to grow their own crops and raise their own livestock now that supermarkets are just down the street.

Instead of the deadening fill-'er-up model, some other approach is desperately needed. What's desirable is a system that capitalizes more on the learner, that develops and exploits what the learner uniquely brings to the party, and that makes use of everything now known about how children learn. In short, we need an approach that cultivates the native curiosity and drive of kids, rewards their remarkable persistence and perseverance, and does not trample their motivation or inclination to experiment. Such a system would breed a willingness to use knowledge creatively, to problem-solve, to innovate, to take some risks—precisely what is needed now in our forever-changed fast and flat and fluid global marketplace.

SEVEN

From Scrutiny to Fragility

For all of us, adults as well as children, life is always a dance of close-ness and distance, of approach and withdrawal, of engagement and detachment, of connection and individuation, of dependence and independence. We first learn the basic steps of this intricate and immea-surably varied dance, and most likely acquire an enduring style, in the sorties of attachment with parents early in life. Some lucky souls are intro-duced to the movements with such fluid grace that they seem to traverse life in a lilting waltz with little apparent effort. For others, every step is awkward and halting, and still others seem to engage the world clutched in a dark and driven tango of needs.

How we are exposed to these first steps and what kind of guidance and monitoring we experience will enduringly influence the self we carry and our patterns of advance and retreat in the face of life's inevitable chal-lenges . . . and the very paths we take through life. Some will be moti-vated to approach life in search of positive experiences and achievement, others will be motivated to avoid negative possibilities and failure.

Bringing Out the Worst

In his now-famous studies of how children's temperaments play out, the Harvard psychologist Jerome Kagan has shown unequivocally that what creates anxious children is parents hovering over them and protecting them from stressful experience. About 20 percent of babies are born with a high-strung temperament. They can be spotted even in the womb—by their accelerated heartbeats. Their nervous systems are innately pro- grammed to be overexcitable in response to stimulation, constantly send- ing out false alarms about what is dangerous. Or perhaps pathways from perception to alarm reaction have been conditioned by experience to overrespond. They have what's known in the psych biz as behavioral inhi- bition. Because of their overexcitability, their initial behavioral reaction to unfamiliar people, objects, and settings is to avoid and withdraw.

As infants and children, the behaviorally inhibited experience stress in situations most kids find unthreatening, and they may go through childhood and even adulthood fearful of unfamiliar people and events, withdrawn and shy. At school age they become cautious, quiet, and intro- verted. Left to their own devices, they grow up shrinking from social en- counters. They lack confidence around others and are consequently easily influenced by them. They are sitting ducks for bullies. Drawn into their inner turmoil, they are on the path to clinical depression.

Yet Kagan found to his surprise that the development of anxiety disor- ders was scarcely inevitable despite apparent genetic programming. While their innate reactivity seemed to destine all these children for later anxi- ety disorders, things didn't turn out that way. Between a touchy tempera- ment in infancy and persistence of anxiety stand two highly significant things—parents. The key factor lay in the degree to which the parents were involved in the infants' lives.

None of the overexcitable infants wound up fearful at age two—as long as their parents did not hover and overprotect but allowed the chil- dren to find some comfortable level of accommodation to the world *on their own*. By contrast, at age two, over 40 percent of highly reactive in- fants typically are behaviorally inhibited, displaying avoidance, ceasing activity, crying, and generally showing distress in the face of unfamiliar people, objects, and events.

Those parents who overprotected their children—directly observed by conducting interviews in the home—wound up with fearful kids. "Overprotectiveness brings out the worst in kids," observes Michael R. Liebowitz, clinical professor of psychiatry at Columbia University, former head of the Anxiety Disorders Clinic at New York State Psychiatric Institute and director of the Medical Research Network. He has found that an unusually high proportion of panic patients reported having had overprotective parenting in childhood.

True, behaviorally inhibited kids experience stress in situations most others find unthreatening. But shielding them from stressful events is hardly the solution. The evidence makes a compelling case for requiring the child to adjust to the world, by gradual exposure to fearful stimuli. That provides a child with the opportunity to extinguish the fear response.

A small percentage of children seem almost invulnerable to anxiety from the start. But the vast majority of kids are somewhere in between. For them, overparenting can program the nervous system in such a way to create lifelong vulnerability to anxiety and depression. And the lessons begin early—at birth.

Start-Up Stress

We are literally born *into* stress, our birth kicked off by a rising tide of cortisol, the mother of all stress hormones, in which we are actually bathed. It gives our liquid-laced lungs a last-minute booster shot to prepare them for the waiting air, and then shoves us out the door of our very first home. Launched by cortisol, we arrive into the waiting arms of our mothers. And that makes all the difference in the world. From there on in, our ability to tolerate stress and—this is critical—to cope with it constructively, to handle threats and challenges, to engage in exploration despite the risk of uncertainty, is shaped just after birth, with the way we are touched and handled and fondled by our mothers.

The ongoing studies of the neuroscientist Michael Meaney at McGill University are the instruction manual of this emerging story. But we can cut right to the denouement: how mothers touch and fondle their infants sets off permanent changes in the gene activity that regulates our behavioral and hormonal response to stress. The love that we receive as newborns is inscribed in the DNA of our nervous system and sets its tone for life, testament that early experience affects our lifelong behavior, that it becomes encoded in our personality, that outer events sculpt our innermost being.

What maternal care does is alter the chemical environment of genes for the receptors of stress hormones in specific areas of the brain. In switching genes on or off, it permanently affects the level of receptor activity and thus stress reactivity. Early handling creates a lasting increase in the number of stress-hormone receptors in the hippocampus, for example, a deep structure of the brain that is crucial to transferring short-term information into long-term memory and to spatial navigation. This "handling effect" was first observed in studies of rats, but Meaney's team has extended the research to people and confirmed its applicability.

In his studies, rat pups that were well licked and groomed by their mothers grew up to produce low levels of the hormone cortisol in response to stress. And they did not panic in the face of stress. They were more stable and less timid than siblings unlicked. Like all other rats, they respond to the stress of a sudden noise—say, a sharp clap of the researcher's hands—by freezing, but they quickly resume activity and take to actively exploring their surroundings. They never lose their penchant for exploratory behavior. The offspring of less-attentive mothers produce much higher levels of the stress hormone and remain immobilized long after the aversive loud hand clap.

High levels of cortisol are toxic to the hippocampus, inhibiting growth; prolonged bouts of stress are known to cause the hippocampus to shrink, changes that can impair the way the brain processes information. Learning and memory are directly affected; Meaney found that the ability to consolidate memory—a process known as long-term potentiation—was significantly reduced in the ungroomed pups. The hippocampus also turns out to be critical in sending out signals that shut off the body's production of cortisol; the well-licked pups, with their low levels of stress-hormone receptors quickly sated, can quickly tell the hormone control center in the pituitary: thank you very much, we've already had enough.

The ability to pay attention is also reduced in the ungroomed pups. Researchers have found that pups that fail to get the physical stimulation of licking grow up with more attention problems than well-cared-for littermates. It's the tactile contact that counts.

Translated to humans, the handling effect is likely transmitted through touch and through tickling, through stroking and pats on the head. Yes, babies need to be fed and bathed, their cries heeded and their diapers changed. But it's the affection transmitted through touch that will shape them forever.

Stress vulnerability, you could say, is a developmental disorder. The developmental perspective also acknowledges that what the infant acquires at one stage of life prepares him for the next. Growth is not just an automatic linear unfolding of capabilities; it's more a kind of relay in which the baton is passed from one set of emerging abilities to the next, and as they take their lap, they reorganize the entire process, giving rise to an increasingly comprehensive and complex elaboration of abilities. In the dialectic of growth, what the infant needs at two months sets in motion internal processes that become the foundation for what is next required. So what the infant needs at two months is not what the child needs at five years, or at fifteen. Normal development prepares creatures for the world they will inhabit. The processes of attachment and caring that govern early growth set the stage for what must come next: exploration and, eventually, independence.

Encouraging Adaptation

Kagan's studies at Harvard hold a profound lesson for all parents. Those who allow their kids to find a way to deal with life's day-to-day stresses by themselves are helping them develop resilience and their own coping strategies. "Children need to be gently encouraged to take risks and learn that nothing terrible happens," says Liebowitz. "They need gradual exposure to find that most of the world is not terribly dangerous. They need to be gently encouraged to climb a tree or meet new kids and find that nothing terrible will happen. Having overprotective parents is an added risk factor for anxiety disorder because children do not have opportunities to master their innate shyness and become more comfortable in the world." They never learn cognitive tricks and techniques they can use to dampen the alarm signals that might otherwise catapult them into panic or into a downward negative spiral of helplessness and depression.

Teaching children how to cope with the experience of stress is important. "Overprotective parents actualize the tendency to anxiety disorder." Of course, notes Liebowitz, you can't throw such a kid into a situation where he gets overwhelmingly aroused, because that would result in negative reinforcement. "You need to help them attempt positive reinforcement in situations where they are initially fearful. Overprotection fails to encourage them to face things they are reluctant to face. There's also a higher than expected rate of anxiety disorders in the parents of those children. Their anxiety leads them to see the world more negatively, to see it as more dangerous, which reinforces that perception in the children."

Encouraging children to adapt to the world, rather than overprotecting them, seems to be a general principle of healthy functioning even among frankly disabled children. Studies of children with disorders ranging from asthma to epilepsy and bowel disease show that kids function better, with fewer emotional and social problems, and have fewer complications when parents treat them as normal.

According to Nathan Fox, head of the Child Development Laboratory at the University of Maryland, parents who are oversolicitous and over-responsive to their children, providing help in situations when the child does not need it, may actually be reinforcing child anxiety or shyness by rewarding the child's initial signs of anxiety or distress with parental warmth. At the same time they are preventing the child from using and developing self-regulatory skills.

Among the children, the inclination to express negative affect such as fear or distress in response to unfamiliar or challenging events not only is reinforced; it influences voluntary attention and other self-regulatory processes. The pattern of negative reactivity to novelty in a sense trains attention to focus on negative affect or to stay focused on threatening stimuli. So it ramps up its own reactivity.

Much like the deer caught in the headlights and frozen by fright, be-haviorally inhibited children with overprotective parents stay physiologi-cally in alarm mode, vigilant to the unfamiliar or whatever threatens them, unable to disengage their attention from distressing stimuli, unable to shift attention or diminish arousal, and thus unable to engage with their environment. One of the primary goals of healthy attachment is the development of self-regulation in the infant. When parents contingently engage and disengage the attention of the infant to manage his level of arousal, they are gradually teaching him to use an external source to regulate his own arousal and gain control over his own reactive tempera-ment. Over time, if allowed, the child takes over the task of self-regulation. The trouble with overprotective parenting is that it's anything but contingent on the child's needs and it doesn't grant autonomy to the growing child. But parents no longer just worry *about* their kids; they worry *for* them.

Intrusiveness Under the Microscope

Jeffrey J. Wood is a smart, young psychologist at UCLA who gets to see on a daily basis what overprotective parenting looks like in action. In an effort to gauge its effects on school-age children, he has come up with a clever way of bringing out a parent's proclivity for intrusive behavior and assessing its nature. He brings parent-child pairs into his laboratory one at a time, assigns kids a moderately difficult task, and then observes, and videotapes, what the kids and the parents do.

Each kid is given an adjustable belt with a small case attached to it containing a ten-ounce metal weight. With the parent sitting in the room, the child is asked to put the belt over his or her shirt and instructed, "It doesn't have to be tight. You can probably do it by yourself." Parents are then told, "But, Mr. Smith, you can help Jason if he needs it." Parent-child interactions during the belt-buckling process are videotaped and observed remotely by a research assistant. Wood deliberately designed the task to be just difficult enough for most participants so that parents might be inclined to offer some degree of assistance. Just how much assistance, and how it's offered, is the real focus of the study, although parents and children are told that the belt contains monitoring equipment that will gather data for some other purpose.

The task solves many informational problems that have long bedeviled the assessment of parenting. It obviates the need for different informants—say, teachers as well as children and parents—to assure reliability of information. It focuses on specific behaviors (for example, "Mom enters my room without knocking") rather than on vague concepts (for example, "Mom invades my privacy"). It focuses on a short, specific, yet meaningful time frame. And best of all, it is an observational approach. Trained observers can go over and over the videotapes to catch interactions that might have been missed during direct viewing.

Observers watch the entire belt-buckling episode twice. On the second viewing, they record the total number of seconds the parent spent engaging in intrusive physical help or touch, such as wrapping his arms around the child to help put the belt on, sitting the child on his lap while wrapping the belt around the child, picking the child up to put him in an optimal position to attach the belt, or initiating moderate or intense physical affection (such as a kiss) before completing the task. Make no mistake: physical affection is by no means an overprotective activity in itself—but it *is* intrusive and distracting during a task that requires a child's full attention. The context is important. Two separate observers count the total number of seconds of intrusive physical help or touch.

In developing the belt-buckling task, Wood found that the amount of intrusive help or touch parents proffered was totally unrelated to the level of difficulty children experienced with the task. Some kids struggled or requested help during the belt-buckling task, and some did not. There were no statistically significant differences between the two groups in the amount of intrusive physical help or touch—suggesting, says Wood, that in providing help for their children, parents were responding to something other than the children's needs.

The coding system Wood developed is formidable. It notes parental encouragements of independence and children's refusals of help, whether they walk away from an intrusive parent or verbally declare, "I can do it," or, "No, I like it this way." Parental touching or giving of physical help of any kind merits a higher (worse) score than offering verbal help ("I'd try sitting down to do that"). But the very highest (most intrusive) score goes to those parents who take over the task for the child without permitting his further efforts to put on the belt—while the child typically becomes passive and uninvolved. The coding system measures the length of time before a child struggles with the task, or a parent first offers "help," or encourages independence. And it records the frequency of all actions and intrusions.

Please Knock Before Entering; or, What's with This Internet Monitoring?

"Parents who act intrusively tend to take over tasks that children are or could be doing independently," says Wood, "and they impose an immature level of functioning on their children." Among school-age children, parental intrusiveness can manifest itself in at least three domains: unnecessary assistance with children's daily routines (such as dressing), infantilizing behavior (using baby words, excessive physical affection), and invasions of privacy (such as when parents open doors without knocking or monitor Internet use). Among adolescents as well as grade-schoolers, intrusiveness can take the form of doing homework or term papers for children, monitoring of e-mail and Internet use, monitoring children by cell phone or other electronic device. High on the list are parents who call teachers—even professors—and lobby for a grade change or exceptional treatment in a specific situation.

"When we look at the linkage between intrusive or overinvolved or overprotective parenting and anxiety problems clinically, we really see a strong connection," says Wood. "The more intrusiveness that parents engage in, the more likely their children are to have an anxiety disorder and really be impaired by anxiety. Either a strong biological predisposition or a very stressful environment—or both—lays the groundwork for being at risk of a specific anxiety disorder. There's certainly no predestiny even in the face of children's genetic disposition." Perhaps the largest environmental influence children experience is parenting. "Overinvolved parenting plays a big role. It's not just one study that shows it," says Wood. "It's across many studies."

Wood pauses to remember one particular child, a fourth grader who typically came home most days between 8:00 and 9:00 p.m., after a series of extracurricular activities, quickly had dinner at the coffee table, kissed his mom and dad good night, and that was pretty much it:

> In our interview with him, he definitely turned out to have multiple signs of intrusive parenting. His parents were extraordinarily involved in all the activities, didn't grant him very much autonomy in what he was doing. There was this enforced practice attitude, where "you have committed to do all of this, so now you really have to put your all into it, so you have to devote time to practicing and becoming perfect at it." The seeming paradox is that the parents are involved in a lot of the children's daily routines, like dressing and bathing, which is surprising considering that the children are so competent in so many sophisticated activities. There is the sense that they would be quite capable of engaging in all their own self-help skills and having more independence in their daily lives without all the supervision. It's really a level beyond supervision—worried monitoring and worried involvement. It's quite discordant with what these children are able to do.
>
> "What does it mean that my parents are giving me all this extra assistance and direction? Does it mean that I am incapable or incompetent in some way?"

In fact, that appears to be just the interpretation kids make. "Having those feelings and thoughts typically does lead to certain emotional problems," says Wood. "There is lots of research showing linkages between a sense of self-efficacy and anxiety and depression. That's how I got into it—learning about the parenting patterns in middle- to upper-middle-class families and recognizing there was probably a connection with children's emotional adjustment."

Missing in Action: A Sense of Self-Efficacy

Forget everything you ever learned about self-esteem. Self-efficacy is different. A sense of self-efficacy—a person's perception of her ability to reach a goal—seems to be the critical factor in emotional adjustment. It's not some global sense of feeling good about yourself for no reason at all except that you exist. No, self-efficacy is a cognitive belief about capability and the expectation of performing capably, and it is a direct outgrowth of experiences of mastery.

A sense of mastery is an almost magical psychological power. A wellspring of both optimism and decisiveness, it is a view of yourself as responsible and capable of achieving goals through your own independent action. It makes people active participants in life. It sets people off on the path of lifelong learning. It gives them courage to experiment and explore and direct their own activities. It allows children especially to go after what knowledge they need, not wait to have it poured into them. It's not a guarantee that you walk on water; it's the belief that you can solve whatever problems come your way. There is a feeling of control over experience, a trust that making the struggle will be worthwhile. It's a sine qua non for resilience, that indefinable quality that allows some people to overcome the most dire adversity. A sense of mastery is a central component of well-being, as it literally lowers psychological and physical distress, conferring near immunity to generalized fearfulness and depression. It isn't, strictly speaking, a cognitive skill. It's even better. It's what allows you to draw on your cognitive resources, especially in a pinch.

There is no formula for acquiring a sense of mastery. And there may be an infinite variety of situations from which it takes seed. What they all have in common is the opportunity for rising solely by oneself to the demands of a challenging experience from start to finish, one where the outcome is by no means certain at the start. A sense of mastery flourishes among innovators and creative types. And yet it is very much at home in preschool. You see it every time a child exercises the freedom to assemble a pile of blocks, stands back, and surveys a towering accomplishment while declaring to no one in particular, "Hey, look what I just built."

Self-efficacy actually motivates people to take on challenging tasks.

The catch is that to acquire a sense of mastery, one has to do things completely on one's own—because the resulting sense of accomplishment is formative and transformative. It burrows deep in the sense of self and strengthens it from within.

The research Wood has been doing for the past five years indicates that the children of intrusive parents lack mastery experiences. They are impaired by anxiety because they "have no self-confidence and their parents have not engaged in the kinds of parenting styles and behaviors to make children feel like they can actually handle situations on their own. Children will inevitably face times when they must be independent—in their social relationships, in school, in dealing with separation situations—times when they can't be with Mom or Dad. If they're not used to that, then the lack of self-confidence turns into anxiety and fear of the situation—fear that something bad or unpredictable could happen and there's no Mom or Dad to be here to stave off the danger. They often develop avoidance."

In one current study of middle-class elementary school children, Wood and his associates have the kids rate themselves in different arenas of self-confidence—how they feel about their ability to handle the academic demands of school, to make and keep friends, to socialize with others, to handle emotional ups and downs, to cope with negative feelings, to take care of themselves, and to act independently when the time comes. They make multiple assessments of the children's anxiety and include the perspectives of parents, teachers, and the children themselves. The researchers also observe the children in frank anxiety-provoking situations like giving speeches. Similarly, they obtain multiple measures of parental intrusiveness. The most revealing, Wood finds, is talking in depth to the children about the degree to which their parents are involved in various kinds of daily activities. Many parents, he observes, engage in elaborate bedtime rituals, often including having the child come into the parent's bed. "They generally provide a lot more comforting and nurturing than the child needs," he says. "This is just really teaching the children that maybe things wouldn't go so smooth or they wouldn't feel so safe if those things weren't done for them."

So far, he's looked statistically at the relationship between self-confidence, anxiety, and parental intrusiveness. And he's found that it's parental intrusiveness that sets off the chain leading to decreased self-confidence, which then leads to increased anxiety. "Self-confidence," he adds, "is an important intermediate factor that explains in part why kids with high anxiety seem to have parents who are more intrusive than average."

Parsing Overparenting

Wood finds there are multiple elements of overparenting that contribute in very specific ways to the development of problems in children. "One key aspect of intrusiveness is that it is really the opposite of gradual exposure [to the unfamiliar or feared situation]—what Kagan showed disarms anxiety even in the face of genetic loading for it. The parents, by being so involved in the minute details of daily activities, are interfering with the habituation process, which leads to a decrease of the different kinds of fears."

Another is excessive psychological control, overregulation of children's activities and routines. It includes parental decision making for children and instruction to children on how to think or feel—the micromanagement of kids' emotions and mood states through the use of coercive or suffocating parenting techniques. The classic is conditional approval, whereby parents show interest and affection only when a child does well or offers a viewpoint that agrees with theirs ("My mother or father is less friendly to me if I don't see things like he/she does"). The old warhorse is guilt induction as a means of discipline: "You're making your mother crazy by getting Bs." It also involves parents telling a child what he is feeling: "You are not really uninterested; you are afraid."

Control encourages dependence on parents, because it essentially communicates incompetence and it inhibits individuation. It also affects children's perceptions of mastery over the environment. Lack of mastery leads to anxiety by biasing children to believe that events are out of their control. Parental control is the direct opposite of the granting or encouraging of autonomy in children, and it inhibits autonomy. What makes psychological control so powerful in crippling children is that it involves manipulation of the attachment relationship. It is a means of creating insecure attachment.

The highly regimented childhoods that today's parents are very active in arranging for their kids leave children with little breathing room of their own, says the social historian Peter Stearns. "I'm not just talking about activities. I'm talking about styles of dress. We think the children are facing a lot of choice, and in some ways they are. But it's usually choice under pretty strict controls."

In a recent professional article, Wood articulated the link between intrusiveness and one specific form of anxiety, separation anxiety in young children. He views it as a proxy for the linkage between intrusiveness and all forms of anxiety.

Among adolescents, the UCLA psychologist argues, the result of intrusive parenting is likely to be social phobia; that's because the normal tendency of adolescents to fear themselves constantly scrutinized by others runs up against and gets validated by actual parental overinvolvement and overscrutiny. In both cases, a kind of emotional reasoning takes hold: "I feel fearful, therefore there must be some grave danger in the situation. Something bad may happen."

"When children with anxiety are obliged to be away from their parents who tend to perform even simple daily routines for them and comfort them excessively (i.e. act intrusively), they are faced with two challenges," Wood explains in the journal *Child Psychiatry and Human Development*.

First, they are separated from trusted caregivers, which due to their parents' typical overinvolvement, is a relatively unfamiliar situation for them. In combination with their anxiety proneness, this lack of familiarity with independence may predispose them to develop catastrophic misinterpretations about such situations. Second, when away from parents who act intrusively, children are often confronted with tasks (e.g. social interactions, daily routines) that their caregivers have normally performed for them, compelling them to attempt activities with which they have had little experience with successful independent action. Vulnerability to anxiety tends to make these unmastered activities highly stressful. And children with a history of intrusive parenting are likely to have low self-efficacy for performing these activities (e.g. unfamiliar daily routines at school), thereby increasing their anxiety. These reactions are directly triggered by facing unfamiliar situations when unaccompanied by a parent. In contrast, the presence of parents provides a cue of safety and success in such situations (potentiating reduced state anxiety); as a result, children are negatively reinforced to avoid separations. Hence, high parental intrusiveness may set the stage for children with high anxiety to react negatively to, and subsequently fear and steer clear of, situations requiring separations from their caregivers.

Because overprotection renders children unable to cope with stressful situations, and unable to cope with the real world, it makes them less able to cope with pain. Researchers have long known that stress exacerbates pain. A recent array of studies suggests that a sense of mastery minimizes both the perception of stress and the perception of pain. The loss of a true sense of mastery may explain why researchers are now finding a generation gap in chronic pain, with younger people experiencing more pain and more pain-related negative effects than older people. Older adults were better able to cope with their pain, had less trouble falling asleep, and had fewer depressive symptoms as a result of pain. The researchers believe that generational characteristics and attitudes, along with life experiences and expectations, may explain the differences.

Anxiety is well recognized as a predisposing factor for depression. So it shouldn't be surprising that invasive parents, who create anxiety in their children, weaken them in other ways as well. "A hovering parent who is closely identified with the adolescent does increase the risk for extreme guilt in the youth if they do not meet the expectations of the parent," says Kagan. "This can increase the risk for depression." For him, the central fact is how a young person interprets the parental behavior. "If the adolescent interprets the protection as motivated by a desire to stifle growth, then the outcome will be undesirable."

How Concern Can Cripple

Halfway around the world, at the University of Haifa in Israel, which has a world-class Center for the Study of Learning Disabilities, the doctoral candidate Liat Feingold is also conducting research that sharply illuminates how parents who mean the best for their children can wind up bringing out the worst in them. Her studies focus on kids with learning disabilities, but the findings embody general principles that likely cut across many domains of experience.

There comes a point, she has found, when concern, by itself, can be crippling. Feingold looked at eighty-five kids, fifth and sixth graders, with reading disability, the most common form of learning disability, and whether, and to what degree, being aware of their disability helps them cope with it. It turns out that the kids exposed to the most learning assistance—who underwent the greatest number of diagnostic and treatment sessions—wound up being preoccupied with their disability, which pitched them into a state of anxiety about learning and led to a decline in academic achievement. There is such a thing as too much time spent dealing with a problem; it can backfire and bring about the very outcome one hopes to avoid.

Awareness of their disability proved adaptive to kids to the degree that they had knowledge about it, understood its implications for their emotional and academic functioning, and were exposed to strategies for coping with it in and out of school. Such kids did well academically. But at some point knowledge about the disability lost its productivity—when awareness created only consuming concern with the dysfunction and detonated negative emotions, such as anxiety and depression. Those emotions used up cognitive resources, disrupted information processing, and destroyed learning motivation. When that happened, reading comprehension suffered, and kids fared poorly academically.

What did such kids in was the child's perception of his or her mother's level of anxiety. "When a child with reading disability feels that his mother worries about his academic success, his anxiety level rises, he thinks ruminative thoughts of his disability, and it relates to low achievement in reading comprehension. The parent's assumption of child incompetence gets communicated to the child."

Parental anxiety was also communicated in the degree of parental involvement with the learning problem and with the child's studies. The more parents sought diagnostic and treatment sessions, the lower the child's intrinsic motivation for learning. The results, says Feingold, flatly contradict the currently accepted wisdom that parents should be as involved as possible with their child's learning disabilities. Continuous parental dealing with the disorder delivered a negative message all its own that was completely unintended. Exposing a child to repeated clinical evaluations and different treatment methods causes a child to think too much about the disability and ruminate endlessly and unproductively over how it will impact his life. The constant parental dealing with the disability transmitted to the child a general feeling of anxiety and was the agent of self-preoccupation.

Under these circumstances, even the best knowledge about the disability and how to deal with it is no longer useful to a child (or any-one), because it is not accessible; anxiety kept the children, as it always keeps people, from making use of their repertoire of cognitive and emo-tional resources for dealing with challenges. Overinvolvement delivers a double whammy. It weakens kids from within, usually by creating anxiety. And then it keeps them from developing or deploying their own coping strategies.

Awareness is always a double-edged sword. Here we see how going to great lengths to help someone else can sharpen the wrong edge of the sword. Such efforts transform awareness into self-preoccupation with the dysfunction, and they interfere with the ability to cope. Good intentions create bad outcomes when those intentions lead to extensive external (parental) involvement in a problem that is largely internal to a child. They vitiate an individual's own motivation to overcome the problem and create dependence on external forces rather than on personal resources. One result among the reading disabled: self-learning efficacy is impaired. Of course, the whole point of helping is supposed to be to stimulate someone's ability to learn, not to impede it.

In the end, we all have to assemble and learn to rely on our own re-sources to cope with the idiosyncratic array of strengths and weaknesses we each have. Help is good when it's not too invasive, when it doesn't de-stroy motivation, when it leaves room for a child (or anyone) to assume some responsibility for figuring out how he best functions. "It's important that children with reading problems know what their learning disability is, what its ramifications are, and how to deal with the problem," notes Feingold. "However, it is important not to spend too much time dealing with the issue."

Hand-Me-Down Dread

If it's so damaging, why do adults engage in death-grip parenting? For many it is an expression of their own anxiety. Just because anxiety exists in both parent and child doesn't mean it was transmitted via genes. The behavioral transmission of anxiety may be far more pervasive.

"There is a high level of neuroticism underlying the actions parents take in setting up many extracurricular activities and being involved in their children's daily routines," says Wood. When he began to work with the parents clinically, he saw their utter fear of the consequences if, for instance, their child didn't do a perfect job of brushing his teeth on his own. Or if he selected clothes that didn't match. "A lot of the basis of parents providing unneeded assistance seems to be parental worries and concerns about untoward effects of the children doing a task for themselves that could end up with imperfect results. Therefore the parents need to step in and take partial or full responsibility to make sure that these things are done just right and the children avoid whatever consequences the parents perceive are possible."

And yet a child's very confidence and independence require a substantial dose of trial-and-error learning—and allowing a child to fail. Wood explains:

> There's an internal motivation on the child's part to succeed, so there's no danger to some failure. It's an important aspect of learning to cope with the realities of life. It allows children to figure out intellectually how things work. And it allows them to develop an internal schema for independence and the other tasks they need to learn. If you put a Rubik's Cube in a child's hands and tell him that the way to solve it is to make five moves to the left and three to the right, that doesn't teach the child the basic rules for solving the geometric problem. But if you give it to a child and say, "Fool around with this," he'll have a hands-on experience learning the properties of the activity or object that teach him something about the world and about what he can do to influence the world. Mastering a concept requires a certain amount of failure and error—learning that certain things do work, certain things don't, and finding out about both.

Failure is a way of figuring things out. It teaches us what doesn't work.

Wood thinks that the inability of parents to accept less than perfect performance comes partly out of fear of the child's future. Imperfection negates their syllogisms of success. Parents worry that one bad grade on a fourth-grade math test is the start of some breakdown in the child's math skills that will keep him from college and the good life, and they resolve to do everything in their power to prevent that. That represents the kind of catastrophic thinking that typifies anxiety.

No Practice Managing Worry

There is no question that parents want their children to be safe. Over the past several years, that desire for safety has somehow come to mean not just the physical safety but even more the psychological safety of children. In implementing that desire, parents basically translate it as not wanting their child to be sad or otherwise upset. Parents have come to feel responsible for the children's emotions. At its most extreme, that overprotective attitude winds up as a belief that "my child can do no wrong."

It is common among today's parents to have outsize fears about letting their children experience distress in any form. They want their children to be happy, and they have the mistaken idea that the way to find happiness is to be happy every minute of every day. Children's happiness and emotional fulfillment have superseded independence as the primary goal of parenting. "Many parents have some strong fundamental belief that anxiety or upset or anger is bad and shouldn't be experienced because it is destructive to kids," observes the psychologist Lynne Siqueland, who heads The Children's Center for OCD and Anxiety in Plymouth Meeting, Pennsylvania. "Their definition of what a good parent is and what a good parent does includes protecting their kids from those experiences."

In itself, she notes, anxiety is not a scary thing. It's a protective emotion; it keeps us on our toes, and it cues us to prepare well. We all need a certain amount of anxiety to carry out our tasks in life. "But when kids get anxious," says Siqueland, "parents drop all demands for appropriate and competent behavior. They're scared the kids are going to have a breakdown or become suicidal. If you hold a view of your child as fragile, the child will come to embody it. He won't have the chance to work through the difficult moments. He won't come to believe he's capable. You can create chronic anxiety in a perfectly healthy child that way alone."

Of course, not only is constant happiness impossible to achieve; protecting children from distress prevents them from knowing what to do when the world isn't going their way. Often enough, the parents of children that Siqueland sees have themselves experienced anxiety. "They feel 'It's so painful for me, I don't want to subject my child to that level of pain.' They themselves don't know how to manage it, they think it's intolerable, and they don't want their kid to experience that. Their intent is good." But they can't even conceive that their child might not feel the same as the parent does.

The effects are crippling. The child never gets to know that he can comfort and reassure himself, never gets practice in managing worry, never gets to know that he can gain a sense of control about the worry— a sense of mastery about coping with strong feelings. "Parents' tendency to take over for a child does not give the child a chance to practice crucial psychological or interpersonal tasks," Siqueland observes. "Excessive helping not only sends the message to children that they are incapable of managing normal situations without parental assistance; it also teaches children that distress, pain, and anxiety are dangerous and to be avoided at all costs."

In the absence of experience of adversity, children gain no understanding of the need for perseverance. One result is that there is no patience for feeling bad. Parents rescue. But parental overinvolvement keeps kids from experiencing minor upsets in doses manageable enough for developing their own coping skills. So they are not being immunized against big bad feelings and just crumble in the face of life's ordinary difficulties.

A Competition of Needs

Yet another way parents contribute to children's anxiety is by modeling catastrophic thinking: "If you don't do well on this math test, how will you ever get into Harvard?" Studies have long shown that such cognitive distortions are not just self-defeating; they are typical of persons with anxiety and its first cousin, depression. Recent studies pinpoint catastrophic thinking as the single most potent contributor to the development of child anxiety, the element most responsible for the transmission of anxiety from parent to child. It leads to the development of a worldview in which bad events and worse outcomes are pervasive, inescapable, and unmanageable.

Parents engage in catastrophic thinking when they describe problems as unresolvable. They make comments about their own lives, the children, or the world that exaggerate dangers, the likelihood of negative consequences, or helplessness, Wood explains. He relayed two examples from conversations he had recently heard: "Mommy, can I go outside and play with Tommy in the front yard?" "No, honey, Mommy is busy right now and I don't want some kidnapper picking you up off the front lawn." And, "Look at the way you're treating your homework this week. You come home and do the bare minimum and you're happy with a 94. You could be a genius, but you're heading for a very mediocre life."

Death-grip parenting is also a means for some adults to get the psychic rewards of closeness. "It's not that the parents find the child 'needs' the help or involvement, but they themselves need the involvement at an emotional level, a social level, or physical level," says Wood on the basis of clinical observation. "Not that long ago, we had a mother tell her twelve-year-old son that 'the reason I embarrass you in public by giving your ten-year-old brother hugs and kisses all the time is because he needs it and I need it. I know it embarrasses you, but I'm not going to stop, because I like it.' She put into very simple terms what we suspected from various other parents in our studies."

Yes, the goal of parenting is to raise an independent child. "But it's as if the positive role parents can play in optimal development is in competition in some way with parents' needs of a largely self-serving nature," says Wood. "They need the involvement at whatever the cost. There is a lot of irrationality in parents' perceptions of why they're doing it and a lot of willingness to overlook the implications for the children."

Some anxious parents create a sense of fragility in their children by seeing their children as fragile and then encouraging their labeling as such. "We have developed some parental practices that encourage kids to think of themselves as sickly," says Stearns. He specifically cites the burgeoning diagnosis of attention deficit disorder. "We're doing this more in the U.S. than otherwise similar societies are doing," he points out. "There is something that goes beyond pure science, something in the culture that makes us unusually eager to identify this; perhaps it is discomfort with children who give us problems. And we have a batch of almost entirely well-meaning experts who are eager to jump in and say they can help. This problem category shows every sign of growing."

Taking away basic experience in almost any domain you can name— even in the presence of a hypothetical or demonstrated handicap—leaves children feeling incompetent. It is the path to victimhood. In a detailed examination of the use of height-augmenting drugs, Stephen S. Hall, writing in the *New York Times Magazine,* came to that conclusion about the psychological effects of short stature on otherwise normal children.

"Often parents think the children have a complex about size, but I think it's the parents who have a complex," one pediatrician told him. Nevertheless, many parents opt to put their children through lengthy and expensive (twenty thousand dollars a year for five years) treatment, with human growth hormone, which winds up adding a stunningly disappointing average of 3.7 centimeters in height. As one researcher explained, "The biggest side effect from growth hormone use is unmet expectations." A major rationale of drug use is to protect children from teasing and bullying as a result of their short stature. But Hall, himself short, heard from many pediatric endocrinologists "that many kids learn to cope with the stress and may be better off in the long run in having learned to deal with the adversity."

The writer concluded: "As someone who now views the psychological distress of short stature as transient and survivable, I also wonder about the long-term psychological side effects of the decision to pursue height augmentation. Does it inadvertently send the message that the resolution of adversity or stress resides in a syringe or pill? Does it imply to a child that we should change physically to accommodate the biases of society? And do we accidentally diminish a child by focusing on height rather than on helping him bulk up his emotional muscle and resilience—muscles that will always prove useful in adulthood?"

The protectionism that takes all the risk of life for kids rests on the assumption that children are easily bruised. It becomes a self-fulfilling prophecy. The fact is that too much protectionism *creates* frailty. Not only do children fail to develop coping skills for life's vicissitudes, and fall apart when they hit a speed bump, but kids come to think that something must really be wrong with them if they need so much protection. They are deprived of real opportunities for learning about themselves and for growth.

The End of Independence

Sensitive and responsive parents know that sensitivity and responsiveness change with development, and they are sensitive and responsive to their child's burgeoning independence. Behaviorally inhibited children become less inhibited over toddlerhood if they attend preschool or are exposed to nonparental caregiving for at least ten hours a week. It could be that they gain from interacting with unfamiliar peers.

Children who go to day care, observes Nathan Fox, may be more likely to receive parenting that fosters independence. In addition, they also likely gain experience and practice interacting with unfamiliar people, thereby reducing their fears. Others, like Sarah's daughter, who stay at home, are particularly likely to receive parenting that is oversolicitous and overcontrolling. "A parent's own anxious or fearful personality may lead both to the decision to keep a child at home and to an overprotective parenting style" that maintains the child's tendency to behavioral inhibition.

"It smacks of a parent who has no confidence in the child's ability to be safe, to handle any situation independently," adds Wood. "It's hard to imagine that the child would not pick up on those sentiments in multiple ways and have their sense of efficacy seriously damaged by that type of superinvolvement." The UCLA psychologist says he is surprised at how prevalent is the attitude of never wanting to leave a child with a caretaker or babysitter—even among families that can afford high-quality care. "Clearly the parents' rationale is 'the reason we are staying together all the time is because something bad could happen to you if we didn't.' It implies that there is something dangerous to be avoided. If that gets communicated to the children in some way, that is not leading to a realistic or positive view of the world as a fairly benign place. The underlying cognition common to all anxiety disorders is that there is a real lot out there to fear."

Then, too, the insecure attachment created by death-grip parenting can generate anxiety in offspring through its own direct means. It literally alters the stress reactivity of the infant and, acting through the hormones of the stress response, sets the emotional alarm center in the nervous system so that it is highly reactive—as if the child were born behaviorally inhibited. The insecure attachment gives rise to anxiety de novo.

Death-grip parenting may originate in parents' anxieties about the world they find themselves in and a misplaced need for control in a world that seems constantly in flux, but it is encouraged by a widespread misinterpretation and misapplication of the attachment literature as it is filtered down to parents. There are media pediatricians who advocate "attachment parenting"—as if attachment didn't occur naturally, as if attachment benefits from the conscious imposition of control. As advocated by the pediatrician William Sears and his wife, Martha, a nurse, attachment parenting is a prescription for natural childbirth, wearing the baby in a sling, constant availability to the child, and forgoing babysitters, the use of pacifiers, swings, strollers, and other "material" soothers instead of oneself. In fact, it is a kind of regiment that violates the fundamental spirit of attachment—mutual co-regulation—which involves both sensitivity to a baby's varying needs and allowing for a mutuality of influence.

Intrusive attachment owes something, too, to rapid technological change and the expansion of knowledge. The sped-up information society has created a culture in which children can no longer be dependent on adults for information and wisdom. "Kids tell us all the time that their parents are clueless," says Sudbury Valley's Dan Greenberg. "Their knowledge and experience are no longer relevant. What's left is emotional dependence. It's the only claim parents today can make for having a hold on their kids. It reflects the anxiety of desperation."

Parents have such trouble separating themselves from their children that they are increasingly unwilling to send their kids to residential summer camp, a place that traditionally gave children a chance to escape the scrutiny of parents but still provided the watchful eyes of adults. And it gave adults a usually very welcome break from parenting and time to renew adult relationships. But summer camp has been transformed from a summerlong experience into, most commonly, a one- or two-week stint, usually involving some kind of skill training. One writer recently expounded on the need for children and parents to experience separation and confided that she was flooded "with separation anxiety so intense that it radiates down my arms as I type"—as she sent her daughter off for a grand total of six days. "As a parent, I fully realize the anxiety each mother and father feels in placing the welfare of their children in the hands of another," goes the greeting on the typical camp home page. Most camps now have Web sites that allow parents to monitor their children from afar by way of photographs and videos that are changed daily. Parents scour them so closely that noticing a small Band-Aid on a child's knee now is cause for a parent to call the camp to find out what went wrong.

The purpose of the attachment system is to free a child to explore the world *on his own,* figure out how to make his own way through it, and feel secure enough to take some risks. It is predicated on the fact that eventual separation underlies the growth and development of individual identity, of abstract knowledge, of problem solving, of coping skills, and of resilience. Love isn't doing everything for your child; that's narcissism. Love is allowing your child to try and to fail and teaching him how to pick himself up. In taking away every obstacle, parents are destroying the very things that will

assure the success and happiness of their kids in the future. Intrusive attachment is as much a distortion of developmental needs as too little; it
keeps kids dependent and sets them up for lifelong fragility. The tragedy is
that with the best of intentions, parents today may be crippling children—
especially those children who have the most resources behind them and
would otherwise have the greatest shot at success.

Fallout of Invasive Parenting

Invasive parenting undermines children in still other ways. Being looked
at all the time makes children extremely self-conscious, says the child psychologist David Anderegg. As a result, they get less communicative;
scrutiny teaches them to bury their real feelings deeply. And most of all,
self-consciousness and constant reminders of the dangers lurking everywhere remove the safety to be experimental and playful. "If every drawing
is going to end up on your parents' refrigerator, you're not free to fool
around, to goof up or make mistakes," he points out. And if all the bumps
are taken from the path, then children wind up with a kind of chronic low-
grade depression. Parental hovering, however, is why so many teenagers
are so ironic, he notes. It's a kind of detachment, "a way of hiding in plain
sight. They just don't want to be exposed to any more scrutiny."

Irony is just one of the defenses kids develop in response to parental
invasiveness. An online language all their own is another means young
people have devised to escape parental scrutiny. Codes like Leet Speak
and coinages like P-911, for parent alert, are attempts by teens—and
highly creative ones at that—to find release from parental control and
create some breathing room of their own, although determined parents
can now find online dictionaries and translators to help them decipher
the information.

Even protectiveness in the form of using parental connections on behalf of one's children undermines kids' sense of self-efficacy. Says
Anderegg: "When you cheat on their behalf to get them ahead of other
children"—by pursuing accommodations and recommendations—"you
just completely corrode their sense of self. They feel 'I couldn't do this on
my own.'" A child comes to think, "If I need every advantage I can get,
then perhaps there is really something wrong with me." A slam dunk for
self-doubt and depression.

Overparenting encourages people to grow up with an exaggerated sense of their own importance. That contributes to their growing difficulties in getting along with others. In the hothouse of child rearing today, children rule.

An educational inspector, the Danish psychologist Bent Hougaard stepped into a nursery school playground one morning to observe whether the daily routines of the school were congruent with its educational objectives. All the children were outdoors, playing. Behind a small shed, five-year-old Jack was throwing sand at some younger girls. Hougaard asked the boy to stop. "You're not in charge of the nursery," Jack shot back. The visiting psychologist took the bucket and spade from Jack, put them on the roof of the shed, and headed into the school for a planned meeting with the staff. Suddenly the boy was right behind him. "You old asshole," Jack shouted, "you don't rule over me." Hougaard was stunned; he had seen a lot in his years as a psychologist, but never this. "I had to force myself to think, 'Bent, remember you are a child psychologist. Don't hit or kick; he is the child.' Before I knew it, the little master was asking for his bucket back. He got it when he promised not to throw sand at anybody again." But the promise was short-lived. Within seconds, Hougaard got a kick in the behind and a couple of spadefuls of sand thrown right in his face—along with a triumphal "You don't rule over me."

The tragedy is that hothouse kids never learn to rule over themselves. They make enormous demands on everyone but themselves. They experience the most trouble coping just when they are put in environments where they have to function on their own—leaving for college or entering the workforce.

EIGHT

Crisis on the Campus

ollege is where the fragility factor is having its greatest impact. By all accounts, psychological distress is rampant on college campuses. The young are breaking down in record numbers and showing serious forms of distress in ways previous generations did not. The hottest place on college campuses these days is not the local brew-pub, the athletics center, or the famous-architect-designed student union. It's the campus counseling center. Once backwaters of the mental health system, dealing primarily with roommate problems, relationship issues, and schedule stress, campus counseling centers are now the new front line in the battle against mental illness. Through their doors are likely to march about 10 percent of the student body in any given year. In 2005, 9 percent of all college students sought counseling on campus; at some schools the rate exceeds 50 percent.

The severity of student mental health problems began rising in 1988, dramatically so in the 1990s, according to an annual survey of campus counseling center directors conducted by the psychologist Robert Gallagher of the University of Pittsburgh. The University of Michigan Depression Center, the nation's first, estimates that 15 percent of college students nationwide are now suffering from clinical depression alone. In a 2005 survey conducted by the American College Health Association, 19.6 percent of students reported experiencing depression in the past school year; 13.4 percent had anxiety. More than 90 percent of the forty-seven thousand students surveyed reported feeling overwhelmed at least once during the school year; 28.6 percent had the feeling on eleven or more occasions. Over 45 percent of students felt so depressed they said it was difficult to function. The collective forms of distress on campus affect from 10 to 20 percent of students in any given year, depending on the school. In addition to those students seen clinically, rates of self-reported depression are climbing, surveys show.

Relationship problems haven't gone away; instead, their nature has dramatically shifted, and their severity has escalated. Colleges report ever more cases of obsessive pursuit, otherwise known as stalking, leading to violence, even death. In the past fifteen years, sexual assaults have quadrupled. A survey of 366 counseling centers in 2005 recorded 375 cases of obsessive pursuit, with 92 students being injured and 4 killed by their pursuer. Anorexia or bulimia in florid or subclinical form now allegedly afflicts 40 percent of women at some time in their college career; female athletes are especially prone to eating disorders on campus. There's no sign of letup in sight; experts report that eating disorders are on the rapid rise now among preteen girls.

Eating disorders have become so much a part of the collegiate landscape that disparaging one's body is now regarded as a norm of female behavior. As one former college official explained, "I have a friend who is a first-year dean at an Ivy. She told me that the residence halls have serious plumbing problems caused by the prevalence of bulimia among the female students." She admitted that she herself couldn't vouch for the story—but that she believed it. Maybe it *is* apocryphal. But it brilliantly captures the situation.

Emotional distress is rampant on U.S. college campuses, and it is openly discussed and, often, well recognized. But sometimes the biggest danger is actually hidden from view. The psychological fragility of students is damaging the mental and physical health of individuals. But it is also corrosive to the collegiate infrastructure. The mental state of students is now interfering with the core mission of the university, says Steven Hyman, provost of Harvard University and a psychiatrist who was formerly director of the National Institute of Mental Health.

The vast majority of the nation's college counseling centers report that they are under siege, trying to meet the demands of unprecedented numbers of students with a wide range of serious and—this is important—increasingly complex psychological problems. From major and manic depression to eating disorders to self-harm to substance abuse, campus mental health centers are dealing more and more with acute conditions that have, in their extreme form, life-and-death consequences. Shedding their reputation as the Rodney Dangerfield of college services (because they get so little respect), counseling centers are more and more seen as critical to the core mission of the university—relieving the mental burdens that impede students from learning and incubating the next generation of civil society.

As a result, the issues that campus counseling centers now face reach into the highest offices of higher education. There isn't a meeting of college presidents where the subject of student mental health doesn't come up, observes Hyman, as provost the second-highest officer of Harvard University. "It's an important, nationwide problem in higher education," he says. Adds Kevin Kruger, associate executive director of the National Association of Student Personnel Administrators, the organization of college student affairs officers: "It's one of the top five critical issues on campuses." "By the tenth or eleventh week of the semester," says Russ Federman, director of counseling and psychological services at the University of Virginia, "we are near saturation. All appointments are filled up—and we are strongly resourced. But students don't stop coming." Although they are struggling to manage swarms of students with serious depression and anxiety disorders, colleges are also reluctant to keep expanding services for fear that they might cross some invisible line and transform themselves into therapeutic communities.

The middle of the night may find a SWAT team of counselors calming down a dorm wing after having crisis-managed an acute manic episode or yet another incident of self-mutilation. Morning will certainly find the staff administering psychotherapy to students struggling to overcome histories of trauma such as childhood sexual abuse, relationship problems, including date violence, and that dormitory staple, eating disorders.

Did we mention substance abuse? Attention deficit disorders and learning disabilities? At one elite institution, 10 percent of students report problems with binge drinking. Rare is the college that has not experienced a student suicide. A ten-thousand-student campus can expect one student suicide a year. That doesn't count all the highly disturbing attempts.

Hospitalization, a court of last resort, is commonplace. Ninety-one percent of counseling centers hospitalized at least one student in 2005; one hospitalized a hundred. On one five-thousand-student campus where

most students are commuters, three to six students are typically hospitalized a semester, primarily for suicidal gestures and first psychotic breaks.

In 2001, 85 percent of North America's student counseling centers reported an increase in "students with severe psychological problems" over
the past five years. Thirty percent of them had a student suicide; 60 percent of them dealt with obsessive pursuit cases (fifty persons injured, five
killed). By 2005, 96 percent of counseling centers observed that the percentage of students with significant psychological problems was growing.
Just between 2004 and 2005, counseling center directors reported increases in self-injury, the number of students with eating disorders, sexual assault cases, and students reporting previous sexual abuse. They also
found themselves facing an increased demand for crisis counseling.

"Every director of every college counseling center is reporting more
hospitalizations, more serious problems, and taking care of sicker students," says Richard Kadison, a psychiatrist who heads Harvard University's counseling center.

"The world isn't getting crazier," observes Pamela L. Graesser, director
of counseling at Rivier College, a small Catholic institution in New
Hampshire whose students are primarily from blue-collar families. "College is just getting more like the real world around it." College is available
to more people than it used to be. The problems Graesser saw twelve
years ago when she worked in a psychiatric hospital "are the same ones I
now see on campus." In 1965 there were four million college students in
America. Today there are fourteen million. And more of them live off campus, not as tightly tied to the campus community as students once were.

It may be that colleges are seeing the true prevalence of mental disorders that exists in the larger world. There simply is not as much surveillance in the outside world, and college is more available to more people
than it was a generation ago. Still, their counseling services overtaxed,
schools are responding by triaging cases, rationing counseling, and, some
say, over-relying on medications to get kids through what may, in the end,
prove to be an unusually difficult (but not necessarily permanent) transition to adulthood in especially confusing times. "Counseling centers are
struggling with doing brief crisis stabilization versus addressing fundamental issues to effect change," laments Federman.

Schools literally can't afford to have anyone fall through the cracks;
student suicide presents huge liability issues and is highly disruptive to
the whole campus. At the same time, parents are pressing colleges to take

on even more responsibility for student safety, well-being, and success. "Universities feel the need to respond in an ethical way," insists Joseph M. Behan, head of counseling at the School of the Art Institute of Chicago.

No one's sure when the demand for counseling and more intensive psychiatric services will begin to level off. Or where, or even how, to draw the line between academic and therapeutic community. But this much is clear: lots of students in college today have lots of psychological needs beyond traditional adjustment and developmental issues. "Through 1996," reports the psychologist Sherry Benton, assistant director of counseling at Kansas State University, where 40 percent of seniors have used the services at some point in their four years, "the most common problem students came in with were relationship issues. That is developmentally appropriate." But in 1996 anxiety overtook it. And it has remained the top problem ever since.

The Prozac Payoff

Although it lands on their doorstep as one more problem, colleges are in fact the new beneficiaries of what many consider one of the great successes of medicine. Call it the Prozac payoff. Colleges are reeling from the number of students arriving already on antidepressant and other medication. A decade and a half of improved drugs has encouraged earlier diagnosis. By minimizing symptoms, early treatment of depression—along with institutional accommodation of disability—has enabled students to stay in the academic system who in other eras might not have made it to college, or would have dropped out after a semester or drifted into community colleges. Today they are attending the nation's elite institutions, where academic, living, and developmental demands sometimes overwhelm the coping skills they have yet to acquire and the drugs don't deliver. Many require psychiatric monitoring and care—care that they don't always get or that they actively reject.

The American Academy of Child and Adolescent Psychiatry reports that about 5 percent of American children under age eighteen are seriously depressed. The prevalence of anxiety is 13 percent for children ages nine to seventeen. Some experts believe the figures for depression in children are higher, that one in four will experience a serious episode before turning eighteen. Although antidepressant use has recently been declining because of warnings regarding children, antidepressant prescriptions doubled between 1998 and 2004.

"Many who wouldn't have gotten to an elite college before are getting here because they were treated when younger," observes Harvard's Kadison. "They need ongoing, intensive care," which not every school has the resources to supply. Many students fall apart given the looser environment, erratic sleeping patterns, and added stresses of college.

Although colleges are now reaping the Prozac payoff, college being what it is, they must also deal with Prozac rebellion. In many cases it is the real trigger for a depressive episode. A significant proportion of students attempts to go off their medication once they get to college. Many figure that now that they are out of the house, where problems first arose, their troubles should be over and they can manage on their own. "They think college will solve their problems," observes Rosemarie Rothmeier, director of student counseling at Austin College in Sherman, Texas. "They say, 'My parents were the problem.' Or, 'I had no friends before, but now I do.' They go off their medication, and indeed, they don't feel bad immediately. It takes some time for symptoms to return."

Others seek to escape the possibility that they may have to be on medication for the rest of their lives; they see medication as pathologizing what they are feeling. They think, "I want to be like everyone else." Still, David Mednick, co-director of counseling at Fairleigh Dickinson University in New Jersey, reports that his "biggest concern is the number of depressed patients needing medication who have not yet followed through filling a prescription. They do not like the idea of being on medication; they share the public prejudice against needing medication to feel well."

Still others slip back into depression surreptitiously. They fall prey to a more disorganized lifestyle and experience the return of symptoms because of disrupted dosing schedules. And then there is that stark fact of campus social life. "Many students stop taking their antidepressants in order to drink," reports Rothmeier.

Today, 14 percent of college students filling out their prematriculation health forms indicate they are actively being treated for clinical depression. That's *before* they get to campus. Many more are diagnosed on campus. When 134 colleges recently sponsored a depression screening day, 12,999 students showed up; 5,199 were referred for treatment.

One index of the upswing in depression on campus is prescription patterns. The number-one prescribed drug for college students is not the birth control pill or an acne medication. It's Prozac. In second place are antianxiety agents, significant because depression and anxiety are now considered two faces of the same disorder. The number-three spot goes to all other SSRIs combined. Of two thousand students entering Harvard's student mental health system in 2001, more than one thousand were given prescriptions for one of four leading antidepressants. That doesn't count other antidepressants or prescriptions given to students by outside physicians. On average, over 25 percent of campus counseling center clients now take psychiatric medication, up from 9 percent in 1994 and 17 percent in 2000.

Prozac, however, turns out to be proxy for a number of problems. "It's an indirect indicator that lots of psychiatric illness is being treated on college campuses," says Morton Silverman, a professor of psychiatry at the University of Chicago, former head of its counseling services, and current senior adviser to the national Suicide Prevention Resource Center. Like many working in the college setting, he is more apt to use a diagnosis of depression than any other. The destigmatization of mental illness has proceeded only so far. "Depression is more accepted than schizophrenia or bipolar illness or personality disorder. It's still not okay to have a more serious psychiatric problem," especially among graduate students in law and medicine, for whom such a diagnosis might eventually pose licensure problems.

Spring Break(down)

April is the cruelest month. College counseling centers feel the crunch, giving a whole new meaning to "spring break." Students who put off counseling all year suddenly realize they're going home soon. "They're going back to the situation that made them crazy in the first place, or back to the abuser," reports Rivier's Graesser. Seniors flock in with anxieties about confronting the real world.

And there's a whole new rite of spring. It starts just after college acceptance letters go out. Parents call the counseling centers at the schools where their offspring have been accepted. "They say, 'My son or daughter has a serious eating disorder' or 'has been hospitalized for depression; what can you do to support them?' " reports Mark H. Reed, counseling director at Dartmouth College. They're footing the bill; access to mental health care is now one of the factors they weigh before writing a check.

In addition to handling more cases of depression diagnosed before college, counselors find that they are picking up many more new cases of depression in college. "There are increases in both undergraduate and graduate students carrying a diagnosis," reports Silverman.

"More students are coming to college predisposed to developing depression," he observes. There are more students with a family history of the disorder. And there are many more students with prior sexual and physical abuse, both of which increase the risk for depression. "The incidence of sexual and physical abuse was on the rise ten years ago," he says, "and that generation is now coming to college."

Many looked forward to college as a place where they could be free to get the help their families discouraged—or made necessary in the first place. Although many students come to college openly declaring experience with depression, large numbers do not make it known—until a crisis erupts. Reed worries "most about the students we don't see."

Cases of moderate to severe depression are rising also because depression often—and increasingly—co-occurs with other problems, such as alcohol and drug abuse and personality, eating, and anxiety disorders. The compounding of disorders renders conditions hard to treat and even suggests that some more fundamental disturbance is dysregulating numerous systems of the brain and body at one time. It may be that the seeds of disorder are sown early in development by the hormonal chaos of insecure attachment. In ways both subtle and profound, early experience shapes the neural pathways that underlie lifelong susceptibility to anxiety, depression, and personality disorders; it shapes their architecture, their excitability—and their responsiveness to later efforts at change. "We're seeing more depression because more other disorders are arriving and present as depression," explains Silverman.

Most college counseling directors confess to being surprised by the number of students turning out to have bipolar disorder. It typically presents dramatically, with an acute manic episode. "We are seeing more first episodes of mania every year," Silverman reports. "It's very disruptive. It generally means hospitalization for the student. The number of hospitalizations for psychological reasons is going up each year, and the percentage attributable to bipolar disorder has risen." In 2005, 366 campus counseling centers hospitalized a total of 2,462 students for psychological reasons, up from 2,210 in 2004.

The boom in bipolar disorder may be an outgrowth of too-liberal use of antidepressant medication; antidepressants can stimulate mania. And it may also reflect wanton diagnosis of attention deficit disorder in school-children. "It's difficult to tell the difference between ADD and bipolar disorder in kids," says Reed. "Lots of ADD turns out to be bipolar disorder."

The trouble is that the kinds of stimulants that work for attention problems, not to mention caffeine—that mainstay of college life—are precisely wrong for bipolar illness and can trigger a manic episode. "The first manic episode is related to a stressor, such as sleep deprivation," Reed explains. "Almost always some substance is also on board." He believes it is often an attempt by a student at self-medication.

Perhaps the clearest index of the campus mental health crisis is the weekly appointment calendar of a college counseling psychologist. The National Survey of Counseling Center Directors reveals that in one typical week, one college mental health counselor sees:

- 6 incest victims (2 suicide attempts)
- 3 drug and alcohol abuse cases
- 2 prepsychotic—on meds and supportive counseling
- 2 rape victims
- 1 physical abuse victim
- 2 eating disorder cases
- 2 depression following death in the family
- 1 schizophrenia in remission
- 1 child of alcoholic parent
- 1 married grad student with homosexual urges
- 3 traumatized by broken relationships

Drinking to Oblivion: Why Passing Out Is In

There is a September ritual every university faculty member and administrator has come to dread. "Every fall," reports John Portmann, assistant professor of religious studies at the University of Virginia and author of *Bad for Us: The Lure of Self-Harm*, "parents drop off their well-groomed freshmen, and within two or three days many have consumed a dangerous amount of alcohol and placed themselves in harm's way. These kids have been controlled for so long they just go crazy."

Students around the globe have long been known to bend an elbow, and rare is the university without its share of brewpubs near campus. But the nature of student drinking has changed dramatically in recent years. Once a means of social lubrication, drinking has acquired a darker, more desperate nature. In the first two weeks of the 2006–7 school year, one well-regarded eastern university issued sixty "alcohol-related conduct violations"—in a freshman class of thirteen hundred. "The number is way up," said a vice president. "Something has changed. Something is going on in the high schools." The conduct violations primarily involved fistfights, sexual assaults, and roommate conflicts. The administrator couldn't help noting that this was the brightest class the school had ever admitted, as measured by SAT scores, and their extracurricular experience was pretty spiffy, too.

Like the students who do it, the drinking today is highly goal directed, and the new goal in drinking is exceedingly blunt: to drink as much as possible as quickly as possible. Binge drinking is defined as consuming more than five drinks (four drinks, for women) at one sitting. Campuses nationwide are reporting worrisome increases in binge drinking over the past decade, with alcohol-related hospitalizations commonplace. A major football rivalry, with its party atmosphere, can send dozens of drinkers to the hospital with acute alcohol poisoning. Tied directly to the increase in alcohol abuse is a rise in violence on campuses. Its most significant manifestation is an increase in sexual assaults.

Alcohol is the drug used by most young people in America. Overall, more than 40 percent of collegians report binge drinking. In its 2005 survey of over forty-seven thousand students at seventy-four colleges, the American College Health Association found that 40 percent of students consumed five or more drinks in one sitting at least once in the prior two weeks. A total of 37.2 percent of students reported that as a result of their drinking, they did something they later regretted. And among the students who drank, 30.4 percent forgot where they were or what they had done. Binge drinking is rising fastest among girls, and they are especially drawn to alcopops, a kind of Kool-Aid with a kick. Alcopops are sweet, fruit-flavored drinks that hide the taste of alcohol—there are 1.5 ounces of spirits in every 12-ounce serving. They're marketed almost exclusively to the young and widely seen as a "girlie drink."

Since picking up a glass—and bending an elbow to bring it to the mouth—can impede the process of getting drunk, students have turned to technology to support speed drinking, relying on an external device to leverage the efficiency of their efforts. Hence, their invariable party prop is the beer bong, about as blunt an instrument as you'll ever see—essentially a quart-size or larger funnel borne aloft, the outflow channel being a short hose that is inserted in the mouth. This crude device—trash technology—resembles nothing so much as an intravenous infusion setup. Nothing comes between you and your booze. You just have to open your gullet. You can hold the tubing aloft yourself and dance ecstatically while drinking. Or you might boogie up to a communal beer bong, whose large reservoir feeds multiple hoses at one time, and latch on. Some enterprising wag always manages to roll a large, portable multiuser beer bong onto the beach at spring break—you don't even have to be an engineering student to rig one up.

Of course, there's no law requiring the reservoir to be filled with beer; wine, alcopops, or hard spirits work just as well, especially for women, ever mindful of beer bloat. In Ann Arbor, Michigan, home of one of America's foremost research universities and its largest stadium, football Saturdays are famous. So is 914 State Street, site of the three-story beer bong—hung outdoors from a balcony via thirty feet of tubing—that is a frequent stopping-off point for students. The highly public nature of participation, often before a large gathering of bystanders, only serves as encouragement.

The beer bong might be the ultimate emblem of shifting patterns of student social life. One-on-one dating is a quaint relic of the 1950s. Socializing among the young today takes place primarily in groups. And large parties are far more frequent on most campuses—and off campus—than they used to be. Once confined to weekends, they now occur every night of the week on some campuses. Group socializing puts a great demand on social skills. Alcohol rushes in where social skills leave off.

The resemblance of the beer bong to an infusion apparatus goes beyond appearances. It totally obviates the need for voluntary action. You just have to be there. Intention is not even in the equation. Drinking from a beer bong removes the possibility of pausing even to think, "Should I order another?"—a step that, by comparison, now seems the social equivalent to soul-searching. This is not a case of judgment impaired. Judgment is circumvented altogether. By its very nature the beer bong holds decision making in contempt of the party spirit and evades it entirely. Once you latch onto the beer bong, gravity does all the work. The beer bong bypasses the brain. And in doing so, it disconnects you from your own self.

Beer bongs are not the only change in drinking patterns over the past decade. Hard liquor flows furiously, too, and most binge drinking now involves distilled liquor. "Power hours" are popular, in which students down as many shots as possible in a limited amount of time. And "twenty-one on twenty-one" is a new rite of passage; turning twenty-one is the occasion for a celebration in which you are given two hours to down twenty-one shots just after midnight on your actual birthday.

High spirits can quickly turn to dead spirits. The new desperation that fuels binge drinking is reflected in a rise of mean violence on campus. Binge drinking is strongly linked to sexual assault and rape. Each year, more than seventy thousand college students are victims of alcohol-related sexual assault or date rape. An estimated fourteen hundred college students die each year from alcohol-related injuries. That doesn't count the half-million students who are injured each year under the influence of alcohol.

After the party's over, students often come to class inebriated or hung over, if they get there at all. The heaviest drinking occurs, of course, on weekends, which now begin on Thirsty Thursday, but the effects increasingly hang over the whole week. In a 2002 survey of 772 Duke University undergraduates, researchers found that 51 percent of those who drank at all had had at least one blackout in their drinking lifetimes. Researchers were shocked to find that blackouts—a lack of memory of events that occur during a period of heavy drinking without a loss of consciousness—were so common. Members or pledges of fraternities and sororities are twice as likely as their non-Greek classmates to get drunk at least weekly, and are at significantly higher risk of being injured—falling out a window, getting burned—or injuring someone else.

The Duke study suggests that heavy drinking by students is not a pastime to wink at. Drinking prior to full brain maturation damages neurocognitive functioning in many ways—it impairs decision making in the executive center of the brain, boosting preference for short-term rewards and desensitizing people to long-term losses. But the most troublesome outcome of all may be that it especially undermines the structures that allow people to impose voluntary control over drinking in the future. Sure, it impairs learning and memory—and the adolescent brain is more sensitive to memory impairment than is the adult brain—but it also increases the risk of later alcoholism by close to 50 percent. "The Grim Neurology of Teenage Drinking," blared the *New York Times* headline, reporting that "47% of those who begin drinking alcohol before the age of 14 become alcohol-dependent at some time in their lives, compared with 9% of those who wait at least until age 21."

One popular cocktail is any kind of alcohol mixed with so-called energy drinks like Red Bull. But it packs a particularly mean punch. It significantly reduces the perception of impairment—without reducing alcohol-related deficits. The disconnect students experience between their perceptions and objective measures of their abilities may actually cost more of them their lives—because they believe they are unimpaired when they get behind the wheel to drive back to campus.

But why has binge drinking become such a serious problem only in the past decade? It has to do with the changing nature of social life, insists the psychologist Bernardo Carducci, a professor at Indiana University Southeast, where he is founder and director of the Shyness Research Institute. Students, he finds, increasingly lack garden-variety social skills, the kind acquired over time in repeated face-to-face encounters, first with adults and then with peers, the kind that breed sensitivity to others, the understanding of often-subtle interpersonal cues, and the ability to resolve conflicts. Heavy drinking has become the quickest and easiest way to get accepted. "Much of collegiate social activity is centered on alcohol consumption because it's an anxiety reducer and demands no social skills," says Carducci.

"Plus, it provides an instant identity; it lets people know that you are willing to belong." Whether it is your usual style of socializing or not, "everyone binges the first few weeks of college," reports a professional observer of student life who is not long out of college herself.

"You have this transition period," explains Carducci. "Anytime there is a period of transition, there is a period of uncertainty. And uncertainty leads to conformity; uncertainty makes us turn to others. When you're turning to others, when you're trying to affiliate, you turn to people who are most like you. And when you are uncertain, you are much more likely to be subject to social influence. People get you to do things so that you will feel like you fit in."

Social anxiety is so great among the young that it has given rise to the new custom of pre-gaming, the act of quickly consuming a large amount of alcohol even before going out to a party. "In college," reports Greg Moore of the University of Kentucky, "the students often find they cannot deal with conflict and are often anxious about social situations—anxiety they often treat by multiple shots of vodka before they head out the door."

Today's students drink, contends Joyce Bylander, provost of Dickinson College, because they are so fragile. "It's the fragility of today's students that creates the need for them to be medicated and anesthetized in some way with alcohol, to be able to be social, to be out there. It emboldens them to be on display in some ways; to have a certain numbness they are less self-conscious. But it also decreases their capacity for good judgment. They may think they're more open, but they are, in my opinion, more vulnerable."

The new patterns of alcohol consumption are fueling a "substantial increase" in students seeking treatment as a result of acts of violence, observes Isabel Goldenberg, head of student health at George Washington University. "Only a few years ago, this would have happened only two or three times a year. We feel it is linked to fewer coping skills, little experience in conflict resolution and little experience in community living. Alcohol is also a large part of this. Last year, through October, we had 36 hospital admissions for acute alcohol intoxication. This year we have had 76 admissions."

A veteran of three campuses, Bylander has "never had to hear a sexual assault case on any college campus I've ever worked where alcohol was not a party to the assault." She tells of the e-mail that "fell into our hands, in which a group of young men were describing a party they wanted to have. They wanted to make sure there was plenty of alcohol there and that the women got plenty of alcohol because, they said, 'it's the only chance we have for having sex with them.' Right off the bat that's a violation of the law, because the law says that women who are incapacitated by alcohol cannot give consent. If that's not predatory behavior, I don't know what is."

The shocker is, Goldenberg adds, that the more alcohol abuse among college students increases, the higher their test scores or GPAs. "Is this a function of increased intelligence, increased competition or increased stress? We don't know, but it means that as many of our schools become more competitive, we are selecting a higher risk population of students."

Binge drinking appears to go far deeper than group validation and stress relief. The psychologist Paul Joffe of the counseling center at the University of Illinois at Urbana-Champaign believes that students engage in binge drinking as a misguided, but readily accessible, way to put meaning in their lives. From extensive interviews he has conducted with students, he contends that binge drinking is, at bottom, a quest for authenticity and intensity of experience. It gives young people something all their own to talk about, and sharing stories about the path to passing out is a primary purpose, a pathway to bonding.

The MySpace phenomenon has underscored the need to have a story to tell—and even show. Edward Spencer, associate vice president for student affairs at Virginia Tech, a man who spends a great deal of time around students, told me that "the enormous quantities of alcohol" so many students are increasingly willing to drink really mystified him—until he began sitting down and talking to students about it. "Students now see getting drunk as an opportunity to be onstage and tell your story on MySpace," he reports. The performance element is a recent addition to the alcohol culture. "The binge is a moment to preserve on MySpace, a moment to tell people about. It's an opportunity for intensification, preservation, and demonstration for others."

In a world of the young dominated by text messaging, the need for story-centered narratives—even narratives of getting "wasted"—may be greater than ever. Still, it's an inverted universe in which drinking to oblivion is the way to feel connected and alive.

Down on the Pharm

If alcohol abuse is a quick bulwark against anxiety over lack of social skills, students also have their own instant solution for feats of performance on demand—"pharming." Students openly sell and share prescription drugs. Drug abuse is widespread—especially with prescription drugs.

There was a time not long ago when the most popular shortcut to success was CliffsNotes. Today the shortest path to achievement is Modafinil (a drug used to treat narcolepsy and other sleeping disorders). Or Ritalin or Adderall, prescription medications that act as stimulants and are widely used to treat attention deficit disorder. Students call them "study drugs." They boost mental focus and sharpness.

CliffsNotes at least maintain the power of achievement squarely in the student. Drugs put the power of success on the pharmacy shelf. They work in the short term, making users feel sharper, but their long-term value is unclear. They totally disconnect students from their own sense of purpose or motivation. They may cause subtle—and possibly permanent—

disturbances in still-developing brains. But that isn't their worst subversion; they keep students from developing skills of self-regulation. If you never have to confront your own demons of distraction, you never learn to subdue them.

The Social Fabric Unravels

The consequences of the mental health crisis on campus are far-reaching. The ripples can already be felt—and can be expected to influence life in America for years, if not decades, to come. Along with the military, the university is a major front line of cultural assimilation in America, the place where the increasing ethnic and cultural diversity of the population finds common ground and diverse groups become more or less integrated. What the university experience is about—implied by its very name—is providing and promoting a sense of community, shaping and molding a cohort as it prepares them to meet the demands facing their generation. It is supposed to be a place of face-to-face interaction academically and socially.

But college officials report that mission is, in the words of one, "getting challenging." One major effect of depression and other mental health problems is to break down the sense of community. Depression is a disorder in which one of the most prominent and identifying symptoms is social withdrawal. Further, even when it isn't manifest in clinical disorder, the perception of being under stress, so widespread on campus as well as off, discourages people from making the extra effort it sometimes takes to communicate effectively across differences of religion, ethnicity, gender, gender identity, or background.

Given its core population of those on the verge of adulthood, the university can be thought of as a leading indicator of societal and perhaps political trends. By this index, it's not unreasonable to expect increasing polarization in years to come.

In 2004, there was a perceptible drop in interaction between students from differing backgrounds, according to the annual survey of incoming freshmen conducted by the Higher Education Research Institute at UCLA. Fewer friendships or study groups crossed any lines at all; 67.8 percent of the 300,000 incoming freshmen surveyed reported that they frequently socialized with someone from a different racial or ethnic group, down from 70 percent in 2001. What's more, a growing number of students appeared unlikely to have a diverse set of friends in college, with fewer of them expecting to socialize with people outside their own racial or ethnic group. This was the lowest percentage recorded since the question was added to the survey in 2000. Further, fewer students than ever care about promoting ethnic understanding: 29.7 percent in 2004, versus 46.4 percent in 1992.

Resignation, Not Rebellion

Marissa, the Yalie we met in Chapter One, first became aware of how constricted her life was during high school. "I loved poetry and photography and all this 'weird' stuff. But I felt like I wasn't allowed to explore. I was typecast as the one who'd do the best on all the tests. I was class president, star lacrosse player. I didn't do it because I wanted to; it's just what everyone expected me to do. I had to get the best grade on the test because I knew everyone was expecting it. I didn't care. I played that game. It was like, 'Whatever . . . next.'"

Whatever. Marissa shrugs and delivers the expression that virtually defines her generation. Apathetic. Dismissive. Compliant. Without passion, affect, or energy. It's the sound of hostility and resignation rolled into one locution. It recognizes that their lives are regimented and directed by others—parents, coaches, pricey professionals hired to train them—but they don't see a way out. They don't have the courage to rebel or the skills to stand on their own. Because they've never had to grapple with the kinds of unhurried and unstructured experiences that breed coping strategies and resilience, they collapse when they encounter pressure, adversity, or simply unexpected circumstances.

Marissa just wanted someone "to ask me what I really loved or who I really was. No one seemed capable of that. I realize now that it was my fault. I should have screamed: 'Let me take photography.' But in my very competitive all-girls school you just didn't do that." She applied to Yale for early decision and "cried for three weeks afterward. I was so sick of having to excel and be this person that I just didn't want to be. I had a dream of dropping out and running around the country in this Jack Kerouac type of existence. I longed for a much more organic experience." For Marissa as for many, it took a breakdown to jump-start her sense of self, to give herself permission to abandon premed and start on more personally meaningful studies—and to develop a tolerance for human frailty.

Hanging on Through High School

Why is it that kids like Marissa who seem to do well through high school fall apart in college? (Hint: it has to do with the removal of external structure and routine, and exit from the programmed and protected cocoon of home.)

It's a mistake to think that today's college students are really just a bunch of privileged brats who've had it way too easy and merit little sympathy for their problems. Or to dismiss them because they are suffering from homegrown pressures to compete and perform, and the psychic stresses and social-emotional deficits engendered by such pressures. They do in fact have to prepare themselves for a world far different from the one most of today's adults emerged into. A constantly changing, anxiety-provoking, overstimulating, and, yes, more highly competitive world. The world impinges on these kids in ways generations before never dreamed of, and it has from an early age.

Moreover, not everyone is so privileged.

One psychologist told me of receiving a call from a daughter of privilege who had been a client while in high school. Now a freshman at college, she didn't like the food on campus. She prevailed on her parents to set her up in an apartment. All that was lacking was a letter from the psychologist authorizing the need for a move off campus into an apartment where the girl could live with reference to her own needs exclusively. The psychologist refused.

Isn't a university *supposed* to gather many people of many different backgrounds? And isn't half the challenge of college learning to live with others and discovering how strange are the customs and rituals of the little tribe your family represents? Is it a privilege to live alone off campus? Or a sentence to loneliness and depression? A refusal to learn social skills? An unwillingness to help her own cohort forge a common context for their lives?

I have talked to counselors and directors of campus counseling centers across the country. From every single one I heard horror stories of sexual and physical abuse and also a kind of privileged neglect—in the face of parental anxiety and overinvestment—today's students had been subjected to. But here's what confused me. A lot of the kids seemed to do well enough in high school to get into some of the country's "best" colleges. How is it that kids who seem to be functioning well until college have difficulties once they get on campus? Aren't they survivors? Wouldn't they have developed resilience?

Not necessarily, says the psychologist Marie van Tubbergen of Ann Arbor, Michigan. Van Tubbergen spent a year of predoctoral internship at the University of Massachusetts, in its counseling and testing center. Sometimes, she says, the students are just holding things together until they get to college.

"I encounter this a lot among the traditional college student (age eighteen to nineteen at time of freshman year)," she told me.

> My personal theory is that [in high school] students are able to tolerate an enormous amount of stress and family conflict because (a) they have no choice about where to live, (b) they have enormous external structure: school, family rules, et cetera, and (c) there is some sort of cognitive setup that believes that they just need to "get out of the house" or "be on their own" or "out of high school" and then they will be free of their problems.
>
> Students survive brutal family environments in high school with the presumption that if they can just live it out, it will be over. Then they get to college, and after a couple of months or a couple of years they discover that (a) they do now have choices about where they will live and who they will see, (b) they have only their own resources to set/maintain a structure and routine to support them, and (c) their problems did not magically go away even though the reasons for their problems are not now part of their daily life. This leads to the terrifying insight that their problems may never "go away."

Van Tubbergen told me that she constantly hears "heartbreaking stories of abuse, neglect, and family conflict. These kids held it together in the belief that it would be over soon. Then they leave home and it isn't over. And there's nothing left to blame. They discover the emotional fact that if you leave the stimulus, it doesn't mean your problems are solved. And they experience sadness and rage. 'If it's over and I'm still unhappy, then it's just me.' Their family relationships affect all the relationships they are in now."

Suicide on Campus

Since depression is the single biggest risk factor for suicide, and since the severity of mental problems on campus is increasing, it might be expected that the number of campus suicides would be skyrocketing. But that is not the case, although a few highly publicized incidents at Harvard, MIT, and New York University have fostered a general perception that ivory towers are for jumping.

It is more likely that the social structure of college protects people in some way—or the traditional structure of college has in the past—and that colleges have been doing a pretty good job of keeping suicide attempts from being successful. The suicide rate is actually lower on campus than among same-age people outside.

"Suicide is not a good marker for the rise in mental disorders in colleges," insists the University of Chicago's Silverman. "Every suicide is a personal tragedy. But it's not a reflection on university policies or procedures."

Every suicide is also enormously disruptive to an entire campus. So counseling centers make a big effort to prevent problems by reaching out to students with programs of information. "We're no longer just 'mental health professionals,'" says Harvard's Kadison. "We're marketing directors, trying to figure out how to connect with students who might need our services." The only problem is that outreach programs, such as after 9/11, work too well. Where Harvard's mental health service was seeing 240 new cases a week in January 2001, it was up to 280 a week in January 2002.

MIT is still reeling from a suicide in 2000, when a young woman a month from her baccalaureate and entering a graduate program set herself afire in a campus dorm. Her family sued the university, on the grounds that parents should be notified if a student is suicidal, and the lawsuit, ultimately settled in 2006, was allowed to proceed against specific administrators and medical staff on the grounds that they should have prevented her death, inasmuch as they knew she was troubled.

"We can't do that," says Kadison. The trust that help seeking will be kept confidential, often particularly from their families, is what encourages students to come in in the first place. "The students are adults at age 18. We are all seeing suicidal students. We'd just be a switchboard calling families all the time."

For the year 2004, 366 campus counseling centers reported 154 student suicides, three-quarters of them among males. To the extent that it was known, 45 percent of the students were depressed, and 27 percent had relationship problems. Some 13.5 percent of the students were troubled by grades.

One chilling effect of the MIT lawsuit has been the adoption by some universities of mandatory leave policies for students who present a "serious threat" of suicide. But it's not yet clear whether such policies are legally and ethically viable, and they may conflict with federal disability and privacy laws. Nor is predicting who is at high risk of suicide, even among students with serious conditions such as bipolar disorder, an exact science. Schools are bending over backward to do all kinds of outreach on campus—online surveys of suicidal ideation, e-mail counseling, depression screening, stress-reduction clinics—in hopes of finding distressed students and persuading them to seek treatment before disorder declares itself in suicide. In 2005, Harvard even created a new administrative position, widely dubbed the "fun czar," to help students counter a "depressing social" scene and create a climate of happiness on campus.

Birth of the Blues: Age of Risk

What accounts for the increased vulnerability of young people to mental disorders today? Certainly, there has been no shift or drift in genetic makeup. More likely, many factors combine in ways subtle and overt to create susceptibility that becomes a headlock in the presence of performance pressures and the absence of very basic coping skills.

A major reason for the surge in serious problems on campus may be that college is the age of depression—along with many other mental disorders. Increasingly, mental health professionals recognize that depression, anxiety disorders, bipolar illness, personality disorders, and schizophrenia are conditions that first arise in late adolescence and young adulthood. Ages eighteen to twenty-five are now recognized as prime time for the eruption of mental illness, making college, with its concentration of eighteen- to twenty-five-year-olds, the prime place. Catching disorder quickly is critical, as early management strongly influences how illness plays out over adulthood. And so it is that in every imaginable way, colleges are the first, best hope for rescuing the minds of America's future.

A *Cumulative Burden of Stress*

Young people today do live in a far more complex world than their parents inhabited. That alone can set the stage for overloading abilities to cope. In the face of novel problems, the young are indeed on their own. There is no acquired or accumulated wisdom that their families can hand down to the next generation; there is no model of successful behavior for the kids to absorb at the breakfast table. The very thing they need most—the freedom to experiment and make their own adaptations to life as it confronts them—is largely denied them in their overcontrolled hothouse upbringing.

Today's college students have faced competitive pressures from an early age, and they are carrying a cumulative burden of stress. "It's more stressful to be a kid growing up these days," says Dartmouth's Reed. "These students experienced competition to get into kindergarten. They are on a treadmill, develop portfolios, and cultivate a few narrowly specialized 'areas of excellence' to get into the best prep school."

By the time they get to college, some lose their love of learning. "Many are on a treadmill with blinders," he adds. That does more than rob them of childhood. "Most of their self-esteem comes from a few areas of excellence. They fail to develop an internal system to sustain them in all environments." Like Marissa, "they've sunken under the weight of obligation at an early age."

It isn't the competitive orientation by itself that is so damaging. It's the *chronicity* of the competitive pressure that is most harmful. Competition per se can be good. It is energizing, mentally clarifying, a stimulus to peak performance. But even marathons are finite, and the regimen of preparation is reasonably clear-cut. Constant competition, on the other hand, is a chronic stressor. Like all chronic stressors, over time it depletes resources. Worse, it has its own direct negative effects. It is specifically damaging to centers of learning and memory in the brain.

For those students not at a first-tier college, the pressure, ironically, may be especially intense. "They really suffer a crisis in confidence about their future," observes Michael Doyle, head of student psychological services at Loyola Marymount University in Los Angeles. "They feel like they lost out already. So, many feel more pressure to succeed."

What's more, in previous generations, troubled students just disappeared from campus. "Now we're seeing the opposite end of the spectrum," says Austin's Rothmeier. "Parents have too much of an investment. They don't want students to take off time." She often encourages students to lighten their course load, especially if they are on medications. "But these are kids who are used to juggling. The suggestion to slow down is difficult to accept." They're afraid their transcript might be affected and that will put them at a disadvantage for graduate school.

Family Failings

Backgrounds of family dysfunction—even in economically privileged students—contribute to the increasing incidence and severity of student psychological problems. "More students have a family history of mental disorder," reports Silverman. "More have a history of sexual or physical abuse. And we're seeing more kids from troubled backgrounds." A disproportionate number of troubled students come from divorced families and received bad parenting, he says. "They lack the social skills to function in group settings and they lack affect-regulation skills, which make them volatile and act out."

Lacking a supportive family base, young people grow up unbuffered from stress—before they have learned how to handle it. Living in fractured families can lead to greater instability in their psychological lives. It's hard for young people to focus and define themselves if the ground is always shifting beneath their feet. "You have to have an internalized sense of stability to draw on when under stress," points out Linda K. Hellmich, staff psychologist at the counseling center of the University of Kentucky. "Otherwise you become overwhelmed and the bottom drops out."

For those coming out of abusive families, college presents distinctive internal challenges. "It's confusing," says Rivier's Graesser. Living with nonfamily, they suddenly realize "there's a whole other way of being in the world. Once out of the unhealthy system they get a good look at it for the first time. And they typically have crises around going home, beginning with just before or just after Thanksgiving. It's not easy for them to break free of a whole system of thinking that made it normal for them to clean up their mother's vomit after school every day."

Lite Sustenance

The big issue for most students is how to separate successfully from their families, moving from dependence to independence. That's a challenge under the best of conditions. It's especially difficult for the large number who never got what they needed at home or who suffered abuse or neglect at home—or whose parents remain overinvolved in their lives.

The current generation of students was completely formed by the culture of consumption. The means of gratification today's kids learned while growing up doesn't sustain them in moments of challenge or crisis, which are really developmental opportunities and require looking inward rather than outward or backward for solutions.

In addition, they are carrying a cumulative burden from the fact that adolescence begins earlier and lasts longer. In the media-rich world that today's kids live in, they are exposed to a lot of stuff before they have the cognitive and emotional tools to deal with it. For example, they no longer have to discover their sexuality; it's thrown at them from the time they sit in front of a television screen or pass a billboard while safely strapped into the family car. Not many know what to do with it.

Brain Drain

If there's one distinguishing feature of the current crop of college students—indeed, the current dynamic of college life—it is a lack of critical thinking, decision-making, and problem-solving skills, all skills located in the frontal cortex, the executive portion of the brain. These skills hinge on reflection, inner intellectual processes that include evaluating the relevance and validity of information, probing for more information where needed, analyzing and marshaling evidence, developing hypotheses, making reasoned judgments, assessing ambiguity, constructing arguments to persuade others (and ourselves), formulating inferences, calculating likelihoods, envisioning alternative strategies, generating new ideas. They are absolutely essential for analyzing problems and identifying solutions. They don't just operate in some disembodied intellectual sphere; there is, in fact, no such realm. They are the same skills required for maintaining balance when the emotional alarm circuits of the brain are activated—say, when a student gets dumped by a boyfriend.

This is a generation that is used to excessive parental involvement in decisions, often via cell phone, unusually receptive to prescription remedies, and often conditioned to external rewards rather than contemplation. Their experience favors external solutions to problems—pre-gaming, substance use—rather than self-searching. Reflection is not promoted, or even valued, in their goal-directed, achievement-oriented young lives. The general lack of discussion and debate in classrooms on such formerly hot-button topics as, say, ethics is mute testimony of contempt for critical analysis.

Contemplation is a mental skill that, like all skills, must be cultivated and practiced. It both demands and builds the ability to regulate one's emotions so as to not get sidetracked by them—the ability to tolerate internal states. It requires concentration, the ability to focus attention and maintain the focus despite momentary unpleasantness or confusion of thoughts, a way to maintain objectivity about subjective experience.

There is nothing inherently wrong with the capabilities today's young have grown to acquire. It's just that they are not the skills most suited to identifying and removing mental stumbling blocks to happiness. And they may even foster them. Without well-oiled skills in reflection and the development of some mental discipline, there is no core sense of self to call on in a crisis, and it is easy to be overwhelmed by emotion. Given their impatience and intolerance for imperfection, they are sitting ducks for turning to alcohol, medication, or even cutting rather than navigating a tide of disappointment with self-analysis or confidence in their own brainpower to see them through.

There's No There There

Most of all, perhaps, they lack a sense of self. Or they are totally disconnected from themselves. The disorders of perfection from which many suffer—such as anorexia and bulimia—are signs they are driven by pleasing others and meeting the standards of others. Performance-enhancing drugs disconnect them even from their own success. In part they have no identity because they have no challenges to develop themselves on. Like Marissa, they feel empty.

Nil on Skills

With their narrowly specialized hothouse childhoods, many students today come to college lacking the very skills that would help them cope most effectively with whatever challenges they encounter. Counseling center directors cite widespread shortage of social and emotion-regulation skills among students.

"Kids need more connection to healthier relationships with friends and professionals," says the Chicago Art Institute's Behan. "Lots of students learned pathological ways of relating to others, not only in their families but in their peer groups. Healthy connections to others are for most students the primary way to work out their problems. Getting people connected is the solution to the isolation and loneliness students feel that precipitate their crises."

"Many students lack acceptance of internal events like sadness, anger and anxiety," says the psychologist Jacqueline Pistorello of the University of Nevada, Reno. Like others in her field, she sees such widespread problem behaviors as drinking and self-cutting as attempts by students to dissipate sadness, anxiety, and frustration. "I see large numbers of students who don't know how to handle anger," said one counseling director who didn't want his school identified. Such students may get particularly disturbed by a bad grade.

Diversity Can Be Daunting

Many universities today pride themselves on the diversity of their student populations and are unusually welcoming to students of many backgrounds. These may include immigrants from all over the world as well as minorities within the United States. Speaking across different cultures enriches the experience of college, a time of expanding minds. But it requires relationship skills at a moment when those seem to be in short supply.

It takes time for most students to make the intellectual, social, and cultural adaptations to diversity, and that puts a burden on students for which not everyone is equally prepared. Although such learning is critically important for the future of the country, it puts a special stress on negotiating differences among people with different views of social relations and different degrees of social skills—a special stress at a time when they are making all their other adaptations to college, including being away from home. "Diversity is a big challenge," reports one administrator. "The crossing of religious, ethnic, and racial lines is not as easy as we would like, and I'm talking about friendships and study groups, not dating. It takes effort and energy."

Yes, it's exciting to encounter people from all different cultures, says Christine M., a junior at Duke University. But "diversity puts more stress on negotiating differences. Different groups bring different ideas of how to make relationships work." As a result, there is widespread failure of relationships—between the sexes as well as between races and ethnic groups—that is "a big contributor to unhappiness on campus."

the widespread lack of social skills is compounded by a paucity of decision-making skills. It's hard to know how to make decisions on your own if you've never been in a position to do so. "I see a lot of kids who are unhappy because they are making bad decisions," Christine observes. "One girl, for example, was miserable because she was sleeping with forty different guys a month. But then they go to their parents, say they're depressed, and wind up getting medication for their unhappiness without learning to make better decisions." College does not provide close-enough models of successful adult behavior to learn from, she adds.

The Underground

Substantial as they already are, the problems currently plaguing students and taxing college resources may be just the tip of the iceberg. Students themselves point to a huge amount of mental anguish still underground. This may be particularly the case in the most elite schools. "In the atmosphere that is established at a competitive university," says Sarah C., a graduate of one highly competitive university who received her master's degree at another, "it is often difficult to express personal vulnerability." And while suffering is almost always isolating, there is a particularly painful twist to it at the most selective schools. Students there compound their private pain by believing they are the only ones experiencing problems. "Indeed," observes Sarah, a former peer counselor, "many students look around them and see others effortlessly finding success and happiness at college. And they feel as if they are the only ones who aren't happy or who are having trouble finding friends or achieving academically."

Once, students might have gained comfort from talking to each other. But today "the dorm community of a competitive university is not a 'safe' place to expose personal weaknesses," she says. The climate is just too adversarial. Students even compete over their eating disorders, vying at the dinner table to see who can eat the least. Generally, however, students go to great lengths to keep their problems private. "In my opinion," Sarah adds, "this has created a culture of suffering in silence."

Here's the irony: problems that get talked about with peers often get normalized and put in a manageable perspective. What's more, talking among peers opens an opportunity for others to pass on helpful information in a casual way, as peers are likely to freely offer suggestions for handling issues they have also struggled with. At the very least, airing problems with peers can eliminate the sense of isolation that often encourages distress to fester and grow in the rich soil of silence.

You might think that college athletes have an automatic advantage in this regard; they play on teams and team camaraderie encourages sharing of problems. But athletes are now among the most distressed students on any campus and experience an array of pressures, including performance pressures, scholastic achievement pressures, the pressure to maintain a competitive weight—along with the cumulative burden of years of competition. And, as coaches find, they tend to keep their problems to themselves, until they're in a crisis that visibly impairs performance—or keeps them from showing up at all for a scheduled competition or practice. Like the ivy-clad dormitories with rotting infrastructure invisible to even a practiced observer, today's college athletes are not anywhere near as healthy as they appear.

A Generation Makes Its Mark—on Itself

Perhaps most puzzling of all the mental health problems on campus is the rise of self-injury—deliberate cutting or cigarette burning or other repetitive mutilation of body tissue. Cutting seems to be the most common type of self-injury. Cutters often use razors, utility knives, scissors, needles, broken glass—whatever they find—to make repetitive slices on their arms, legs, or other body parts. Some people burn themselves with cigarettes or lighters, others pull out their own hair.

Whatever the form, self-injury is making dramatic marks on campus life. Because self-harm is not a diagnostic category, data on its prevalence are virtually impossible to come by. But there appears to be an absolute increase in its occurrence among the young. No one knows whether it's a sudden epidemic or has been rising gradually. There used to be a great deal of secrecy about such strange behavior. Alarmed at the rapid rise of campus incidents of self-harm, colleges themselves are focusing attention on the problem. "It has now reached critical mass and is on all our radar screens," says Russ Federman. In 2003, nearly 70 percent of college counseling center directors reported increases in cases of self-injury. Women are about twice as likely to engage in it as men.

It's highly disturbing for a student to walk into a dorm room and find her roommate meticulously slicing her thighs with a shard of glass or a razor. And it winds up becoming highly disturbing to the whole residential community: self-injury always mobilizes a crisis response, so that it can be distinguished from a suicide gesture. The self-burning or bloodletting has the outward appearance of a suicide attempt. Or a cry for help.

Self-harm is, however, the polar opposite of suicide—a gesture, bizarre though it is, that is highly functional and actually life affirming. It specifically enables people to cope—it's just that they don't know any other way to alleviate intolerable states of mind. "These students go about cutting their wrists or burning their hands very matter-of-factly," says one campus counseling center director. "It's the best coping mechanism they can come up with. Most are seeking relief from unpleasant affect."

Cutting and other forms of self-harm may well be the emblematic activity of the psychically shielded and overly fragile. The signature stigma of the psychologically stunted, self-mutilation, carried out in isolation, reflects the inability of the young to cope with or even to articulate the distress of intense negative emotions or numbness, or to speak out in many ways. It is, in short, the almost inevitable collision of limited problem-solving abilities and emotional dysregulation among those who have been deprived of their own self-authenticating experiences in the world.

In a random sampling of 3,069 students at Cornell and Princeton, conducted in the spring of 2005 over the Internet, 17 percent of them—20 percent of women, 14 percent of men, many of them graduate students—reported that they had cut, burned, or harmed themselves at least once in the course of their lives. The average age at first incident of self-injury was between fourteen and fifteen. But 41 percent of the self-injurers started between the ages of seventeen and twenty-two—most likely when they were already in college. This "increasingly popular method of regulating distress," said the researchers, enabled most of the self-injurers to function well enough to go undetected.

Where Is the Self in Self-Harm?

How do I know I exist? At least I know I exist when I cut.
—*Post on an Internet message board for those*
   who self-injure

Self-harm is a serious symptom, says Federman. An extreme one, even. But of what? "It isn't about taking their life," he says. "It freaks others out, and people are agitated by it. But rarely does cutting constitute imminent danger to the self. There's not usually suicidal ideation." Most often, self-destructive students are acting out problems of relationships, and incidents often follow an experience of personal rejection. "The primary reason for self-injury is emotional regulation," insists Pistorello. "These people do not have the safety of a trusting relationship, which is how one learns to regulate emotion. As a result they withdraw and use themselves."

A sense of searching for authenticity and self-validation runs through accounts of self-harm. Many women grew up in families where their own feelings were dismissed. Or they experienced sexual abuse and had no way of articulating their feelings of pain and shame. Cutting becomes a way to express one's self. Because so many young people are detached from their self, have been deprived of the kinds of experiences in which they might discover it or even trip over it, self-harm can be the way to anchor oneself, as the psychiatrist Keith Ablow puts it, "to some sort of reality—the reality of the flesh."

In another dark way, says John Portmann, self-harm may have positive ramifications. It spares others. "This is the first generation of adolescents to really mutilate themselves in significant numbers, males as well as females. Most people, especially guys, when they are frustrated harm others. It also is a continuation of narcissism. Part of the reason why we're in the midst of the wimp phenomenon is that young people are accustomed to thinking only of themselves, seeing themselves as the center of the universe. But when they get frustrated, instead of harming people around them, as people always used to do, their first thought is of themselves once again, and they harm themselves instead of the people around them, because they mean more to themselves than anyone else does."

A Dangerous New Remedy for Anxiety

Most people go to great lengths to avoid blood and pain; it's difficult to understand how harming can be constructive. A pure paradox, morally, biologically, psychologically, self-harm is simply baffling to those who've never done it. Self-mutilation is an extreme way of making inner distress visible, mainly to themselves. Those who have been most shielded from hurt harm themselves to feel real and alive. "When there is no feeling when you are dead inside, the pain, the blood, it proves I am alive. The blood is so red and beautiful and I can feel again," one cutter confided to British researchers.

"There's a euphoric element to it. It's an impulsive act done to regulate mood," observes Armando Favazza, vice chairman of psychiatry at the University of Missouri and author of *Bodies Under Siege: Self-Mutilation in Culture and Psychiatry.* "Those who do it want to live. They do it to feel better." It is, he contends, an extremely effective treatment for anxiety. People who do it report it's "like popping a balloon." There's an immediate release of tension. Students say, "The slate is wiped clean." It's not very different from the way people with bulimia feel after purging. Favazza says it provides rapid but temporary relief from feelings of depersonalization, guilt, rejection, and boredom, as well as sexual preoccupations and chaotic thoughts.

"It's basically a home remedy for anxiety, and a very effective one at that," adds Arthur Nielsen, a Chicago psychiatrist and an instructor at Northwestern University. Supporting the assertion that self-injury is on the rise is evidence that rates of anxiety are dramatically increasing and that average U.S. children today report more anxiety than psychiatric patients of the 1950s.

Driven to Distraction

There is definitely a cultural component to self-harm, Favazza insists, pointing to culturally sanctioned practices of self-mutilation such as body piercing and tattooing, even religious and cultural scarification rituals. The more acceptable body mutilation practices are in any context, the more likely they are to be used pathologically. Even divorced from cultural rituals, the behavior is not new. Judy Garland, he says, was a "big-time cutter." Princess Diana admitted to episodically harming herself. "It was always around. The interesting question is why it is coming out of the closet *now.*"

Physical pain helps people disconnect from intense emotional turmoil, says Federman, but the effect lasts only a few hours. Yet the physical pain becomes a way of giving objective reality to the overwhelming emotional pain or intolerable numbness. "As the blood flows down the sink," one cutter wrote in an e-mail to a British researcher, "so does the anger and the anguish. It's a way of transferring scars and wounds inside onto a visible object, in my case my arm (once my leg and once my chest). It's easier to deal with it on the outside and it's a way of communicating the pain within."

Not to be overlooked is the sense of power it confers. In a way, self-harm is all about control. "It allows people to take control of painful processes they feel are out of control," says Federman. For those who have been regimented and told what they want since birth, who have lived under the anxious scrutiny of their parents, and for whom the world has been painted a risky place, self-harm is a way to actively assert control over the domain of the body. It provides the illusion of control over themselves. "It's a way of persuading oneself that 'I can control my world,'" adds Portmann. What's more, those who cut usually control the information surrounding their act; they almost always keep it secret, and they usually wear clothing to hide the telltale scars.

Although most cutting is a highly private act, Favazza reports that he now knows of cutting parties—groups of girls who get together to cut in each other's presence. And some female students, he says, like to hang out with cutters. That has given rise to "pseudo cutters"—those who cut not to gain release but to belong to the group.

No Outlets Beyond the Self

No one is sure why self-mutilation was rare just a generation ago but seems commonplace now. "Forty years ago there were huge movements of social change students could act on," Federman points out. Today students are more inward-turning; the self is seen as the primary arena for action.

Here lies perhaps the ultimate paradox of scarification: self-harm reflects the inability to find something else to do that makes one feel more alive. Earlier generations sought meaning in movements of social change or intellectual engagement inside and outside the classroom. "But young people are not even speaking up or asking questions in the classroom," reports Portmann.

At least to some degree, the pattern of psychic unrest afflicting students today reflects a constriction of cultural outlets for anger and anxiety. Growing up in a consumer culture, young people are forced to focus on themselves rather than direct their energy outward to the world. "There is such a passivity to disorders such as self-harm and bulimia," observes Joseph Behan. "You have to ask, why are students not acting out more progressively to help society? Why are they not raging against the things that have neglected or abused them? There's no dialogue in the culture today for being socially focused."

The lack of cultural outlets for anger and anxiety "leads to things like self-cutting as a form of protest," says Federman. So constrained and stressed by expectations, so invaded by parental control, today's students have no room to turn—except against themselves. Their self-absorption makes it logical that they would use themselves as a stage of operations. Emotional well-being directly suffers when there are few distractions from egocentric concerns.

A Design for Dewimping

Favazza considers it imperative that self-mutilation be stopped as soon as it's discovered. Otherwise, the impulsive cutting can become more repetitive and take on a life of its own with addiction-like qualities. Episodic cutting may take place three or four times a year. But those for whom the impulse to cut has become more autonomous may cut themselves three or four times a week. Treatment of self-mutilation often involves psychotherapy plus antidepressants, which decrease the impulsivity behind most acts of self-harm.

But increasingly, the most effective treatment for self-harm is dialectical behavior therapy, a blending of Eastern and Western psychological strategies with an emphasis on the learning of emotion-management skills in both individual and group settings. "Dialectical" because it grapples with the fundamental paradoxes and contradictions of self-harm— and of life itself. It also recognizes that cutters are doing the best they can to cope—but holds their toes to the fire to do more. It was developed by the psychologist Marsha Linehan at the University of Washington in the 1980s specifically for those who self-harm, and it has been applied to an expanding range of disorders ever since. In some ways, "dialectical behavior therapy" is a misnomer; it's much more than a therapy. It's a corrective worldview that sees the interrelationship of health and understanding, and views both not as static things but as ongoing processes hammered out through a continuous Socratic dialogue with the self and with others.

As much philosophy as psychology, dialectical behavior therapy sees self-harm as making perfect sense in psychologically constrained circumstances—a learned coping technique for unbearably intense and negative emotions among people whose very sense of self was somehow invalidated by earlier experience. Over the course of a year, it trains individuals to balance life's tensions and complexities as an ongoing, dynamic process that accommodates the constant flux of real emotions without getting overwhelmed by them. Mimicking the conditions of life, it teaches coping skills in a group setting, where people learn basic principles of asking for what they want, responding to challenges, and using negative feelings constructively rather than as a signal to shut down.

What is so remarkable about dialectical behavior therapy is that it is a veritable instruction manual for redressing the psychological fragility that characterizes the nation of wimps. It addresses a range of deficits that appears to be almost generational. In acknowledging complexity and contingency, in recognizing distress and pain as facts of life, in reducing confusion about identity, in teaching emotion-regulation techniques and interpersonal effectiveness, in its understanding of individuals in contexts, in balancing acceptance and change, self versus other, and thoughts versus feelings—in accommodating the nature of modern reality—dialectical behavior therapy aims to develop perspective and coping skills that so many have been deprived of. It is presented as a yearlong course requiring classroom interaction. Colleges would do well to transpose dialectical behavior therapy from the clinical to the academic, present it as a course in basic life skills, and require it of all new students.

NINE

Arrested Development

Adolescence Without End

The end result of cheating childhood is to extend it forever. Despite all the parental pressure—making children overly precious, depriving them of their own experience of the world, eliminating play, pushing them into narrow performance grooves, burdening them with a heavy load of parental expectations—and probably because of it, kids are pushing back, in their own unique way. By every measure of adulthood, they're taking longer to grow up. It may be a kind of millennial version of *Groundhog Day*; if they keep at it long enough, at some point they may get it right and move on.

According to a recent report by a team of sociologists led by the University of Pennsylvania's Frank F. Furstenberg, "Adulthood no longer begins when adolescence ends." There is, instead, a growing no-man's-land of post-adolescence from twenty to thirty, which they dub "early adulthood." Using the classic benchmarks of adulthood—leaving home, finishing school, getting a job, getting married, and having children—65 percent of males had reached adulthood by the age of thirty in 1960. By contrast, in 2000, only 31 percent had. Among women, 77 percent met the benchmarks of adulthood by age thirty in 1960. By 2000, the number had fallen to 46 percent.

Furstenberg contends that the lengthening road to adulthood reflects new economic realities: it takes at least an undergraduate education to achieve or maintain middle-class status today, and it takes time after that to find a full-time job that supports a family. Nearly two-thirds of young adults in their early twenties get economic support from Mom and Dad, many even after they start working.

This lengthy period before adulthood, often spanning the twenties and even extending into the thirties, is now a period devoted to further education, job exploration, experimentation in romantic relationships, and personal development. There is no one pathway into and through adulthood, and the whole trip at this point becomes much less linear and predictable than the regimented childhood many were ushered through.

Family therapists might add another step toward full adulthood—dismantling the hierarchical relationship to parents and reestablishing a bond as peers, in essence, "firing" one's parents and reconnecting to them in a new and more equal, adultlike way. It's not so much a question of how the child sees them or what he calls them, but more a reflection of how he sees himself. And that doesn't seem to happen much before age thirty. It takes time to gather the necessary prerequisite—an identity we can call completely our own. For young adults to begin an adult relationship with their parents, they have to be fully differentiated from them. There's no magic to the age. It requires the time to become economically independent and well established in an intimate relationship. Becoming a parent is part of the requirement, too; having kids brings to the surface issues in the family of origin that must be resolved. With this definition, adulthood may be as far off as forty.

Boom Boom Boomerang

Independence isn't abetted by pressure for success when those demands are at odds with the requirements of child development. "It's hard to know what the world is going to look like ten years from now," says Tufts's David Elkind. "How best do you prepare kids for that? Parents think that earlier is better. That's a natural intuition, but it happens to be wrong."

Combined with the lack of free play, a steady march of success through the regimented childhood arranged and monitored by parents on their timetable creates young adults who need time to explore themselves. "They often need a period in college or afterward to legitimately experiment—to be children," says the social historian Peter Stearns. "There's decent historical evidence to suggest that societies that allow kids a few years of latitude and even moderate [rebellion] end up with healthier kids than societies that pretend such impulses don't exist."

One classic benchmark of adulthood is marriage, but its antecedents extend well back into childhood. "The precursor to marriage is dating, and the precursor to dating is playing," says Indiana's Bernardo Carducci. The less time children spend in free play, the less socially competent they'll be as adults. It's in play that we learn give-and-take, the fundamental rhythm of all relationships. We learn how to read the feelings of others and how to negotiate conflicts. Taking the play out of childhood, he says, is bound to create a developmental lag, and he sees it clearly in the social patterns of today's adolescents and young adults, who hang around in groups that are more typical of middle childhood.

It's not possible to ignore the fact that the drama of development today plays out against a backdrop of continued high levels of divorce. And that, experts agree, confuses kids considerably. The instability of social bonds appears to be one of the major factors responsible for the rise in anxiety among the young. It takes them longer to find an identity, longer to figure things out, especially relationships. However, they're not using that time to gain the social skills that will help them enter and sustain relationships, the primary pillar of well-being and increasingly defined even by young people as a key component of life success. The difficulty in relationships is a decisive factor in avoiding independence; commitment is just too big a risk for the psychologically fragile.

Ties That Bind . . . and Bind . . . and Bind

It's bad enough that today's children are raised in a psychological hothouse where they are overmonitored and oversheltered. But that hothouse no longer has geographical or temporal boundaries. For that you can thank the cell phone. In little more than five years it has become one of the most ubiquitous accoutrements of student life. Even in college— or perhaps especially at college—students are typically in contact with their parents several times a day, reporting every flicker of experience. "Kids are constantly talking to parents," laments one Cornell student, which makes them perpetually homesick. "They're not always focused on school; they're always looking back. And telling their parents they want to be home.

"There is a constant reference to parents. Being close to your parents today is more acceptable; there is a much smaller generation gap than when my parents were growing up." The continuing ultraclose attachment to parents combined with perpetual access to them, however, keeps kids emotionally focused on their parents long after they should be loosening their primary attachment to them and reconfiguring their attachment mechanism for a romantic partner.

A counseling staff member at a large northeastern university reports, "The number of students I have seen who talk to Mom or Dad five-plus times per day is remarkable." He argues that such students are not developing the capacity to manage their own emotions and "therefore we are seeing classic unhealthy self-soothing behaviors increase, namely binge drinking, self-mutilation, and eating disorders."

But the cell phone does something even more subversive; the perpetual access to parents infantilizes the young, keeping them in a permanent state of dependency. Whenever the slightest difficulty arises, "they're constantly referring to their parents for guidance," the Cornell student observes.

Think of the cell phone as the eternal umbilicus. It is the new and pervasive instrument of overprotection.

The Eternal Umbilicus

Leaving home for college is the beginning of the end, the first substantial taste of independent living most young people get. It presents a major opportunity for children to develop their sense of self—the process of individuation—outside the direct influence of parents. College is in fact unique in allowing young people to test out identities, assume responsibility for themselves, and perfect their self-regulation skills in a setting that provides considerable safeguards and regular feedback. It is an important stop in the journey to adulthood. The move from parental regulation to self-governance does good things for developing minds; it's linked to lower levels of depression and decreased involvement in risky behavior. At least that's the way it was until around 2000.

Today kids move away from home physically—but not emotionally. Actually, Mom and Dad go off to college with the kids—they sit in Matt's front pocket or Alexa's purse, constantly available, instantly accessible by cell phone. All the kids have to do is activate speed dial. Cell phones have radically transformed parent-child communication, and likely the entire parent-child relationship, in a very short time. Speaking to parents from the dorm was, just ten years ago, a very occasional thing, and often a hurried and public thing at that. Now talking to parents is an everyday occurrence and, often enough, a several-times-daily experience. What gets shared, and when, seems to have shifted responsibility in ways that are only now beginning to be understood. Cell phones keep young people tied to their parents—relying on them for advice, decision making, problem solving, emotional comfort, and sometimes much more—when they should be making their own moves toward independence.

In 2000 only 38 percent of college students had cell phones. By the fall of 2004, 90 percent did. Cell phones certainly make social life more fluid. That's a huge plus in a changeable world. But they do a few other things that no one has even begun to grapple with yet because everyone, and most institutions, are still reeling from their rapid adoption—faster than with any other technology in history. According to the University of Zurich sociologist Hans Geser, the failure to understand what cell phones are doing to public and private experience is part of "the larger tendency to ignore the impact of technologies on the unspectacular aspects of everyday life," even though they are leading to fundamental transformations in individuals' perception of themselves, of the world, and how they interact with that world.

In most cases, students now go off to college well versed in cell phone use, as the average age of cell phone adoption is about twelve and dropping rapidly. While cell phones enable almost constant peer-peer contact, they also fortify ties between parents and children, single-handedly reversing the conventional pattern of adolescents lessening their interactions with family as they get older. In fact, researchers have found that older teens are now more likely than younger teens to maintain regular phone contact with their parents. "Under such conditions," says Geser, "parents have cogent reasons to buy mobile phones for their youngsters, and even to pay most of their bills. First of all, they hope to keep a certain control on the whereabouts of their offspring." Second, they use them for coordination purposes, helpful for arranging pickups on the fly and accommodating schedule changes. Third, they use them for security—for assuring themselves that the kids are safe and well. In this case, it's the children who wind up paying the bill of parental security. The cost is their autonomy. As one recent graduate put it, "When do you depend on you?"

Kids report every blip and flicker of experience immediately as it happens, without engaging in reflection or otherwise processing the experience. They are especially prone to report to parents their negative encounters, because it is a neurobiological fact that young minds overweight negative experience. They report little lumps and bumps to parents, and the parents, fed the negative totally out of context, overreact to it. As with most emotional encounters, listening may be all that is needed for the solution of problems. But distance and the desire for distress-free kids collude to push parents into overdrive. So the dean gets a call from a parent protesting a grade. Just that morning he had received a call from a parent who had booked a hotel room on campus for a month because his precious one was changing majors. The father never even considered just telling the kid to work it out himself.

The advent of cell phones on college campuses is so new that universities have not had time to formulate policies on their use. Minutes after a class lets out, professors and deans can be swamped with calls from parents of students unhappy with a grade or a schedule change. Maybe a kid is unhappy with the playing time he's getting in his sport. Did we mention roommate disputes? These turn out to be just the tip of the iceberg—exchanges that are blatantly intrusive. But there is a whole range of insidious consequences that have started to generate deep concern. In addition to changing the developmental trajectories of a large proportion of students through its impact on independence, individuation, and self-regulation, the cell phone is altering the entire college experience and the nature of the university as well.

Attachment Undermined and Overdone

As rattled as faculty and administration may be about calls from parents, by far the most profound effect may be on what happens inside the heads of young people. The main problem with having your parents in your jeans pocket is that you never have to activate the mental machinery for independence—the mental representations of Mom and Dad inside your brain. As a result, you never learn how to guide yourself through the making of decisions on your own or come to rely on your own judgment. It's hard to become independent when you're on the phone with people who make decisions for you several times a day.

The internalized image of Mom or Dad is packaged in the neurons and activated by separation. This parent-within is the agent by which regulation is handed off from flesh-and-blood parents early in development to the child later in development. Activated by absence, the internal working model of Mom becomes the source of comfort and guidance whenever we find ourselves faced with uncertainty or difficulty. It is the true, original, all-terrain crisis-management system, our primary source of security in life.

But when Mom and Dad are on speed dial, "cell phones keep kids from figuring out what to do," says the psychologist David Anderegg. "They've never internalized any images; all they've internalized is 'call Mom or Dad.' "

A Mutual Embrace

Barbara Hofer is an associate professor of psychology at Middlebury College who has begun formally examining how technological changes are influencing the transition to adulthood. She had been taking informal surveys of students in her classes about student-parent communication and was "shocked year by year at how much that increased." Armed with a National Science Foundation grant, she recently set out to try to quantify the issue.

In particular, she says, she is interested in how frequency, type, and content of contact between parents and college students are related to students' developing autonomy and self-regulation—and how contact affects how students learn to become self-regulating learners. "Developmentally, the college years have always been a period in which individuals began to take more responsibility for their academic and personal lives. Ideally, individuals during this period of 'emerging adulthood' learn to become autonomous while remaining connected to their parents. Our concern has been whether the availability and ease of communication through cell phones and e-mail may be impeding this process. If parents are still calling, talking about paper topics, and editing students' papers via e-mail, et cetera, then students are not accepting the responsibility they need to accept to become autonomous learners."

Enlisting the help of a senior—given the lightning-fast evolution of features and usage patterns, she felt it important to involve a student in the design of a questionnaire *for* students—she posted a Web-based survey on the college orientation Web site in order to collect data from both students entering the class of 2009 and their parents. The adolescents were asked to reflect back on their high school experiences, particularly in terms of parental involvement in their academics and other behaviors, and to look ahead and anticipate their communication and involvement with their parents during college.

All 156 students and 39 parents who completed the prematriculation survey were resurveyed at the end of the semester, when additional questions assessed satisfaction with college, changes in autonomy and in both self-regulation and parental regulation, and satisfaction with parental relationships and communication. In addition, all 550 entering first-year students answered a short set of questions about their expectations. A small group of 46 students filled out questionnaires on a weekly basis throughout the first semester so that Hofer and her student Elena Kennedy could track communications throughout the term, get more information about the content of the conversations, and find out who was initiating the conversations, what type of advice was offered by parents, and whether it was solicited or unsolicited. The research findings were presented at the 2006 annual meeting of the American Psychological Association, and Kennedy was one of a handful of students selected to present the work at a Council on Undergraduate Research conference on Capitol Hill in Washington.

Hofer admits that both she and Kennedy were "particularly surprised by the frequency of communication during the first semester of college, which is even greater than we suspected." It was even greater than students expected before they got to the college gates. Queried in August before arriving, students reported that they expected to communicate with their parents—by e-mail, cell phones, text message, or whatever, all combined—an average of 3.3 times per week while at college. In reality, they were communicating 10.4 times a week during the first semester of college. Not only were the vast majority "not dissatisfied with this—which also surprised us"—28 percent of the group said that they actually wanted *more* contact, especially with their fathers. They wanted to know more about their fathers' lives.

Disturbingly, parents initiated much of the contact. But not all of it. "Our study implicates both students and parents" and shows both are "deliberate in their communications," Kennedy said. It is a decidedly mutual embrace. "Our hypotheses are that parental regulation can thwart autonomy development during these years and that college students need to move toward self-regulation of their behaviors and academics," Hofer explained. "So it may not be how much students and parents talk but what they talk about and the degree to which parents give students room to grow and experiment, make decisions and choices, and learn to seek help from other sources."

Overall, students made developmental gains throughout the first semester. But those who initiated contact with parents three times a week were more likely to remain emotionally dependent on them. At the end of the first semester, they scored lower than other students on measures of autonomy, indicating greater emotional dependence. Such students were more likely to go to a parent than another authority figure or a friend to talk over a problem or to get advice. Technology makes this contact easy, says Hofer. "If there's a daily phone call, it's obviously much harder to work things out on your own."

A Whole New Take on "Homeschooling"

The dependent students didn't rely on their parents just for advice on personal issues, such as relationship problems—they used them to help with academic work. In focus groups Hofer had conducted with students before the study, she was "astonished" to discover the extent of parental involvement in collegiate academics. One student announced that his mother had all his course syllabi and called to remind him each time he had a test. "I was pretty shocked," Hofer said, but she soon found out "it's not uncommon at all." The student researcher was less shocked.

Fully 30 percent of first-year students reported seeking or receiving academic help and advice from their parents. "Not only are parents and emerging adults communicating much more frequently than any previous data has documented," Hofer found, "but the communications involve a high level of parental involvement in and regulation of academics. These two findings alone indicate the need for a critical examination of the role that parents play in students' lives at colleges and the effects of their involvement."

The findings of widespread parental involvement in student academics give a whole new meaning to "homeschooling"—and cut right to the dean's office of higher education. Parents may be paying, but who is doing the learning? "We really want to track this behavior," Hofer says. "I've been meeting with people on campus about our own honor code, because we've never specified whether that's a violation or not." Her concern extends beyond the Middlebury campus to all of higher education. But she can't specify how the Middlebury findings compare with what is going on at other colleges and universities, because her study is one of the first of its kind.

"These are issues that colleges need to work on clarifying," she insists. "What is an appropriate level of help, to what degree should parents be involved in academics, and how do we provide the support for students to become more in charge of their own academics and to go to more appropriate sources of help—the writing center, a faculty member?" Perhaps not surprisingly, the study also found that students who take more responsibility for their academic lives were more satisfied with their academic performance and overall college experience. It's hard to be happy in one place if you're constantly oriented to another.

Hofer thinks that the best kind of support parents can give is helping their college student children learn how to utilize available resources and how to take that initiative on their own—whether that's finding out why they got a disappointing grade, getting help on test taking, talking to the career services staff about careers, or negotiating a room change. Such nonparental resources are, after all, cultural capital, and parents who are concerned about the future well-being of their children would be wise to show them how to exploit it. Despite delivering their kids to institutions that are asked to assume the responsibility of first-line caretaker, parents are still asserting that role and allowing or even encouraging their children to turn toward home for it. Perhaps the cell phone has suspended parents and almost-adult children alike in what could be called the permanent present.

Living in the Permanent Present

But wait. There's more. Although there are far too many variables to definitively establish clear cause and effect, reliance on cell phones and the instant access they provide undermines the young just as insidiously by destroying the ability to plan ahead.

"The first thing students do when they walk out the door of my classroom is flip open the cell phone," observes Carducci. They scroll down a list of contacts, all hovering in a permanent present tense, and click one. "Ninety-five percent of the conversations go like this," Carducci reports: " 'I just got out of class. I'll see you in the library in five minutes.' "

There's no planning involved. Absent the phone, you'd have to make arrangements ahead of time; you'd have to think ahead. As Zurich's Geser puts it, "The cell phone effects a transformation of social systems from the 'solid' state of rigid scheduling to a 'liquid' state of permanently ongoing processes" of coordination and rescheduling where "everything happening is conditioned by current situations."

What may seem on the surface like a harmless phenomenon may actually be establishing a possible pathway to clinical depression. The ability to plan ahead and set goals and hold them in mind—critical to being an adult—resides in the prefrontal cortex, home to the executive branch of the brain. It operates through the same neural circuits involved in depression. The prefrontal cortex is a critical part of the self-regulation system, and it's deeply implicated in depression, a disorder increasingly seen as caused or maintained by unregulated thought patterns—lack of intellectual rigor, if you will; cognitive therapy owes its very effectiveness to the systematic application of critical thinking to emotional reactions. It's in planning and the setting of goals and progress in working toward them, however mundane they are, that the circuitry of positive emotions is activated and positive feelings are generated. From such everyday activity, patience, discipline, and resistance to depression are born in brain circuits that, at college age, are still undergoing maturation.

Cell phone communication creates depression vulnerability in other ways, too. It adds to a cumulative burden of psychological stress by forcing people to instantly switch roles and redirect attention at any unforeseen moment—an established source of stress.

What's more, cell phones—along with the instant availability of cash and almost any consumer good your heart desires—promote fragility by weakening self-regulation. "You get used to things happening right away," says Carducci. "You not only want the pizza now, you generalize that expectation to other domains, like friendship and intimate relationships." You become frustrated and impatient easily. You become unwilling to work out problems. And so relationships fail—a powerful experience that often paves the way to depression.

An Instrument of Regression

Perhaps most counterintuitively, the instrument that seems the very embodiment of modernity is actually a powerful force of social conservatism—no, make that social regression—at a time when young minds should be expanding. Cell phones promote a kind of tribalism that is nothing so much as premodern—verging on prehistoric. They don't just keep young people firmly embedded in their family; they constrain their social exposure as well and arrest social development. The cell phone actually strengthens ties among people who are already familiar with one another. After all, phone numbers are not published in a directory; they're given out only to a small circle of friends, and caller ID means that no calls have to be taken from unpredictable new sources.

As an instrument of "regressive social insulation," Geser and other observers find, the cell phone allows people to shield themselves from their wider surroundings "by escaping into the narrower realm of highly familiar, predictable, and self-controlled social relationships with close kin or friends." In the process of strengthening already existing relationships, mobile phones discourage the young from enlarging their social interactions. One major effect: "public space is no longer a full itinerary, lived in all its aspects, stimuli and prospects," while the predictability and uniformity of existence are emphasized. By fostering tribalism, no matter how nomadic, the cell phone *closes* social fields, favors parochialism, and perpetuates traditional relationships.

Because the cell phone "emancipates" people from their common local setting on campus, there is scarcely any universe in university anymore. Professors and other educators are highly unlikely to look upon it as liberation; what they are more likely to see is a cacophony of young people cultivating and populating their own private spheres in what looks to the adults like common space. There is more chaos of competing conversations, less of a shared cognitive challenge. Between the perpetual ties to parents and old friends, the walls of the university may be on their way to becoming too porous for it to accomplish its twin missions of socialization and education.

Even at the moment of academic encounters, cell phones limit intellectual immersion and learning on campus. There is very little direct conversation of any kind—let alone discussion of projects or debate about topics raised in the classroom or lecture hall—among students exiting a classroom. Cell phones thus create an intellectual vacuum on campus. "Students don't talk to each other anymore about class work outside of class," a University of Michigan professor told a recent conference. "They flip open their cellphones or hurry straight to email." In fact, one of the measures he was using to gauge the effectiveness of experimental programs promoting engaged learning was how much impact the programs had on post-class student-student interaction about class work.

It isn't just that social and intellectual worlds close prematurely, before they have a chance to impact and even expand individual thinking and behavior. Geser argues that cell phones can also be "psychologically regressive" instruments promoting "complexity avoidance" and bringing a certain dulling uniformity to existence. They flatten the emotional landscape. By keeping users tightly connected to loved ones at home, they cushion "traumatic" experiences in novel environments—and serve as "pacifiers for adults." Users never get to feel loneliness or uncertainty, never learn to tolerate their own thoughts or figure out how to cool off their emotions, fail to discover their own inner resources, and never get to engage in reflection, without which an identity can't be built. Thus young people actually delegate their autonomy—and lose the capacity to develop an autonomous personality. As a result, young minds become emotionally flaccid, less prone to develop the ability to react adaptively to unpredictable encounters, to form quick impressions, and to rely on their own inner judgments. "Given the constant availability of external communication partners as sources of opinion and advice, individuals may easily unlearn to rely on their own judgment, memory and reflection, thus regressing to a state of infantile dependency," says Geser. "Human existence is certainly enriched by feelings of longing or homesickness, by experiences of anxious insecurity about what others may be doing, by sadness when a loved one leaves and joy when he/she finally comes back. Cell phones tend to level out such emotional oscillations."

Counterfeit Connection

Like instant messaging and the Internet in general, cell phones can be deceptive in creating the illusion of connection. "You're always able to trick yourself into thinking you're connected," a young psychologist in training told me. "There is a general movement to disconnection. We have all the tools, but we don't feel connected internally."

"It used to be you'd call someone because you had a reason to call," a graduate student at American University said. "Now you call because you're bored waiting for the bus to come. It's almost a noise pollution." Time is an empty vessel that must be filled with calls. The communications expert Leysia Palen of the University of Colorado at Boulder refers to such usage as "grooming calls." They're devoid of content, and information isn't even the point. With the thresholds of access lowered, the calls are a way of communicating that the relationship exists and will continue in the future.

It's not that cell phones are inherently distancing; they're not. But they are commonly used by the young in ways that promote, rather than alleviate, alienation and disconnection. There's no forethought required for calling and being in touch. "You don't have to put effort into it," the psychologist in training observed. You just scroll down your contact list and call while you're on your way to doing other things. "People made time more when they weren't technologically connected. They had to plan." And as a result of the planning, making contact required effort; it led to genuine pleasure in part because it was the payoff of planning and in part because genuine social contact is always rewarding.

Another way in which the cell phone impedes psychological development is that it provides an excuse for first-year students not to have to get out and make new friends and new connections on campus. They are still in touch with their friends from home and in touch with them through the same medium as they were when they were geographically closer. The technology erodes their ability to adjust and to deal with the realities of college life. And so socialization is restricted to comfortable old networks. You never have to learn how to get along with others or—God forbid—learn *from* others.

The cell phone story is not, of course, relentlessly negative. Mobile phones are amazing devices that enable much of modern life. But some uses may be better than others, and the effects may differ by age-group and setting. Middlebury's Hofer sees some light as she points to the 71 percent of parents who say that they communicate more or much more with their college kids than they did with their own parents at the same age, and the 76 percent who say they are closer or much closer with their children than they were with their own parents when they first left home.

Seeing one's parents as people, as individuals outside of their parental roles, is one of the more advanced markers of the transition to adulthood. She thinks that the frequent communication cell phones encourage could actually be enhancing this aspect of autonomy—provided the students are having conversations with elements of mutuality and are learning more about their parents' daily lives and concerns.

The side effects of cell phone use are just beginning to be understood and to get serious attention. We're only entering the first stages of "cell phone society." And perhaps the closest comparison to the confusing situation we find ourselves in is the disarray in the streets before stoplights were erected. Norms about phone usage and social controls have yet to be established. Cell phones may be far less subversive in some settings than in others. While psychologists and sociologists can scarcely keep pace with the technology in studying its effects, they do know this: cell phones especially lend themselves to creating dependency in young people; they also weaken the power of place-based institutions to penetrate the minds of the young and to affect their behavior. The classroom no longer retains the power it had by existing in communicative isolation.

The End of Trust?

The very same cell phone additionally equipped as a tracking device may make it a far more intrusive call.

The newest generation of cell phones has global positioning technology built in, a requirement so that emergency callers to 911 systems can be immediately located. The GPS-equipped cell phones are, in the right hands, lifesavers. But they are now being marketed to fearful parents for general use to monitor their children. In the hands of already overprotective and overcontrolling parents, the GPS cell phone is poised to undermine independence and self-confidence. Adults are not marching in the streets to protest this intrusion of surveillance into a very private relationship. Their own anxieties about their children make this a welcome development. Who needs to worry about Big Brother? He's slipped in under the radar disguised as Big Mother.

A device of pure control, the GPS cell phone couldn't be better designed to inhibit the development of autonomy and infantilize the young. Some devices act like an electronic prison or dog leash, beeping when the child strays from a preset zone. Some automatically activate a call to parents under such circumstances. In some cases, parents at home or in some other remote location can directly follow on a screen their child's movements. For the children, there is literally no private space away from watchful eyes.

It's no exaggeration to say that GPS cell phones used as child minders have the potential to undermine civil society. At the very least, they cultivate a culture of distrust between parents and children. First and foremost, to use the cell phone for that purpose is to outsource trust, to delegate it to a device. But trust is one of the fragile, primary interpersonal links that by definition cannot be delegated or transferred. It is an irreducible and unconditional interpersonal phenomenon. Trust is an essential belief in and reliance on the competence of another; it is an internal state that is built through person-person experience. Trust entails expectation, a prediction about how someone will behave, and since it is future oriented, it is predicated on optimism. Monitoring devices of all kinds are antithetical to trust; surveillance is *not* trust. Surveillance is cynicism embodied.

The catch is that trust *presupposes* risk—there's that pesky word again—and uncertainty. It accepts risk. If there were not uncertainty involved, the relationship would boil down to mere promise.

Trust is not just the interpersonal high wire one must walk to independence; it is the bedrock of the social contract. Civil society operates on trust generalized. The development of autonomy requires that the relationship between parent and child build particularized trust over time through experience. Surveillance is a vote of no confidence, an act of fundamental mistrust. It is an ipso facto demonstration that the world is a mean place and that a child cannot learn to navigate his way through it on his own.

It is hard to understand how a device that sacrifices trust could *not* corrode the future fabric of society. For some parents, a child's ultimate independence is not too high a price to pay for their own peace of mind and emotional security.

Prying Parents Loose

At many colleges around the country, there's a new course, and it fills up as quickly as it's scheduled. It's not even for the students; it's strictly for the adults. It's parent orientation, and it teaches the parents how to let go of their babies. After pouring their emotional, professional, and financial resources into their kids, hitching their dreams and identities to them, even cultivating a kind of liminal lust popularized as "maternal desire," they can't suddenly shut it all off, even at the moment of their children's emancipation. Nor do they want to. Separation is not something they have prepared themselves for, or welcome. They've spent years pursuing closeness.

One of the most salient facts of college orientation today is that parents have to be pried away from their children. The Harvard College Handbook for Parents is not alone in having to spell out how to back off:

> Early in the fall term, [freshman students] phone home sounding frustrated and unhappy, and parents are often tempted to call advisers or administrators or even rush back to Cambridge to "make sure" that problems are quickly solved. In fact, these well-intentioned efforts to "take over" communication with roommates or instructors or College administrators invariably slow the process by which freshmen learn to take responsibility for their dealings with individuals and institutions. Parents can best help by encouraging students to discuss their concerns with [the Freshman Dean's Office] staff members who can help to clarify issues and work with new students to identify how most effectively to address problems here.

Colleges spend days instructing parents in how to let go. They tell parents to adjust their roles, to be prepared for but resist cries for involvement, to expect bouts of homesickness, to encourage kids to problem-solve for themselves. They instruct parents about the wealth of college resources and help centers, so the parents can redirect their children to them; they advise parents not to "push" e-mail or cell phone contact because "a stream of encouraging communiqués, though well-meaning, can sometimes actually hinder a student's personal development." But it may be that college entrance is way too late for the information. The process of independence is supposed to be gradual, and it should have started years before.

Sometimes the parents have to be forcibly separated from their kids. The University of Vermont had to train senior students as "parent bouncers" to keep the adults away from orientation classes meant exclusively for the young—say, on matters of registration or course selection, even sexual education. The university has conducted parent-student orientation sessions that were attended by more parents than students. At other schools, parents have shown up *without* their children to register them for classes and meet with academic advisers on their behalf.

Letting go is in fact undergoing a gradual shift from natural event to traumatic experience. At college orientation sessions, campus counseling center staff are being brought in as reinforcements, helping administrators come up with advice for the hordes of permaparents bereft at having to tear themselves away from their aging adolescents. "For parents who are really struggling with the absence of a child, work at turning your negative energy into something positive," the head of Colgate University's Counseling and Psychological Services advises parents. "Put together a care package or write a thoughtful letter. Your son or daughter will be happy with the gift, and you'll feel like a million bucks for doing something nice for your child."

A whole organization has sprung up specifically to advocate for parents of collegians, and one of its first acts was to acknowledge the difficult time college departure is for them. The College Parents of America, ten thousand members strong, most of them parents of freshmen or sophomores, actively promotes parental involvement so that the adults "feel that they are part of the college community." In 2006 its first survey of "college parent experiences" spun their "hovering habits" not as intrusiveness but as a positive signal that parents are simply eager to be involved in their children's college lives. It also confirmed that the cell phone is their instrument of choice. More than a quarter of the parents said they feel the colleges themselves are not doing enough for the *parents*. The organization has announced that it will be giving colleges periodic report cards assessing their performance—from the *parents'* perspective.

The Harvard parents handbook offers this final bit of sage advice:

> For parents, the freedom that freshmen enjoy can be hard to accept. So can recognizing how little you can now appropriately and directly do to shape the daily round of your son's or daughter's experiences or his or her lifestyle choices, curricular, or career plans. When the aspiring medical student since twelve tells you that high school teaching is now the plan; or when the sure-to-be Olympic swimmer you drove through rain and snow to age-group swim meets swaps varsity swimming for Harvard theater; or when the one who was cer-

tain to major in economics, go to business school, and take over the
family firm, decides instead on English, don't take it as deliberate
hurt or as a rejection of all you have done together as parents and
children. Almost always, it is neither. A young person is setting out
on his or her own life's course. Don't try to hold the course you set
and have been sailing together for seventeen years. It is very hard to
sail a ship with two pilots.

Economic forces may be doing their share to thwart independence,
but permaparents are only too happy to welcome their darlings home after college, or even after a career is under way. Yet one more thing that
maintaining a tight parental bond does is impede young people in the
development of close emotional bonds to others, bonds that should be
forming in young adulthood and that become the basis of romantic part-
nerships. "No one gets married right out of school anymore," says one college student. "Because you're still attached to your parents, the switching
of attachment bonds from parents to peers to partners happens much
more slowly. The progression has changed and it's choppy." In fact, overattachment to parents, along with the continued omnipresence of parents
by cell phone, may be one of the hidden forces behind the distressing
phenomenon of hooking up; it's a way young adults can satisfy their sexual needs without having to acknowledge any emotional attachment to
partners. "Everyone hooks up, and they never see the partner again. That
leads to less emotional security." But it is, under the circumstances of extended adolescence, also strangely functional: it preserves the primary
emotional attachment to parents. And that, the same student observes,
"may be adaptive." Because of debt, competition for jobs, and the high
cost of housing, "we may have to live at home after college."

Sociologists have a name for it—in-house adulthood. Others refer to
"start-up adults" or "emerging adulthood." Whatever the term, the meaning is clear: the boundaries between adolescence and adulthood are
fuzzier than ever.

Infantilization

Although it does not mandate that adults remain overly emotionally attached to their children, the expanding role of higher and graduate education in the middle class is one element that keeps young adults

dependent on their parents. But it works in league with a number of other factors to infantilize adolescents and young adults.

The regimented childhood created for children and the peer culture they've been consigned to guarantee minimal integration of children into adult society. This is very different from childhood in the past, and the effects on children and on adults are just beginning to be recognized. Dwelling almost exclusively in peer culture has left teens with a lack of meaningful work, inside the house or outside, such as internships might provide, where young people could make a real contribution and learn something about themselves and their abilities and interests, have positive contact with adults who are not their own doting parents, and begin to understand that there are a variety of pathways to success. Peer culture might even be contributing directly to disorders such as anorexia and bulimia by warping the ability of young girls to appraise their attractiveness; they see themselves competing for attention only against nubiles like themselves, not the full range of womanhood, which might give a young girl a more balanced view of her charms; it also might attune her to the value of character strengths.

One significant result for adults of the immersion of their children in peer culture is that they lose touch with what children are really capable of—which disposes them to believe that children cannot handle difficult situations. "Middle-class adults," says Peter Stearns, "have a tendency to assume that if the children start getting into difficulty, you need to rush in and do it for them rather than let them flounder a bit and learn from it. I don't mean abandon them, but give them more credit for working things out."

In most of human history and in many developing countries today, observes the psychologist Robert Epstein, author of *The Case Against Adolescence: Rediscovering the Adult in Every Teen,* young people were integrated into adult society very early. They might, for example, be working beside their parents in the fields. The child-adult continuum was pretty much intact until about a hundred years ago, when the legislative consequences of industrialization began what Epstein calls "the artificial extension of childhood."

"Young people are not operating in optimal ways young people did through most of human history," explains Epstein. "Adolescents today are heavily restricted." It's not the first impression one takes away of highly fashionable teens armed with electronic devices of all kinds, but Epstein and a colleague, Diane Dumas, dug under the surface by developing a scale of infantilization, basically measuring specific ways that the behavior of teens is restricted. All in all, there are forty-two measures on the test, which asks, "Since you were 13 years old, have adults regularly or routinely restricted your activities in any of the following areas? Listened in on your phone calls? Searched your room without your permission? Restricted your use of the Internet? Forced you to take medication? Required you to get certain grades? Required you to take certain courses in school?"

The researchers asked a hundred teens between ages thirteen and seventeen in seven locations around the United States to complete the forty-two-item checklist. Respondents said they "regularly or routinely" experienced just over twenty-six of the forty-two restrictions.

To Epstein's surprise, American adolescents had far higher scores—indicating far more restrictions—than U.S. marines and incarcerated felons, two populations that are very tightly controlled. Noninstitutionalized adults scored near zero. "No one can make a decision for an incarcerated felon about religion or education. But for teens, such restrictions are commonly in place. There's something very disturbing about this. There is no question that teens are subject to many restrictions that are typically associated only with young children."

At the same time, Epstein and his colleague gave the teens a test that measures psychopathology. The researchers found a positive correlation between psychopathology and infantilization. "Based on a collage of information from various sources, it is reasonable to conclude that one reason teens are dysfunctional is because they are infantilized. They are, for example, given less choice over their courses, their paths. One of the most bizarre changes in higher education in the last several years is that parents get involved." Epstein contends that the restrictions commonly placed on adolescents are the primary markers of the artificial extension of childhood.

"Young people in American culture are almost completely isolated from adults and have no models of adult behavior," he says. "We end up with young people who don't know the adult world in any way and adults who know nothing about young people. This is new; there is nothing old or natural about it. We adults try to prevent our offspring from making the same mistakes we made. We tend to do this not by running a tight ship at home but by getting our legislatures to do our bidding. When we restrict the rights and activities of young people, in some sense we throw them away."

Writing in the *Boston Globe,* Thomas M. Keane Jr. singled out an attempt by Massachusetts legislators in 2006 to raise the driving age from sixteen to seventeen and a half as blatant infantilization that defies not just common sense but statistical sense—although, he suggests, it meets the emotional needs of today's parents. According to the Insurance Institute for Highway Safety, teenage driving fatalities declined by almost 50 percent from 1979 to 2004. So why the sudden pressure to ban teenage driving? "It has more to do, I suspect, with our own fears as parents," said Keane, pointing to the driver's license as the most concrete symbol of growing independence. The rising number of adult children living at home leads the ex-legislator to believe that the real motivation for a change in driving age is the desire to keep kids dependent just a little bit longer, to postpone their budding autonomy. Wouldn't it be better to teach kids about risks and responsibilities than defer driving age until kids were at college, where their first critical years of driving solo would likely mix with alcohol and drugs? "Sure, raising the driving age may help us sleep better at night. But our most important obligation as parents is not to keep our children dependent but to help them grow up." A reader termed the proposed driving-age curb an attempt to enforce "learned dependence." The case may not be closed. A 2004 USA Today/CNN/ Gallup poll shows that 61 percent of Americans want to take away the right of sixteen-year-olds to drive.

Even though teens don't necessarily *behave* in a competent way, they have the potential to be every bit as competent as adults, Epstein observes on the basis of a test of adultness that he and his colleague also developed. They measured fourteen competencies that people need to function as an adult in America and found no difference between teens and adults on any of them—from love and sex to verbal and math skills to citizenship. The *potential.*

TEN

Born to Be Stressed

Why are so many young people these days experiencing severe distress? From overprotection to under-experience, from lack of play to lack of challenge, from overscrutiny to ties that always bind, from an excess of expectations to an absence of experimentation, elements of everyday activity have powerful effects on minds and brains. There are many ways that common experience may be impacting the brain circuitry that underlies despair, especially at critical times of neurodevelopment.

How do people develop identity and find meaning and happiness—qualities distinctively missing among the nation of wimps? These are all things that cannot be pursued directly. They are by-products of other activities—of challenge, of struggle even, of working toward goals. The evidence from neuroscience is pretty clear. The prefrontal cortex, the epicenter or coordinating hub of motivation and goal direction and all our cognitive high-wire acts, is the affective processing center as well as the wrestling arena of cognitive control.

The prefrontal cortex is critical for shifting mood from one state to another. Our heads are filled with numerous representations, images of people and events that have stood out in our experience. By summoning up internal pictures that represent the material world, we are able to think abstractly. As we visualize our goals and hold them in attention and work toward them over time, we activate the circuitry of positive emotions. Movement toward goals—striving, working hard—also generates opioids in the brain; that is, it sparks the production of endorphins, creating feelings of well-being at a neurochemical level.

Similarly, the deeper dopamine reward system in the brain is set up to recognize active pursuits. As far as the brain is concerned, there is a big difference in the sense of satisfaction you get if you actively *do* something versus passively being given something. Moreover, the sense of reward in the brain is activated *in anticipation* of achieving a goal. You get the biggest high, the biggest sense of reward, when you are doing something challenging and have *not yet* achieved your goal. And that sense of reward becomes the intrinsic motivation to keep on going.

When people overvalue success itself and define a narrow path to it, what's lost is tolerance for trial and error, for mistakes, for experimentation, for messing up, even though it is from trial—and especially error—that all of us learn. Removing all the lumps and bumps from experience, downgrading all the challenge and difficulty, keeps the brain locked into despair. The implications are obvious: feeling bad is sometimes good—or at least necessary.

The Shriveled Quest for Happiness

In part we're creating a nation of wimps because parents want their children to be happy, and they want to be the ones who make their children happy. If their child is unhappy even briefly, they take it as a sign they're not doing a good job of parenting. In this confused climate, they come to believe that one way to make their kids happy is to make things easy for them, so they don't have to struggle or suffer.

A teaching assistant in the University of California system recounted the experience of a friend, a former resident adviser for the dorms, now a lecturer. "The housing office is down the hall from laundry facilities; with the door open, it's in the direct line of sight. My friend received a call one afternoon from a parent whose daughter was on the other line with her; the washing machine had eaten the girl's quarters. The mother was calling so that the resident advisor could go help her. When the RA asked why the student didn't just come down the hall to get someone, the mother replied, 'Oh, well, it's just easier if I do it for her.' "

Another Californian, the stepmother of two girls, insists that the aftermath of divorce has something to do with it, "because each household is competing with the other to be the favorite to the child." Her husband shares fifty-fifty custody of both girls with his ex. "There is *no* responsibility for household chores in our home since there are never any at the mother's. Spitting at their mom is allowed at their mother's house, so yelling at us is allowed in ours. Things need to be smoother, easier, nicer, cleaner for the girls, but with no input from them. My husband cleans their rooms for them and their bathroom, makes their lunches and breakfast, wakes them up in the morning. We make dinner and, afterwards, wash the dishes while the girls watch TV."

It's not that happiness is a terrible goal or an inappropriate desire for one's children. But we have misled them—and ourselves—about what constitutes real happiness and how it is achieved. Believing that never feeling bad or having to endure a moment of discomfort will translate into sustained happiness radically misrepresents how the mind achieves happiness. As if that weren't bad enough, we compound the error by depriving kids of their own self-generated experience of the world, which keeps them from finding out—or even seeking—the truth on their own.

If contemporary parental attitudes were expressed as an equation, it might go something like this: life minus feeling bad equals a shot at happiness. But a better equation would tell the lumpier truth: life plus doing something difficult and tolerating the discomfort of the process and the uncertainty of the outcome equals a shot at happiness; it also supplies deeper meaning and identity.

Our contemporary quest for happiness has pretty much shriveled to a hunt for hedonic bliss. But it takes more than momentary pleasure to live the best possible life. There is a deeper, more satisfying, and more durable state of mind that enables people to positively thrive; researchers generally characterize it as well-being. The two brands of happiness—hedonic and eudaemonic—have remarkably different effects on the brain, and the differing brain structures they involve may help explain why real happiness comes from the search for purpose, meaning, and mastery, and that often entails a struggle. In this emotionally enriched iteration of happiness as eudaemonic well-being, something that animates every fiber of being, adversity can be a passport to the good life and feeling bad is sometimes good.

How the brain establishes and maintains positive feelings is a story just now unfolding in science. Human emotions take shape in a neural circuit involving several key brain structures, including the hippocampus, the amygdala, both deep in the "old" brain, and the prefrontal cortex, the executive center of the thinking brain, the keeper of all our goals and the hotel suite of our mental representations.

One seminal spot in the circuitry of feelings is the prefrontal cortex (PFC), the brain area just behind the forehead. That's where emotion regulation takes place. According to the neuroscientist Richard Davidson, professor of psychology and psychiatry at the University of Wisconsin, two of the PFC's most important functions are restricted to one side or the other. His studies show that the left side of the PFC is crucial to establishing and maintaining positive feelings, while the right is associated with negative ones. Depressed people appear to have a power failure of the left PFC. The failure shows up both in electrical studies of brain response and in PET scans indicating decreased blood flow and metabolism. The depressed simply don't activate the machinery to process positive emotions or respond to positive stimuli.

Specifically, the left PFC is instrumental in what Davidson calls "pre-goal attainment positive affect"—what you and I might call anticipation or eagerness, the positive emotion that arises as we approach a desired goal. Because this circuitry connects widely with other brain actions, it can spread joy into every fiber of being. Depressed individuals can't mentally hang on to goals or keep themselves attuned to rewards. The result: lowered capacity for pleasure, lack of motivation, loss of interest, whole-being lethargy.

The left PFC doesn't just activate positive feelings. Davidson finds that it may also be crucial in inhibiting negative emotion that gets in the way of sustaining positive goals. In this, the left PFC draws on its connections to the amygdala, an almond-shaped structure deep in the center of the brain that pumps out negative feelings.

With the emotion-processing activity of the prefrontal cortex lateralized, the brain operates on a binary code of behavior. The left side of the PFC contains nerve circuits that color psychological events positively, and the right side colors them negatively. This division of labor leads us to see rewards and pleasures or merely emptiness and hopelessness, and then to negotiate the world either by approaching the stimulus source and engaging it or by withdrawing from it.

Individuals normally differ in the degrees of neural activation of the left and right sides of the PFC in response to emotional messages—or, as Davidson puts it, they differ in affective style. That difference may help account not only for a person's susceptibility to depression but also for more general variations in personality. A peppy left PFC underlies extraversion, while a relatively more active right PFC is linked to inhibition, timidity, and anxiety. Left-sided activation prompts people to approach situations, right-sided activation to withdraw from them.

It isn't clear how asymmetries in prefrontal activity get established to begin with. Although these characteristics of brain function are very stable in adults, Davidson says, they are much less so in children. That suggests to him that activation levels of this circuit are set early in life, after a sensitive period, certainly by puberty.

One clue may be that differences in PFC activation go hand in hand with differences in brain levels of the stress-related hormone cortisol. When the left PFC is highly active, not only do people have a sunny outlook, but their levels of cortisol are insignificant. Cortisol patterns suggest that stress had a hand in there somewhere—enduringly altering nerve circuits that control emotion, permanently exaggerating later responses to stress, readily tilting the brain toward anxiety and eternal vigilance for anything remotely threatening, and creating vulnerability to depression. Early experiences up to the time of puberty establish, for the rest of one's life, the levels of sensitivity for activating internal alarm circuits.

Davidson says he has seen patterns of individual differences in left prefrontal activation early in infancy. "In ten-month-old infants we can predict which ones will cry in response to maternal separation based on a prior measure of prefrontal activation."

By placing experimental subjects in a functional magnetic resonance imager to measure brain activity while showing them emotionally laden pictures—photographs of accidents and of starving children, for example—Davidson has graphically confirmed what many scientists have long suspected: that the amygdala scans incoming experience for emotional significance, puts a flag on negative feelings such as fear, goes into alarm mode, and sends out notice of threat; you feel a pervasive sense of panic. The activity of the amygdala also determines how tenaciously a negative event is held in memory. Studies show that the amygdala is particularly active during states of experimentally induced helplessness—such as when people try to solve an unsolvable task—a precipitant of depression.

Ordinarily, as the left PFC turns on, it simultaneously shuts off the amygdala and dampens the flow of negative emotions from it. But in depression, faulty circuitry begets a power failure both in generating positive feelings and in inhibiting disruptive negative ones. The general failure of activation of the left PFC leaves the amygdala running unchecked, overwhelming the brain with negative feelings, unable to respond to positive ones. On the other hand, Buddhist meditation appears to be a powerful way to regulate emotion and prevent depression. Davidson has done imaging studies of practiced Buddhist monks and seen them literally shift the brain into positive emotional states. He's also tested a group of ordinary folks who were randomly assigned to undergo instruction in meditation techniques. Those trained to meditate showed an increase in left prefrontal activation both at rest and in response to an emotional challenge.

Deep happiness—eudaemonic well-being—lies in activating the left prefrontal cortex, by taking an active role in life and becoming engaged in challenges that require effort, says Davidson. The left PFC is where we hold on to the mental representations of desired goals while we are doing the long hard work often necessary to achieve them. They sit on our minds, readily present, and guide our behavior. Among individuals with a more active left PFC, those mental representations keep them focused on goals and doing what they need to keep moving toward them. As they strive, anticipation builds, giving them the motivational wherewithal to withstand setbacks—and ultimately leading them to experience positive feelings frequently and intensely.

Pushing kids down the path to hedonic happiness encourages them to become overly fragile and self-absorbed but incapable of making themselves happy. Even diagnosis and medication cannot furnish the means of positive feelings; they cannot provide the coping skills and power to endure adversity needed for achieving anything meaningful. Nullifying negative processes is not the equivalent of adaptive functioning.

High on Novelty and Challenge

Struggle and challenge are absolutely necessary to feeling good. As Davidson's studies show, the brain is wired for them. But deep happiness or satisfaction doesn't just fall into our laps. You have to wrestle it to the ground for yourself. "Satisfying experiences are *difficult*," says the Emory University neuroscientist Gregory S. Berns.

In distinguishing hedonic pleasure from deep satisfaction, Berns makes a fundamental division: active versus passive. In his scheme of things, pleasure is a passive domain. The emotions of pleasure happen *to* you, like when something good befalls you. Satisfaction is more active; it arises from something you *do*. That makes all the difference in the world to your brain.

The active-passive distinction, says Berns, arises from everything that has been learned about the reward system of the brain in the past decade. "As far as the brain is concerned, there is a big difference between active and passive rewards. It makes a big difference in terms of the brain's response as to whether you're working for something or whether you just had it given to you."

Satisfaction involves activation in the dopamine neurons of the striatum, a portion of the brain that Berns describes as lying "at the crossroads of action and reward." The striatum, in the brain stem at the base of the brain, atop the spinal cord, is involved both in movement and in executive functions, and is responsive to both reward and novelty. "Dopamine activation is something desirable to have, not simply because it feels good; it's not simply a hedonic signal. It's actually more closely related to motivation. It increases the motivation to do tasks, even if there is no reward, even if it is aversive in some way."

Until recently, it was pretty much assumed that human motivation was governed by the pleasure principle, a term coined by Sigmund Freud. Much of what is now known about motivation has to do with the neurotransmitter dopamine—which until the mid-1990s scientists generally thought of as the brain's pleasure chemical. Dopamine is what gives heroin addicts, for example, their high. For sure, dopamine is released in response to pleasurable activities, like eating, having sex, and taking drugs. But studies by Berns and others have shown that dopamine is also released in response to such unpleasant sensations as loud noises and electric shock.

Actually, the Emory researcher points out, careful studies show that dopamine is released *prior to* the consummation of good and bad activities, acting more like a chemical of expectation and anticipation than of delivered pleasure. "What dopamine does is commit your body to a particular action. Satisfaction comes less from the attainment of a goal and more from what you must do to get there." Getting there is more than half the fun.

Because the biggest kick comes while doing the task, in the anticipation and before the goal is achieved, actually achieving the goal is often a letdown. Any CEO will tell you most of the enjoyment was in climbing the ladder, not in being on top. "That is generally the case with goals that span a reasonable period of time during which you have to work toward them. Dopamine is like a fuel-injection system for action. Without dopamine, you can't move," a fact that explains what goes awry in Parkinson's disease, the movement disorder. Under the influence of dopamine, the anticipatory high serves as encouragement; it stirs the last sprint of activity toward the goal.

What he's really talking about, Berns insists, is the ability to learn. The fundamental reason we have a brain is to adapt to a world that doesn't stay constant. What the brain really wants is a steady supply of information about the world and new experiences so that it can build better models of how the world works and thus make it more predictable. Novel events contain information that you don't already have. Since the brain responds only to changes in information, and not the status quo, it searches for intense challenge, in situations where the outcome is not yet known. "Most nerve cells in most parts of the brain fire only when there is a change in inputs. So in order to stimulate dopamine neurons, you need constantly changing inputs. The neurons then actively release growth factors and sprout more synapses," or nerve cell connections. "That is a good thing for maintaining mental health."

It cuts right down to the molecular level. Novel environments, and especially those that require movement, spur the release of a chemical factor that in turn stimulates the growth of nerve cells. The chemical, called BDNF (brain-derived neurotrophic factor), modulates nerve cell development by regulating both the creation of new nerve cells, called neurogenesis, and the branching of existing nerve cells. The growth and branching of nerve cells foster new interconnections between nerve cells—accommodating more information, more learning, more memory, more links of association, more channels of information flow. The understanding that the brain, even in adulthood, is thus constantly forming new connections, changing architecture, and adapting structurally to the environment is relatively new, and the general phenomenon is termed neural plasticity. It is what literally gives us behavioral flexibility—the capacity to alter our behavior to varying circumstances. BDNF is what's missing in the nerve cells of depressed and anxious people. They are frozen in ruts of thought and behavior; they have lost flexibility of response. Of the therapies that work in relieving depression, including physical exercise, all stimulate production of BDNF. Exercise stimulates neural growth factors because it is doing something that is a challenge.

"Living a life with a lot of challenges and new experiences is absolutely fundamental to brain health," says Berns. "That's a very different philosophy for life than the pursuit of happiness." Pursuing happiness is a hedonic approach in many ways. If that is one's goal, then disappointment will always be the end result. Because we pretty much adapt to whatever we have. That's why winning the lottery doesn't make you any happier. It is impossible to be sated that way. The only way you can keep the brain at the same level of hedonic happiness is to give it more and more—what has been called the hedonic treadmill. "Instead of trying to get more and more of things to get happier and happier, a more rational approach is to do different things and difficult things; this is more a philosophy of self-growth."

Absent challenge, Berns explains, the outcome of events is already a given—a ho-hum for your unimpressed brain. "If I tell you what I'm going to give you for Christmas or Hanukkah and you get it, it's not at all the same as it being either a surprise or something you've worked for yourself. Working for something yourself not only gives meaning to what you do; it lays down a much stronger synaptic trace, a more indelible memory."

Dopamine alone will take the brain only so far. What challenge does is lead to the production of moderate amounts of cortisol, the stress hormone. It's the combination of dopamine and cortisol that transforms euphoria into the state of satisfaction. Berns thinks it's also the recipe for transcendence. "Because cortisol is released most effectively by stressful situations," he says, "the road to satisfying experiences must necessarily pass through the terrain of discomfort."

A *Twisting of Risk*

What brain research suggests about the nature of the good life has a striking parallel in studies of those who have survived adversity and come out healthier and happier for it. As a culture, we are just not tuned in to such resilience. We prefer what the Washington, D.C., psychiatrist Steven Wolin calls a "Damage Model" of the human condition, which we currently portray more or less as a disease. It's what is operating behind the widespread belief that if you grow up in a seriously troubled family—say, the child of alcoholics—or under difficult conditions of any kind, then you are virtually doomed to difficulty yourself, perhaps substance abuse problems or depression or both.

Setbacks and disappointment and inner conflict, Wolin has found, are often the best opportunities we get for growth. Happiness comes not from removing sources of discomfort but in struggling through them. In the Damage Model, he has told me, children are seen as passive and without choices to help themselves. And difficulties are seen, like the human condition itself, much as a disease.

There is a widespread misinterpretation of risk. The focus on misfortune inherent in risk research distorts our perception. It winds up creating a prophecy of doom. Research on risk captures only noxious and destructive influences—and in so doing, it inflates their effect in our minds. It isolates negative influences from the human context and presents a false picture of reality so that we harbor an exaggerated sense of possibility. "There is an increased risk that you will become an alcoholic yourself if you have an alcoholic parent," Wolin explains. "However, the increase in risk is four to five times normal, depending on gender. The risk normally in the population is about 5% for males, 1% for females. If you have an alcoholic parent, the risk that you're going to be an alcoholic is around 20% for males, 5% for females. All tolled, about 85% are not alcoholic." The vast majority are not prisoners of troubled families.

The literature on risk essentially ignores the human capacity for coping. It simply reduces the mass of humanity to a swamp of potential victims. Wolin insists that the 85 percent majority who resist the negative influence of the past have at least as much to teach us as the 15 percent minority who succumb.

One thing survivors do, Wolin has found, is take the psychological initiative. They actively cultivate insight, developing the mental habit of asking themselves penetrating questions and giving honest answers. They maintain independence, drawing boundaries between themselves and troubled parents, keeping their emotional distance. They build relationships, doing the necessary give-and-take work to derive emotional gratification from others outside the family. They are creative, expressing and resolving inner conflict in symbolic form. They cultivate humor, too, finding the comic in the tragic. The strength is in the struggle. And the strengths wind up sticking for life.

It's not that such kids grow up unscathed. They have their scars as well as their strengths. What resiliency suggests is that life is complex and emotional experiences are more mongrel than purebred. Resilient children have an ability to tolerate life with its complexities and ambiguities.

After years of working with alcoholic families and teens from poor families, Wolin, a professor of psychiatry at the George Washington University School of Medicine, has instead developed a Challenge Model. It sees opportunity instead of doom. "Survivors are challenged by the family's troubles to experiment and to respond actively and creatively. Their preemptive responses to adversity, repeated over time, become incorporated into the self as lasting resiliences." Difficult experiences force them to create a repertoire of inner resources that make them stress-resistant and resilient.

Kids come into life with a coping mentality, he contends. Difficulties threaten children's sense of self by making them feel powerless; resiliency develops as a by-product of the challenge to maintain a sense of self—that is, out of an attempt to maintain pride. The fact of resilience suggests that children have much more capability and strength than they are now allowed to exercise—they can protect themselves—potentially threatening the already tenuous hold parents have over them.

The Value of Boredom

The absence of challenge is boredom. A crossword puzzle the first time you do it is challenging and fun. The third time it's boring. The brain knows what's ahead and zones out. The brain has many built-in biases; one of them is to preferentially notice and weight negative stimuli. Another is to quickly habituate to experience, to what it has, what it knows, what it sees—a survival mechanism for our ancestors who roamed the savanna. Real danger could lurk in the grass, behind a rock, in a tree; it was a matter of life and death to swiftly strip the sensation of novelty off the unusual in order to free up attention as quickly as possible. That would allow our ancestors to be hyperattuned to what was new and different in their surroundings. Like other survival-minded adaptations, that legacy is ours today.

What enabled our ancestors to be vigilant in a natural and unpredictable environment—the built-in brain bias for constant novelty—afflicts us in a more structured and routinized world. It makes us more prone to boredom. Boredom is a lot like hunger. Given the completely different conditions under which we live today, this propensity often torments us.

Boredom, again like hunger, is an exceedingly unpleasant provocation that is a biological necessity. It's so aversive it literally warps time; it's the black hole of the brain, creating the perception that time passes more slowly than it actually does. As experiences go, boredom is hard to ignore. It creates a negative feeling state, a state of distress that is so uncomfortable to endure that it drives us to action—eventually. That is its likely evolutionary purpose—to motivate us. It's a signal to go do something to feed the brain—in this case, with some sort of stimulation, some new experience or challenge. Unless the brain is exposed to novelty—the stimulus can come from within, such as the exercise of new thoughts and sheer curiosity, or from without, in the world around us; it doesn't matter as long as it snares our interest and engages our attention—neural pathways lie unused and actually begin to wither. Left to its own devices, boredom will nag at us and prod us to do something—say, read the labels of cereal boxes—to extinguish the unpleasantness. Boredom is thus a path to enlightenment.

But as with hunger, you can't even recognize the cue that boredom is or know how to respond to it appropriately if you have violated the signal too often—say, ignoring it by the brain's equivalent of starvation dieting or overriding it by steadily gorging on junk food, filling time with strictly passive pursuits or reliance on entertainment to fill all the spaces in life. The natural world our ancestors inhabited supplied objects and activities aplenty that captivated their attention; paying attention was, for them, a matter of life and death. The task today is to find experiences captivating enough to attenuate the ennui.

As the direct impetus to seek novelty, driven by the brain's need for challenge, boredom, if allowed to run its course, is the first cause of curiosity, a purely internal motivation. Curiosity is a force to drive exploration—of the world around you, the world in you, something. But when parents emotionally overinvest in their children, they typically transmit a sense of the world as a scary place. Overinvolved parents handicap their children's autonomy, drive up their anxiety levels, and deter exploration—it becomes too frightening to even contemplate.

People normally differ in their susceptibility to boredom, both in their tolerance for the negative affective signal that boredom is and in their response to it. Some are so unable to cope with negative emotional states like boredom—they have a kind of emotional incontinence—that they focus on shutting off the signal; boredom becomes a trigger for drug use or pathological forms of excitement seeking, like gambling. Some studies have found that many who experience boredom fear that they will not succeed. Other research has shown that susceptibility to boredom increases among people who are focused on evaluation and judgment.

Boredom susceptibility is a cardinal feature of ADHD, a disorder characterized by reduced inhibitory control—those who have it are unable to tolerate internal cues or to control the impulses arising from them. Seen in this light, ADHD is not necessarily an inborn defect of attention circuitry but a failure to learn to inhibit impulsivity. Perhaps ADHD is powered by anxiety stripping away impulse control. These are scarcely popular conceptions of the disorder.

Plastic Brains Versus Chemical Destiny

We live in a time when the general model of human behavior that most people adopt to explain themselves is one that scientists have largely abandoned: that the genes you arrived with determine how your brain develops. With the addition of a little early input from parents, genes are seen as the behind-the-scenes puppeteers of behavior. But the new view is that the brain is far more plastic and malleable, even in adulthood, than anyone previously imagined. Nurture is in a constant and dynamic collaboration with nature to build and rebuild your brain, construct new neural pathways, and provide nonstop capability for new functions and new adaptations—generally known as learning.

Genes, far from being inscribed in stone, are susceptible to influence from microenvironments and experiences. A kiss, a touch, exercise, even an e-mail, can turn on and off the brain's genes and stimulate new shoots of nerve cells that pave new pathways of communication, adding whole repertoires of behavioral flexibility.

The old belief is based on some vague conception that our natures and capabilities—especially with regard to the brain—are fixed by genes and we are more or less living out our destiny. Sure we know we control our financial future, for example. But we believe that our brains are different, that they operate by unique laws. In this closed, deterministic universe, disorders like depression arise from any of a number of possible quirks in the genetic machinery, we get our variety of dysfunction diagnosed, we supply the missing chemical our genes fail to produce, and we are, or expect to be, restored to health.

The judgment we passively (and now erroneously) accept of our brains—that they are in some area beyond the reach of human effort—is one we are loath to apply to other domains of our lives. We recognize that hard work may be necessary to change our financial outlook. But our psychological passivity directs our behavior and our surprising unwillingness to control our own minds.

The new view of plasticity arrives just in time to provide the foundation for a new psychology for new times. We now live in a global economy that is very fast and very fluid. But we have yet to adopt a view of human capability and adaptability that puts us in harmony with the changed conditions and technologies that have sent shock waves through the lives of most of today's adults. That disharmony may well be the deepest source of the anxiety parents today experience in trying to raise kids for a world that they know is different from the one they grew up in.

In the new view, we are constantly adapting to and capable of adapting to our environment. There are capabilities that we can acquire; our brains are not a collection of fixed circuits; they are receptive to directed effort and active training. It is necessary to remember that brains are most prepared for endless possibility through play and experimentation. This new, dynamic model of mind is a lot like Wikipedia; the brain is more open system than black box, and its very nature is to change and reorganize, rewiring its connections—in response to challenge. Multiple sources of input are welcome, although nothing happens without active involvement.

To a much greater degree than we ever realized before, we are all sculptors and shapers of our own brains. We do not need to declare ourselves defective or dysfunctional every time we find ourselves in an environment that doesn't fit us like a glove. We can figure out a way to adapt, and even to choose the settings in which we want to apply the effort to make those mental modifications. This is vastly different from allowing ourselves to be summed up by our vulnerabilities.

Born to Be Stressed

We are born to be stressed. "Stress" has virtually become a dirty word, synonymous with trauma, but that's only because so many people don't

handle it well or even understand its function. Stress is a necessary ac-
companiment to daily life. Under normal conditions, we are primed to
tolerate stress, and at manageable levels stress forces maturation and integration. It stimulates self-organization. It is a motivator and encourages
us to reach beyond our current level of accommodation to life.

Making life challenging isn't just an exercise in character building. It
is vital to the goal of raising children to adulthood and to the mission of
education. Challenge is necessary for identity, growth, health, and real
happiness. And risk is essential for challenge; it is what you assume when
you take on a challenge. A challenge is a challenge because it demands
that we summon up all our skills and provides the opportunity for growth.

Brain growth takes place only when there is challenge. If we don't have
challenges and take risks, we are bored. Our nervous systems literally
shrink. Some risk is essential in life. All movement entails risk. But then
again, sitting still has consequences, too. Risk is essential biologically,
neurologically, behaviorally. There are real dangers to removing risk and
challenge from experience. Not only is there no growth without risk;
there is no happiness, either.

Happiness is a by-product of working toward goals where the outcome
is uncertain. Maximum positive feelings are generated not after you reach
a goal but as you approach a challenging goal, in that last final sprint
toward it. All of life involves confronting unexpected outcomes and, as a
result, an unavoidable degree of risk.

The brain has an innate need to reach beyond the status quo toward
the new and exciting—the unknown. Just to keep going at all, the brain
needs changing inputs—novel environments, new information. Such inputs stimulate the release of brain growth factors. Dendrites sprout.
Synapses form. If people don't do challenging things, as far as the brain
is concerned, the outcome of events is already known. There is no
changed input. There is no release of brain growth factors. In that state
you are not only *not* building neurons but not maintaining neural connections. Dendrites wither. Synapses disappear. You lose mental dexterity.
The brain becomes rigid, and people become sitting ducks for getting
caught in the rut of anxiety and depression and obsessiveness. So challenges and new experiences are fundamental for brain health. Study after study shows that the secret to maintaining mental sharpness into old
age is to continue providing the brain with challenge (and risk).

Simply stated, it is challenge and striving that keep people, including students, engaged. It is challenge and striving toward meeting the challenge that put the frontal lobes into a positive affective state and dampen their responsiveness to negative stimuli. It is striving that activates the deep-seated reward and motivation systems. People get something long-lasting from such experiences. It is striving that breeds a sense of purpose and the desire to conquer more challenges. It is striving that breeds an enduring sense of self-mastery. It is striving that breeds a deep sense of satisfaction. These are all the neural correlates of well-being. They are the brain's built-in antidepressants.

Clearing the way for kids to take the easy path is tantamount to destroying their brains.

Call It Experience Deficit Disorder

You could say that a large number of young people today are suffering from what might be called experience deficit disorder. Many of their activities are programmed or managed by adults. But we learn through experience. There is no way around that. When you learn through unfolding experience versus programmed activity, you are completely engaged and the knowledge is indelibly your own.

The lack of experience carries its own cache of psychological effects. In this as in so many other ways, the immune system is the perfect model for the brain. The immune system protects us from succumbing to every pathogen in an environment that's teeming with them—but it does so primarily by having some prior exposure to the bad bug. Sometimes the exposure actually ends up infecting us and we get sick. But the upshot of the process is that we then carry an immunity to that pathogen, usually for the rest of our lives. A reference library of cells has been created that, under a challenge, can rapidly reprint copies and use them to disarm a particular invader, preserving our health. In the same way, but with so many more mechanisms to call on, experience educates our brains by allowing the development of coping skills we can call upon in a crisis.

At issue here are not activities like bungee jumping or extreme skiing but the kinds of unremarkable everyday experiences from which children build, piece by piece, a sense of self-reliance and self-confidence, and a sense that they can have an effect on the world. The following incident is illuminating. A mental health professional who founded and runs an international organization in Washington, D.C., and has raised two successful sons recently welcomed her nine-year-old grandson for a short visit. One morning they took a long walk with his dog, and she planned a route back that went by the local grocery store. There she hitched the dog to a tree and instructed the boy to wait with the dog while she ran in to buy a carton of milk.

Immediately the nine-year-old was thrown into high anxiety. "But, Grandma, what if someone wants to steal me?" he pleaded. "Jack, that won't happen and I'll be out in two seconds." "But what if someone wants the dog?" he countered, trying desperately to rouse her concern. She was undeterred. "I knew his mother would be furious at me if word got back to her," she recalled. "But I felt he should have the experience of learning how to take care of himself and figuring out how to quell his nerves by himself for two minutes in a very safe place. When his father was that age and even younger, he was going to that very same store all by himself on errands." Learning how to handle fear in small doses is how we acquire our own unique ways of managing emotions. Those skills, accumulated via play and other mundane daily experiences, are what allow kids to control their reactions to the world enough to be able to pay attention to it and, eventually, participate in it in their own insightful ways.

ELEVEN

Whose Shark Tank Is It, Anyway?

What if the stressful world of cutthroat competition that parents see their kids facing does not even exist? What if it exists, but more in the minds of parents than in reality—not quite a fiction, more like a distorting mirror? "Parents perceive the world as a terribly competitive place," observes the child psychologist David Anderegg. "And many of them project that onto their children—when they're the ones who live or work in a competitive environment. They then imagine that their children must be swimming in a big shark tank, too."

And what if they've micromanaged their kids' lives because they've hitched their measurement of success to a single event whose value to life and paycheck they have frantically overestimated? No one denies the Ivy League offers excellent learning experiences, but most educators know that some of the best programs exist at schools that don't top the *U.S. News & World Report* list. And that with the right attitude—a willingness to be engaged by new ideas and to work hard—it's possible to get a meaningful education almost anywhere.

Further, argues the social historian Peter Stearns, there are ample openings for students at an array of colleges. "We have a competitive frenzy that frankly involves parents more than it involves kids themselves," he observes, as both a father of eight and a teacher of many. "Kids are more ambivalent about the college race than the parents are."

A Reversal of Reasoning

What parents generally offer as justification for hyperprotective parent-ing—the need to prepare their children for a competitive world while shielding them from the dangers Out There—may really reflect their own perception of a dangerous world, or, more precisely, their stressful expe-riences of dislocation in it. Parental anxiety makes everything stressful. Difficulty, in this case, is in the eyes of the beholder.

The Brown University psychologist Stephen J. Sheinkopf has found that free-floating anxiety in parents makes them see difficulty with their children where it does not necessarily exist. For mothers, their own level of distress determines how difficult they perceive their children to be. A mother's state of mind affects her perception of her child and how she in-teracts with the child.

"Psychological distress affects the degree to which infant behavioral characteristics are experienced as stressful or difficult," Sheinkopf and a team of researchers reported in the January/February 2006 issue of the *Journal of Pediatric Psychology,* after studying close to a thousand children and their mothers, more than a third of whom had used cocaine during pregnancy.

The investigators found that mothers who experience stress from par-enting are more likely to perceive their babies as temperamentally diffi-cult. The infant's behavior at one month of age—as measured by cry analysis and reactivity to stimulation—predicted both the mother's rating of infant temperament at four months and the mother's level of parenting stress. It made no difference whether or not the babies had been exposed to drugs. Across the board, say the researchers, the mothers who felt the most parenting stress were the ones who rated their babies' behavior as more difficult.

"Whether or not a mother had used drugs," says Sheinkopf, "if she felt more stress in her role as parent, she was more likely to view her baby as difficult and more likely to view her baby's behaviors just after birth as stressful. If mothers are highly stressed as parents, this will affect the ways that they think about and interact with their babies." He adds that through such interactions, parental perceptions "can have long term ef-fects on how children develop and how families function."

So perhaps we have the view of causation all wrong, all backward. Sheinkopf's research further suggests that the rise in diagnosis of child psychiatric disorders such as attention deficit disorder may reflect not so much a rise in true childhood pathology as a rise in adult stress.

I recently spoke to a child psychiatry fellow at the teaching hospital of a well-regarded eastern university. The doctor had been asked to see a young new patient—of twenty-two months. The psychiatrist didn't really think it was appropriate to see a child only twenty-two months old.

The parents brought the child in insisting on a psychiatric diagnosis and medication for his wild ADHD-like behavior. After observing the child with his parents for a few minutes, the doctor felt that the kid was suffering from little more than a serious case of the developmentally appropriate terrible twos that needed just a bit more parental supervision and input.

Despite the relatively brief time typically allotted to individual cases in modern clinical care, the doctor was able to interview the parents separately. While he was talking to the mother, the father called her by cell phone from just outside. The mother and the father proceeded to fight loudly. The doctor subsequently elicited a history of severe parental fighting in which the adults would get highly absorbed, leaving their worried toddler to fend for himself during these distressing periods. The parents were oblivious to the fact that in addition to terrifying their child, and neglecting him when he was upset, they were modeling oppositional behavior. Is it any wonder the normally curious child was a bit defiant?

As treatment for the child, the psychiatrist recommended marital therapy for the adults. The parents, especially the mother, were visibly disappointed. They refused to accept the recommendation. The psychiatrist knows they will probably shop elsewhere for a diagnosis that not only takes their parenting skills off the hook but also fits their willingness to make the child a psychiatric scapegoat for their own distress.

The California child psychiatrist Elizabeth Roberts reports similar experiences. "I had a woman bring me an 18-month-old she insisted was bipolar, based on the child's temper tantrums, and needed medications." Not only is it not possible to make a diagnosis at that age, but Roberts believes that "psychiatric drugs play into this whole madness of placating, spoiling and enabling our children into a mentally and emotionally hobbled state."

In a 2006 article in the *Washington Post* titled "A Rush to Medicate

Young Minds," Roberts bluntly labeled "shocking" the changes she has seen in her fifteen years of practice as a child psychiatrist and another fifteen years before that as a teacher. "Psychiatrists are now misdiagnosing and overmedicating children for ordinary defiance and misbehavior," she insists. "The temper tantrums of belligerent children are increasingly being characterized as psychiatric illness." She singles out bipolar disorder, attention deficit hyperactivity disorder, and Asperger's syndrome as the diagnoses particularly favored today "to explain away the results of poor parenting practices." It's simply easier to tell parents their child has a brain-based disorder than to suggest their parenting skills need an overhaul.

"Parents and teachers today seem to believe that any boy who wriggles in his seat and willfully defies his teacher's rules has ADHD. Likewise, any child who has a temper tantrum is diagnosed with bipolar disorder. After all, an anger outburst is how most parents define a 'mood swing.' Contributing to this widespread problem of misdiagnosis is the doctor's willingness to accept, without question, the assessment offered by a parent or teacher." Medicating a child's mind has "now become a widely used technique in parenting a belligerent child." Nevertheless, Roberts believes that "frustration is a necessary experience that helps kids learn coping skills and encourages them to develop a realistic view of the world."

Sadly, too many people benefit when a child is diagnosed with a mental illness. Schools get more state funding for the education of a mentally handicapped student, Roberts notes. Teachers have more subdued students in the large classrooms. The pharmaceutical industry actively promotes it and reaps huge revenues, while the insurance structure definitely encourages it. But in the current cultural climate, parents benefit, too. "Parents are not forced to examine their poor parenting practices, because they have the perfect excuse: Their child has a chemical imbalance."

Only children lose. They have to endure unknown effects on developing brains, real side effects, and a diagnosis of mental illness. Typically, one diagnosis—ADHD—and one drug—a stimulant, to improve attentiveness—are only the start of a whole excursion into pathologizing normal behavior. Most often, stimulant prescription for ADHD becomes an "entry drug." It opens the door to further medication. A November 2006 front-page article in the *New York Times* pointed out that 1.6 million American children and teenagers were given at least two psychiatric drugs in combination—despite a lack of evidence that such drug cocktails provide any benefit.

When, after a diagnosis of ADHD, children's problems persist, the parents, as a result of their positive experience with the use of stimulants, are primed to try other psychiatric medications for their children. "After you get them on one drug," observes Ranga Krishnan, chairman of psychiatry at Duke University, "parents don't seem to mind the second." He himself expressed "grave doubts" about the growing use of psychiatric drug cocktails in kids.

What was most notable about the *Times*'s report was the response of the parents interviewed for the article. "Nearly all recalled being in a store when their child threw a tantrum and feeling that onlookers branded them as bad parents," the reporter observed.

It is strangely ironic that a generation of parents that will go to great lengths to do "the best" for their kids is so willing to do what might be the worst for their brains. That's what anxiety does—it prevents people from thinking through the consequences of their actions. The dramatic growth in the psychiatric medication of children might be the most damning evidence of the degree to which parents will go to put their own emotional needs ahead of their children's developmental needs.

Psychoactive drugs have their uses; some are very good at relieving symptoms. But not one of them imparts the mental tools and coping skills people need to stay healthy. Only good psychotherapy can do that. Treatments like cognitive behavioral therapy and dialectical behavior therapy teach rigorous methods of self-questioning—Socratic dialogue and Buddhist meditation as therapy—that prevent mental slippage into negative automatic thoughts, false beliefs, and other cognitive distortions that underlie depression and anxiety. No pill can deliver that. What's more, in the absence of some preventive strategy to neutralize catastrophic thinking, repeated bouts of disorder, particularly depression, seem to change the brain in fundamental ways so that what started out as episodic tends to become chronic.

Downloaded Dread

The very experience that has done the most to elevate the status of kids is probably also the largest source of distrust of children and childhood. The children, after all, are the only ones who are completely at ease with the new power tools of our lives. They are the new masters, at least digitally, and parents are their servants. As with all servant-master relationships, they are not entirely relaxed in each other's presence. And the servants seem willing to sacrifice themselves on behalf of their young masters. Within the family, this upended power balance has made adults deeply fearful of kids even as they dedicate their lives to them. It is perhaps why they cater to them beyond all measure of reason, beyond what is good for them and good for anyone else.

The ultimate in parenting that caters to kids? It is when you don't just *act* for your kid, you act *out* for your child. Take the case of the Pennsylvania mother who went online to get a fake ID for her college-age daughter. "Because I have more time," was the mother's explanation.

Terror will do that to people.

No one has limned the generational digital divide better than those who established the electronic frontier.

"On the most rudimentary level," John Perry Barlow, lyricist for the Grateful Dead and co-founder of the Electronic Frontier Foundation, wrote so presciently in 1994, "there is simply terror of feeling like an immigrant in a place where your children are natives—where you're always going to be behind the 8-ball because they can develop the technology faster than you can learn it. It's what I call the learning curve of Sisyphus. And the only people who are going to be comfortable with that are people who don't mind confusion and ambiguity. I look at confusing circumstances as an opportunity—but not everybody feels that way. We've got a culture that's based on the ability of people to control everything."

In this new order, Barlow later emphasized, "you are terrified of your own children, since they are natives in a world where you will always be immigrants." It's what the kids know, and we don't, that is piling on the parental anxiety. They're the digital natives, born to the technology, and we're the digital immigrants, the adults, who think text messaging is more of a stress than a cool and necessary way of keeping up with pals. We learned the technology late enough so that it isn't second nature, and we speak with varying degrees of an accent. Like all metaphors, the digital native–digital immigrant metaphor falls apart if pushed too hard, but it makes a distinction that gets at a deep truth.

Unlike the kids, for whom that is simply the water they swim in, the adults not only have to learn to live with constant change but had to completely retool and learn a whole other "language," really a whole new way of doing almost everything. That alone makes people feel invalidated and infantilized in a world now beyond their control. And the nature of the learning curve guarantees that they will be far less efficient before getting back to decent levels of productivity. It's frustrating, especially if there are deadlines to meet, ideas to express. And being a learner at square one makes anyone feel childlike and inept despite whatever professional expertise he or she has. These are not comfortable feelings; they can challenge even a healthy identity, and some people go out of their way to, and can afford to, resist them. I know dinosaurs who pride themselves on having their secretaries print out their e-mail for them. Given the change in technology, and the accelerating speed of change of new technology, it's not hard to imagine why adults are fearful, especially of the children. What will be thrown at them next? And they still don't know what the kids know! Better to rage at the Internet as a minefield of child pornography.

Marc Prensky is a video game creator who insists we have yet to grapple with the full implications of the digital native–digital immigrant divide. "Today's students are no longer the people our educational system was designed to teach," he writes. "Today's students—K through college—represent the first generations to grow up with this new technology. They have spent their entire lives surrounded by and using computers, videogames, digital music players, video cams, cell phones, and all the other toys and tools of the digital age. It is now clear that as a result of this ubiquitous environment and the sheer volume of their interaction with it, today's students *think and process information fundamentally differently* from their predecessors. These differences go far further and deeper than most educators suspect or realize."

The students today, he says, are all "native speakers of the digital language of computers, video games and the Internet. So what does that make the rest of us? Those of us who were not born into the digital world but have, at some later point in our lives, become fascinated by and adopted many or most aspects of the new technology are, and always will be compared to them, *Digital Immigrants*. The importance of the distinction is this: As Digital Immigrants learn—like all immigrants, some better than others—to adapt to their environment, they always retain, to some degree, their 'accent,' that is, their foot in the past."

Changed Childhood

The version of childhood we've introduced to our children is very different from that in past eras. Children no longer work at young ages. They stay in school for longer periods of time and spend more time exclusively in the company of peers. Children are far less integrated into general society than they used to be at every step of the way. We've created laws that give children many rights and protections—although we have allowed media and marketers to have free access to their hearts and minds.

In changing the nature of childhood, we have relegated children to their own peer culture. That very separation from the general adult world has forced the adults to lose track of what kids' real capabilities are. We have introduced a tendency to assume that children can't handle difficult situations or take on responsibilities.

Parents need to recognize that they themselves have created many of the stresses and anxieties children are suffering from, without giving them tools to manage them, says Stearns. Parents also need to remember that one of the goals of higher education is to help young people develop the capacity to think for themselves.

The gulf between children's culture and adult culture leads parents to have unrealistic expectations about children's ability to handle adversity, agrees Anderegg. He explains:

> Parents feel like if they're doing their job, their child will never have to experience any adversity, which is unrealistic. I used to see this all the time when a kid would be mean to another kid at school. Parents would be calling the school demanding some kind of intervention. By the time we got all the parents with their complicated schedules together to have a meeting, the kids involved were walking through the school playground holding hands. People think adversity is bad for children. A moderate amount of adversity is good for children. Children who experience a moderate amount of adversity that has been overcome do better because they understand that adversity can be overcome. They come to know that if something is bad today, that doesn't mean it's going to be bad forever. Parents believe that all adversity is bad for children because they never want them to feel bad about anything. Contemporary parents get really anxious if their children experience any adversity.

What the changed climate has done is left adults, and especially parents, with a distrust of the normal course of childhood—and even of children. The adults have completely lost a natural perspective on childhood.

Parents no longer act as if they believe that children have within them their own desire to demonstrate competence and mastery, that they can trust children to follow their own curiosity as a path to achievement—despite kids' very apparent mastery of the technology. Certainly parents no longer trust children to learn on their own; instead, they apply a massive amount of pressure. They don't trust boredom to serve, eventually, as a natural stimulus for discovery and creativity. Nor do they trust that normal social processes provide a great incentive for children to learn, to transfer information from one to the other. Even computers are suspect, holding an array of dangers but none so much as pedophiles and other perps. In their deep disconnect from children, adults, as discussed earlier, have come to distrust play to do anything constructive for kids, let alone lay the foundation for something as serious as self-regulation; it's simply unimaginable that play, that great time waster, could have an invisible hand in wiring the still-developing brain.

Parents certainly distrust that children can grow up without their own divine intervention and omnipresence, and can't even countenance the idea that their own invasiveness might be what is disrupting the processes of development. And yet I know from talking to parents that they suspect that their death-grip parenting isn't fabulous for kids. Still, their massive distrust serves as an invitation to anxiety; once in the front door, it flourishes in the controlled conditions of the hothouse, where child raising is no longer tethered to the constraints of nature.

No Child Left Behind

Like Stearns, Anderegg is alarmed that parents, pursuing disability diagnoses so that children can take untimed SATs, actually encourage kids to think of themselves as sickly and fragile. Colleges no longer know when SATs are untimed—but the kids know.

The incredible irony is that by buying their children accommodations to assuage their own anxiety, parents are actually locking their kids into a vicious cycle of fragility. As one suburban teacher says, "Exams are a fact of life. They are anxiety producing. The kids never learn how to cope with anxiety."

There *are* many pressures and insecurities that parents are feeling, from the pace of technological change to vanishing job security, from financial uncertainty to the fear of terrorism. But parents are projecting their own anxieties onto children and misdirecting their efforts at solutions; their way of coping with the new uncertainties is not to seek social change but to push ever more strongly for individual advantage.

The Price of Vigilance

Overparenting isn't just bad for kids—it has terrible effects on adults. It threatens to undo the very thing that kids need most—a stable family. "Raising children has never been easy. For today's parents, however, it has become a conspicuous source of anxiety and distress. A recent crop of books and articles give voice to this complaint. Likewise in recent surveys, parents report lower levels of marital happiness than nonparents." So begins the 2006 annual "State of Our Unions" report from the National Marriage Project at Rutgers University. What makes the drop in happiness particularly threatening, say the study's authors, the social scientist David Popenoe and Barbara Dafoe Whitehead, is that marriage itself has changed from an institution in which the whole society once had a stake to a relationship "mainly designed for the sexual and emotional gratification of each adult." Take away the emotional gratification of the adult and what's left?

The hothouse in which children are now raised has transformed family life so much that it's no longer fun for the adults. "I spend so much time being a mother that sometimes I forget to have sex," a Portland, Oregon, woman wrote recently in the *New York Times*.

The primary relationship in the family, the one around which the household is organized, is now the parent-child bond. The disproportionate investment in the children of parental emotions, finances, and time erodes marital bonds and contributes to a continuing high divorce rate. Marriage and family therapists point to it as the big killer of marital sex and a primary risk factor for affairs. Unzipped Web sites such as UrbanBaby.com are crowded with adults lamenting that their medicine cabinets are fully stocked with Zoloft and they can't remember when they last had sex with their spouse.

Marriage remains the nation's fundamental social institution, and most individuals still aspire to happy and long-lasting marriage. But life with children is receding as a defining experience of adult life. For one thing, a growing percentage of women, especially well-educated ones, are not having children. Further, as people live longer, the years of child raising shrink as a proportion of the whole of adult life, sandwiched by years of the good life on either side. "Life with children is experienced as a disruption in the life course rather than as one of its defining purposes," and the entire culture "portrays the years of life devoted to child-rearing as less satisfying." One result is that "many parents feel out of synch with the larger adult world."

Hothouse or Safe House?

In the growing divide between the child-free and the childbearing, it just may be that the best defense is a good offense. Children are, after all, the future of the society and of the species. If no one else is looking out for them, then parents must do all they can—even go to great lengths to clear the path for them.

Against a backdrop of cultural devaluation of child raising, invasive parenting makes a certain amount of sense. It makes good Darwinian eat-or-be-eaten sense—as an adaptation to an increasingly hostile environment. Hostile, of course, though not for the marketers, who, parents well know, are themselves predatory creatures of a certain kind. An attempt by parents to wrest for their children what the culture, left to its own devices, might not be willing to deliver at a time when children have expanded needs—such as for education—and require greater investments of time and money to grow to independence in the knowledge economy. According to the U.S. Department of Agriculture, it now costs an estimated $237,000 for a family with an average income of $57,400 to feed, clothe, house, and educate one child from birth to age seventeen. That estimate does not even count the cost of tutoring, SAT preparation, or college education, or special needs of any kind. Small wonder that parents are anxious. At the same time, the percentage of households with children has declined from half of all households in 1960 to less than one-third today.

Parents erect a hothouse around their children as a way to shield them from a world that likes them less and less, and as a way to expand and elevate the importance of child raising in the culture. And maybe they overidentify with their children because no one else in the culture does. Parents must worry excessively about their children because certainly the child-free (they do not call themselves child*less*) will not protect them or otherwise look out for them. Perhaps we should see the often offensive and laughable gestures of these modern American parents as overcompensation. Or even more: as a measure of the gravity of the situation, a mark of the growing isolation of parents, an accounting of the desperation they feel—even if they can't name it or articulate it—in a culture that is increasingly hostile to their primary interest. If that is the case, their behavior can only be expected to get worse. But they do have a point.

In this perspective invasive parents are far more worthy of sympathy than of ridicule. They are more stressed and depressed than anyone else in the culture, doing their best to cope with an adverse climate.

That is, they *would* be worthy of sympathy—if their efforts were not all so tirelessly, relentlessly self-focused. If the efforts on behalf of their own kids didn't have to come at the expense of all the other kids. Why *aren't* they manning the barricades or marching on Washington demanding more benefits for *all* parents—say, paid parenting and child-care leaves at the front end and more financial support for college education at the back end? Why is it just "I don't want *my* child left behind"?

Adaptations are always well-intentioned attempts to survive in changed conditions. But as admirable and necessary as the underlying behavioral experimentation is, not all adaptations are successful. The eventual cost may be too high.

The efforts of hothouse parents are stunningly misguided. First and foremost, invasive parenting fails the cardinal principle of successful adaptation; it does not increase the survival fitness of children either individually or collectively; in fact, the evidence is clear that it dramatically reduces it.

Hothouse parenting is bad for kids. It violates their developmental needs. The parental anxiety that fuels it restricts children from making their own creative adaptations to the modern world, from playing and experimenting. In making children servants of the emotional needs of parents, hothouse parenting chains children to the past rather than freeing them for the unknown future.

Death-grip parenting is terrible for the adults, too. It undermines their mental health as well as the children's. In a study reported to a 2005 meeting of the Society for Research in Child Development, two psychologists found that parents who base their own self-worth on their kids' accomplishments—what psychologists call contingent self-worth—are more anxious and dissatisfied than parents who base their self-worth on other factors. Over 400 parents (222 mothers, 186 fathers) responded to such statements as "When my son fails I feel bad about myself." At the time of the study over 20 percent answered in the affirmative—but the figure appears to be rapidly increasing.

The researchers found that for parents whose self-worth is contingent on their children's performance, the kids' actual achievements and high grades are irrelevant; they don't boost parental emotional well-being—because the threat of a child's failure is ever present. "Parents who based their self-worth on their children's failure were likely to be prone to heightened ill-being and dampened well-being *even when their children were doing well in school,*" the psychologists discovered. "It's possible that the potential of failure is so threatening to parents with high contingent self-worth that children do not need to actually fail to contribute to parents' negative emotional functioning."

"All parents feel bad when their children don't do well," says the study's co-author Missa Murry Eaton of Penn State University, but only "overinvolved parents feel bad about themselves." They see their child's poor performance as a reflection on themselves. Such parents, she finds, are also driven to exert unnecessary control over their kids—by checking over or actually helping with their homework, even when such help is unsolicited—because it helps reduce their own uncertainty and anxiety by attempting to improve academic performance. The children, for their part, wind up feeling incompetent.

In a separate series of studies, Eaton has shown that parents whose self-worth is contingent on their children's academic performance go to great lengths to control their children inappropriately, through invasiveness. They often try to extract information from their kids ("My mother often calls me at school to check if I am studying enough") and take over tasks, such as checking over homework, when their assistance isn't requested—all with the desperate intent of maintaining their own sense of self-worth. Those parents who didn't base their sense of self on their children's performance were less controlling of their kids.

When family life is focused on the needs of the kids to succeed, and activities are organized around the kids' schedules, parents suffer in other ways. They feel isolated and depressed. There is very little socializing with other adults as adults. The lack of their own intimate or broader social relationships is one of the forces pushing parents to meet their own emotional needs through their children and their performance in school and on the athletic field.

And, of course, "contemporary motherhood now threatens contemporary marriage," says the Rutgers report. "Most Americans marry for lasting love, friendship and emotional intimacy. Achieving this new marital ideal takes high levels of time, attention and vigilance. Like new babies, contemporary marriages have to be nurtured and coddled in order to thrive. The problem is that once a real baby comes along, the time, the effort and energy that goes into nurturing the relationship goes into nurturing the infant. As a result, marriages can become less happy and satisfying."

The irony of the child-centered family is that while it caters to the child, and creates a sense of preciousness, it serves no needs of the child. It only makes kids fragile.

How Parenting Lost Its Allure

"What I notice more than anything," a thirtysomething mother told me, "is how few mothers seem to take joy or interest in any children but their own. There is no common interest or common welfare, no curiosity about another child's energy or spirit. It is just not interesting at all to most mothers, other children. I find this very sad, this myopia. It seems to me that when we become parents we enter a community but these days there is no sense of community." Anxiety keeps parents too tightly wound to worry beyond their own front stoop.

We've made adulthood look very unattractive to children. As they see it in adults' eyes, it is a stress-filled, worry-ridden, joyless place almost totally focused on the children. Why would anyone in his right mind *want* to move past adolescence? Vigilance is enormously taxing—and it's taken all the fun out of parenting.

Parents need to abandon the idea of perfection and give up some of the invasive control they've maintained over their children. The goal of parenting, the University of Virginia's John Portmann emphasizes, is to raise an independent human being. Sooner or later, he says, most kids will be forced to confront their own mediocrity. Parents may find it easier to give up some control if they recognize they have exaggerated many of the dangers of childhood—although they have steadfastly ignored others, namely the removal of recess from schools.

Parenting experts haven't helped. On the contrary, says Anderegg, they've completely overwhelmed parents with data and conflicting opinions. "There is a huge range of expertise, and parents spend an incredible amount of time online doing their parenting homework, trying to figure out the best way to do this and the best way to do that. It doesn't help, because they just become completely overwhelmed and the conflicting information makes people more anxious. The more choices people have, the unhappier with their choice they are when they finally make a choice. That is a lot of what's happening with parenting. It's a sort of unsatisfying job, you collect all this data, but the data doesn't tell you what to do, so you have to collect more data, and you're unhappy with the choice you make."

There are happy parents. Anderegg sees them. But they are the people who are most likely to have the most children. The more children people have, he observes, the more relaxed they get with their younger children. "You understand that they aren't going to break. All the terrible things you imagine probably aren't going to happen. And you understand when you have more children that each child comes with their own temperament; you come to know that your contribution, while important, is not the only one. Parents of first children always overemphasize their contributions to developmental outcomes. If you have five or six children, when you get to the younger children, those parents are pretty relaxed because they realize the kid is going to turn out pretty much the way the kid is going to turn out. We just don't see that as often because few parents are in that situation."

Putting Worry in Its Place

Parental anxiety has its place, but today's parents are not applying it wisely. They're paying too much attention to too few kids—and in the end, the wrong kids. As with the girl whose parents bought her the Gestalt-defect diagnosis, resources are being expended for kids who don't need them. Everyone would be better off if attention to the kids was redistributed.

There *are* kids who are worth worrying about—kids in poverty, kids who witness domestic violence. How about the four thousand American children orphaned each year by parental homicide? "We focus so much on our own children," says Tufts's David Elkind. "It's time to begin caring about all children."

TWELVE

Class Dismissed

I t's every modern parent's worst nightmare—a school where kids can play all day. Or talk. But a funny thing happens. No one takes the easy way out. And graduates seem to have a head start on the information age. Welcome to Sudbury Valley School. Its two hundred kids are having a hell of a good time preparing for the future. And not one student needs a diagnosis of ADHD or learning disability to fit into the program.

"I've learned a lot about how my mind works by paying attention to how I unicycle," Ben declared in preparation for high school graduation. And from the time he was twelve, Ben paid attention to nothing so much as unicycling. When students elsewhere were puzzling over, say, the periodic table, Ben, along with a handful of schoolmates, was mostly struggling up and racing down New England mountainsides, dodging rocks, mud, and other obstacles. His "frantic flights to maintain balance" demanded both deep focus and moment-to-moment planning. But they gave him something missing from most classrooms today—a passion for pursuing challenges and inhaling the skills and information (to say nothing of the confidence) to master their complexities.

At Sudbury Valley School, there's no other way to learn. The thirty-eight-year-old day facility is an alternative institution that works. It is founded on what comes down to a belief about human nature—that children have an innate curiosity to learn and a drive to become effective, independent human beings, no matter how many times they try and fail;

that kids normally seek challenge and are willing to persevere if they are allowed to exercise their own natural curiosity. And it's the job of adults to expose them to models and information, answer questions—then get out of the way without trampling motivation. There are no classrooms per se, although students can request instruction on any subject or talk to any staffer—or any other student, for that matter—anytime about an interest. There aren't even grades. From overnight hiking trips to economics classes to the weekly School Meeting at which all matters—including my visit—are discussed and voted on equally by students and staff, all activities are age mixed.

Some kids start Sudbury Valley at age four, their parents committed to democratic principles even in education and trusting to the byways of self-motivation. Some, like Ben, arrive around age six. "Ben was a kinesthetic learner," says his mother, Pam. "He really learned by doing. I could tell he was not going to sit in his seat at the local kindergarten, where the kids were arranged in rows and raised their hand to speak. We went for a visit and he declared, 'I'm not going there.'" Others land at Sudbury Valley later because they lost interest or failed in conventional schooling, and the place was a last-ditch choice by parents at the end of their tether, desperate to keep the child in school.

All of them spend an inordinate amount of time talking to each other, reading in quiet corners, drawing or painting, hunkered in the computer rooms, and moving around the mansion, barn, and grounds that serve as one of the most alternative of alternative schools in the country. Mostly they spend time playing.

When Jeffrey H. and his wife first heard about Sudbury Valley, they were categorically dismissive. "I mean," he says, "how can kids learn anything without doing much of anything?" That, however, was before the first four of his six kids started school and their curiosity began withering instead of expanding. "After spending many years in the business world, it dawned on me that we learn best what we really want to learn, and you really have to have that spark. When I read [again] about the Sudbury idea of letting kids pursue their own interests, I was ready to buy in." It took two trips to get all four kids their required weeklong trial visit, but when the kids gave the thumbs-up, he sold his house in Nantucket and moved his brood across the state; as with any good neighborhood school, a family has to live nearby in order for the children to attend. "You don't realize until you're an adult how natural it is to learn, how interesting the world really is. We adults think we know how to do it and the kids don't and therefore we have to teach them how."

So ingrained is the belief that children learn only when confined to their seats and explicitly taught in an organized way that most adults overlook even the most obvious evidence to the contrary—that the young struggle persistently against even their own clumsiness to master such formidable tasks as crawling, walking, and talking on their own. "They stand, they totter, they fall down, they may even get hurt—over and over again—but still they are driven to learn how to walk. Learning and teaching have nothing to do with each other," declares Dan Greenberg, who, with his wife, Hanna, is a founder of Sudbury Valley. In traditional schools, he says, teaching is driven by coercion, which breeds resistance. "Learning is driven internally by curiosity. Teaching can only be effective if the person you're teaching has sought you out to teach them." People like to stretch themselves, he adds. "Why do they do it so naturally in their leisure activities but not in school with their mandatory activities?"

Outsiders commonly choke upon hearing that no one even teaches reading. Sometimes insiders get a bit antsy, too. When Ben was in the second or third grade, anxiety temporarily overtook his well-read father, who offered the boy a dime for every fifteen minutes he'd spend reading at home. Ben accepted the bribe long enough to prove he could do it.

But in characteristic Sudbury Valley style, his reading proficiency took a huge leap forward only *after* he began playing with airplanes and then an electronic flight simulator—because that required him to read the flight manual. And that led to discovery of flight simulator communities on the Internet, which led to mock airplane battles, which led to communicating with squadron leaders, which led to wanting to know how to spell and write. All of which got Ben to one of the most competitive and intensive liberal arts colleges in the country, where he has completed his freshman year. "Ben has had a great year at college," his mother reports. "He's thriving on the academics, and gets up to all sorts of zany antics with his friends (such as paddling a two-man bathtub in the Crum Creek Regatta and coming in second place). He's one of a group that revitalized the hiking club. They successfully petitioned the administration to include an overnight hiking trip as part of freshman orientation in the fall, and he'll be one of the leaders on the trip. He's taking logic, linguistics, physics, and calculus next year. All in all, I'd say that although he certainly has had to work very hard this year, he definitely has been equal to the challenge of organized courses and the stresses/pleasures of college living." Says Greenberg: "You don't need to give kids a fundamental education, because they'll grab it on their own."

Explaining Sudbury Valley to family, friends—anyone—isn't easy. It's threatening to people, observes Ben's mother. "It's not what they experienced, and what they lived through is what they think everyone else should do. Giving children a lot of freedom and responsibility really pushes people's buttons."

There is no magical way to expose all kids to all knowledge and have them find which one is their destiny, notes Greenberg. Sudbury Valley trusts that kids (and adults) can sniff things out on their own. "Every individual struggles to make his own integration. No one can do it better."

Sudbury Valley students don't live in a bubble. The doubts that others have about their education weigh on them, too. Kirsten did what many others wind up doing sooner or later for a day or two: she sat in on classes at a nearby high school. "I didn't come away feeling that I had less knowledge," she said. But she was "surprised that the encouragement to think and learn on my own that I was used to wasn't there. I was surprised at the lack of trust."

When Ben was thirteen, guilt over time spent unicycling led him to visit a middle school and take a math placement test. "I placed in the top class and that pushed me over the edge towards continuing at SVS. I needed something to tell me that I wouldn't be behind in a normal school."

Those doubts work two ways, though, drawing to Sudbury Valley sullen and shy teens short on goals and motivation. Stephanie was sinking in her SAT-pressurized public high school when she decamped in junior year for Sudbury Valley (her friends derisively called it "day care") for "the sole purpose of avoiding college." For several months, she puffed and sunned her days away on Smoking Rock. In time, she drifted over to the music barn. There she picked up a flute again and began playing purely for pleasure. Two years later she selected a college specifically for its new arts center.

Jessica was severely depressed in her community's high school. Numerous friends "shared my indifference, but they were content with their apathy. I was tortured by it." Her parents agreed to a change, but adapting to Sudbury Valley was difficult. "It's hard for a kid to be thrown into that atmosphere," says Ben's mother, Pam. "There's nobody telling you what to do. You really have to forge your own path."

Jessica was shy. She brooded. She sat at the edge of the Sewing Room, pretty much the crossroads of the school, a large space on the first floor of the mansion where there's always animated debate or a raucous card game around a huge table. For a long time she just listened. Eventually she began contributing to political arguments, discussions of personal beliefs, "and philosophies of education and just about everything else." Conversation and debate, she insists, were the source of her education. Conversation: the most engaging way that people exchange the content of their minds.

Current educational theory corroborates her assertion. Increasingly, across all the sciences, there is an awareness of social capital. Researchers in a variety of disciplines believe that human interaction is critical for learning and the best learning comes about as a result of social participation. Relationships provide both the deep motivation and the context for acquiring information; people are driven by the desire to understand the perspectives of others. Studies have shown that peer engagement, for example, clicks on both intellectual engagement and learning persistence among students.

School government is a primary route to moral development and self-mastery at Sudbury Valley. "You have to practice responsibility and judgment to be an effective adult in modern society," says Greenberg. At weekly town-hall-like School Meetings, every person has one vote. "Students govern the school completely," reports Jason, a twenty-nine-year-old alumnus. "The fact that a five-year-old has the same meaningful vote as an eighteen-year-old is very empowering. It has a lot to do with the difference between an average public school student and a student as SVS."

Day to day, a six-person judicial council, or JC, enforces the rules legislated in School Meetings. Students of all ages run for a three-month term as clerk—organizing procedures, investigating all allegations of misconduct, keeping detailed records, holding hearings, meting judgments. JC embodies the very idea that you can make mistakes and learn from your errors. A student might be charged with bringing illegal substances on campus or littering; students and staffers alike have the obligation to file a complaint if they know of any infraction; they come to see it as a way of protecting their special community. In two days of JC meetings, I never saw a student defiant or defensive about even serious charges against him. All were keenly aware they had betrayed the trust placed in them. Some calmly presented exculpatory evidence, but all accepted whatever punishment was handed down, from extra cleanup duty to short-term suspensions that could inconvenience their whole family. Over time at Sudbury Valley, almost everyone runs for a term on JC. Getting to judge and sentence one's peers builds a strong sense of justice and creates confidence in the fairness of the school.

There's only one graduation requirement. Students have to write and present to a committee—and defend before their peers—a thesis about how they are prepared to be an adult. It takes time to write, even more time to figure out. "Even kids who've never written before are articulate," says Greenberg, "because they have something to say. Writing skills depend on having something to say."

What Sudbury Valley does for its students is invisible to the unaided eye. It allows for the development of an internal structure of success. Sudbury Valley students are not working exclusively to please their parents. They are not striving to live up to the expectations of others. They have been allowed to struggle and experience failure and come up with their own coping strategies, building their own inner resources. They have been given the opportunity to develop their own authentic motivation and determination.

Students take it upon themselves to prepare for college entrance. They study for SATs, often seeking the help of Sudbury Valley staffers. About 50 percent of students go directly to college. Some choose to travel or try other things first. Many sample college while at Sudbury Valley by taking courses at Northeastern University or Harvard Extension School—sometimes to reassure themselves that they can do the work, sometimes to further a long-standing interest, sometimes for the sheer challenge. They import the information to Sudbury Valley and feed the general conversational din.

No doubt about it, Sudbury Valley students throw college admissions officers into a quandary. "They structure their own education and have no educational documents," laments Martha Pitts, director of admissions at the University of Oregon, "while we need to make sure a student is prepared for success." But she finds that those from a nontraditional background who prove their proficiency do very well there. "So we welcome them."

Most make college a deliberate choice on their own timetable, not something they simply hurtle on to, driven by parental expectations. Parental expectations, in fact, often have to be reconsidered. Jeffrey H., for example, has a sixteen-year-old son who wants to be a marine. "I'm not thrilled. But if in a couple of years he still wants to be a marine, that's something he'll do, because that's something he's got to decide for himself." Another son, a seventeen-year-old senior, has no idea what he wants to do next year. Jeffrey H. isn't worried; it took him two stabs to get through college himself. "He'll probably struggle for a while with some low-level jobs. But that in itself is an education. When he's ready to take on some grander goals, which will probably include college, he'll be ready to do it."

Some choose paths other than college. Students have become lute makers, auto technicians, musicians, equestrian-farmers, dedicated environmentalists. Some have started their own companies at eighteen. Others take retail or service jobs to get money for travel abroad for a year or two. Some continue their education cautiously, going on to community college. They do what they do not by default or by obligation but from a sense of understanding what they're doing and why.

"A parent naturally wants to do the best for their child and somehow comes to assume they know what's best for the child," says Jeffrey H. "But the person who knows best is the child himself. It *does* require a certain amount of faith and patience to allow the kids to figure out who they really are, what they want to be and what their interests really are."

A longitudinal study of over a thousand graduates shows that Sudbury Valley alumni take an increasing amount of time between high school and college. "The opening of vistas of the twenty-first century has affected everyone," says Greenberg. But the students go on to lead deeply satisfying lives. Most are unusually resilient. Almost all feel that they are in control of their destinies. They report that they lead self-directed lives for which they have consciously set their own goals and made their own choices. They grow up with the confidence that they can learn what they want and need.

Since 1991, over three dozen Sudbury Valley–type schools have sprouted around the country, more around the world—all coming to the model on their own; there is no proselytizing. I visited De Ruimte (The Room) in Soest, not far from Amsterdam, in the Netherlands. As at Sudbury Valley, the youngest and longest-term students it attracts are largely children of well-educated families who have the confidence to buck convention. It may be that the positive-oriented and culturally rich environments such kids grow up in at home contribute the lion's share to how they turn out, and the kids would do well in any school so long as it didn't shame unsuccessful efforts or otherwise destroy motivation. It may be that the Sudbury Valley schools work so well because they are all small, their values have a chance to spread by contagion, and bad choices are constrained by the power of social approval. No one can say for sure. Greenberg winces when I refer to Sudbury Valley as an "alternative school." Alternative schools, he contends, have an agenda. "They don't want kids to suffer." At Sudbury Valley, the students face the consequences of their own behavior all the way through. "Kids are naturally critical," he points out.

One element contributing to the vitality of the Sudbury Valley approach is what most other schools are losing—any element of spontaneity. "It's an issue of control, predicting outcome," says Greenberg. The successes of our culture have become our failures, he insists. "We expect everything, including our children, to be perfect. We don't understand that the domains in which we've been successful as a society—the invention of penicillin, say—are a fraction of the domains of life. We have no idea how to deal with perspective, because it is so overwhelming. The human race has won the lottery—and is completely disoriented. We now expect to do everything right away, think we can cure every disease."

The same approach has been translated into education. Schools and parents believe they now have it in their power to create children who are perfect. And if they can't, it is for some specific reason that they can blame. "We must learn to live with the tragic truth of unpredictability," argues Greenberg. The idea of predictability is strictly the result of a now-outdated Newtonian, mechanical view of the universe. "We want to know we've fixed everything. That's why there are now tests for creativity. Exposing yourself to a random event is taking a risk. Parents today do not want to allow children any confrontation with risk. They want everything planned and predictable"—precisely what is flattening their children.

Here is how a graduate summed up the influence of Sudbury Valley on his life:

> Had I gone through a traditional educational system, I think I would
> have turned out very differently. I think that my confidence in my-
> self and my ability to tackle whatever it is I want to tackle in large

part came from having been given the trust to shape my own education and the trust that I would know what was best for myself from
a young age. I never find myself in a situation where I feel like I don't
have the tools to tackle it. Sometimes it takes a while, if it's something new, but I never feel like I don't have the inner strength and
direction and ability to do whatever it is. That's a huge part of how
I see myself.

The Sudbury Valley approach, it could be argued, doesn't pour it all in.
That made me wonder what graduates felt unprepared for in the real
world after they had been exposed to it. I made a point of contacting
Sudbury Valley graduates and asking them that very question. Jason's answer is typical. He attended Sudbury Valley for three years, from 1991 to
1994: "If anything, I felt unprepared for the discovery that most of the
people who had gone to public schools and later college seemed to be so
uninformed about so much that is going on in the world. The vast amount
of people who were being force-fed information that they couldn't have
cared less about really weren't retaining any of the information anyway.
That continues to shock me over ten years later."

Schools like Sudbury Valley are one reason for deep optimism. They
are already giving kids practice thinking for themselves and educating
them for a broader definition of success. They are oriented to the new realities of the world.

Hold on to your hat—so are video games.

Embracing the Devil

Forget everything you've heard about video games. They are not the end
of civilization as we know it. If you believe that, then you would have
thought the devil himself introduced the waltz, movies, comic books,
even the novel—to say nothing of rock and roll. All are forms of activity
that shocked the self-appointed gatekeepers of the culture at the time of
their introduction. If you are liberal and enlightened, you probably still
think of gameplay as bordering on the demonic, a passive activity that re-
cycles violence and destruction featuring Hollywood blockbuster figures.
If so, it's likely you haven't seen a video game in a long time. Stop thinking of video games as primarily objects of consumption; start thinking of
them as tools of creation. And they long ago left their Hollywood envy be-

hind; that was before they realized how much the players themselves could contribute to the game. Rather than robbing children's minds, video games today are instruments of the imagination, of engagement, of challenge and connection and collaboration.

They are also avenues of escape from adult control. Small wonder so many adults speak of them with near hysteria.

In part because they didn't grow up with them and have not followed their evolution, most adults see video games as a vengeful and even sadistic outlet of killing and maiming for the already alienated and socially incompetent. But video games have come a long way since Nintendo debuted in 1985. Sure there are shooting games, but mostly there are highly sophisticated multiuser games in which kids and adults from all over the world—often thousands at a time—participate cooperatively and competitively to construct and advance complex societies and entire fantasy worlds with characters they create and whose social behavior they generate and orchestrate. They make decisions and plot long-term strategies. It's not possible to play without learning about social life and complexity—the infrastructure of civilizations, transportation and communication, government and philosophies of social organization, political structure and leadership, civic and social obligations and relationships, negotiation and collaboration, to cite just some domains of knowledge most such games stimulate. And then you get to experiment, to try out procedures and personas.

It's a long way from Tinkertoy mechanics—in video games children learn largely to manipulate symbols, not building parts. But it's a whole lot to get out of a game, often played over extended periods of time and requiring thought, strategizing, and problem solving while stimulating mental dexterity—the basic tool kit of the knowledge society we now live in.

Increasingly video games are portals of expression and learning, where kids can take on roles and explore their own personalities and set up whole alternative universes. In one major sense, video games are indeed the enemy of adults—they constitute one of the few domains where children safely escape the obsessive control of their parents and freely experiment with and exercise their own sense of themselves. Ironically, adults often see the Internet as the source of robotic attention and activity, but that is a measure of how little they understand what their children are doing on it. Mostly the kids are writing, communicating, gathering information, or playing in some form. They are immersed in paying attention, expressing themselves, and learning—really learning—typically so unaware of how much they are taking in that the video gaming industry refers to the process as "stealth" or "accidental" learning.

If you don't "get" it, console yourself. Gaming experts see it as a completely different kind of learning, one that didn't exist before the Internet shifted learning from a linear event to a dynamic, surround-mind extravaganza. Video games are transdisciplinary by nature, both in production and in play, incorporating cutting-edge elements of all the sciences fused with dynamic art and compelling narratives—whether taking their point of departure from history, mythology, or literature—that the players create in whole or in part. The other reason you don't "get" them is that the act of playing is fundamentally different from the act of observing someone play.

Video games are breakthrough activities because they allow people to experiment with their identities and personalities, capture some of the complexity of the social world we live in while they automatically teach kids—and a growing cadre of adults—how to manipulate symbols and strategies and resources in pursuit of dynamic goals. Some innovators are so enthusiastic about the ability of games to teach so much without any of the standard educational pain that they consider gaming the best—and most inadvertent—kind of job training. "Unlike education acquired through textbooks, lectures and classroom instruction," says John Seely Brown, former chief scientist of the Xerox Corporation, "what takes place in massively multiplayer online games is accidental learning. It's *learning to be*—a natural byproduct of adjusting to the new culture—as opposed to *learning about*. Where traditional learning relies on carefully graded challenges, accidental learning relies on failure. Virtual environments are safe platforms for trial and error. The chance of failure is high, but the cost is low and lessons learned are immediate."

Gamers team up to undertake huge challenges, and they have to marshal the knowledge, skills, talents, and actions that enable success. They learn by doing, complete with immediate feedback. "This process brings about a profound shift in how they perceive and react to the world around them," contends Brown. "They become more flexible in their thinking and more sensitive to social cues. The fact that they don't think of gameplay as training is crucial. Once the experience is explicitly educational, it becomes about developing compartmentalized skills and loses its power to permeate the player's behavior patterns and worldview." Becoming an expert in a game such as World of Warcraft, one of the most popular, is nothing less than a "total-immersion course in leadership." And that appears to be directly translatable to success in the real world.

Not bad for a diversion.

THIRTEEN

"We Didn't Get Here by Rocking the Boat"

Raising children is very much a private matter—and has arguably become increasingly privatized as responsibilities once informally shared by communities and more formally assumed by institutions and their supports have shifted onto individual families. In this atmosphere, raising children has become aggressively private, with adults regularly hovering over their children, taking over tasks for them, and otherwise breaching boundaries between themselves and their kids.

Given the nature of parenting and the immaturity of the young, some fuzziness of boundaries is always inevitable. And no matter where a boundary is, healthy children invariably push against it, seeking to control progressively more of their own development—often on a timetable well ahead of their parents' desire to relinquish control. In all close relationships, nurturing always bumps up against controlling, and the boundaries are, in ways now subtle, now blatant, typically negotiated and renegotiated on an almost daily basis. Among those who are still developing, adjusting the boundary and acquiring autonomy is a nearly constant process—and a necessary one. Families and individuals all have their own styles, often transmitted down through the generations, and the process of granting autonomy can range from the tortured and traumatic to the graceful and seamless.

Today's parents, however, unable to quell their anxieties about outcomes in an implacably dynamic world, regularly overstep and encroach on the physical, emotional, and intellectual space of their growing chil-

dren. What's new and breathtaking about their stance is that it often blatantly overrides the developmental needs of children; the adults justify
invasiveness on grounds of safety or efficiency or invoke some other element of grown-up necessity, but that doesn't make their usurpation any
less subversive of their children's eventual independence or mental health.
By some sleight of sanctimony, overconcern and invasiveness have, in
fact, become virtues, hallmarks of attentive parenting among the middle
and upper classes. In the tug-of-war that good parenting always is, the
parents are now winning, apparently for the first time in history. In other
eras, social historians inform us, children were simply not so obsessively
monitored and had more time by themselves. Or they were more inclined
to resist the incursions on their autonomy.

For all its privacy, however, invasive parenting has significant public
repercussions. Overparenting isn't just bad for individual kids, weakening
them from within and rendering them psychologically fragile; it's bad for
the country as well. A generation that has been led to prefer the safety of
certainty to the possibility of failure inherent in risk taking not only makes
comfort its highest virtue; it imperils the future of the economy that sus-
tains us all. Further, the growing inability of the young to exercise autonomy and make decisions on their own threatens democracy itself.

Of all the features of democracy, none is more fundamental than the
ability of people to make decisions for themselves about their government, its policies, and their own lives. You educate for democracy not by
preaching about it but by practicing it. Good judgment and the power to
make the right decisions don't spring full blown; they have to be trained,
practiced, rehearsed in countless little decisions through childhood. One
assumes small risks in learning to make decisions and, by monitoring outcomes, some of which are bound to be unwanted, and adjusting course
as needed, gains confidence in decision-making ability.

That makes the current climate of cell phone use highly problematic.
As perpetual access to parents becomes a standard—whether encouraged
by adults in the name of safety or demanded by offspring who have never
been allowed to take even a first step toward independence—the young
have little opportunity to assume responsibility for themselves. Through
what has become an eternal umbilical cord, they are tied to their parents
for advice, decision making, problem solving, emotional comfort, or more,
at ages when they should be making their own moves toward independence. They fail to activate the mental machinery of independence that

will guide them through decision making on their own and encourage them to rely on their own judgment.

It is startling enough that college graduates display little interest in cutting the cord and actively encourage parents to accompany them on job interviews as they start down their adult paths. It is downright disturbing that parents accede, when the more responsible and future-oriented approach would be to transfer skills of discussion, negotiation, and judgment to their now-adult children, skills they will unquestionably need for a lifetime of functioning.

Survival Strategies

The emerging psychological fragility of the young will likely shape American culture for decades to come. Consider just one of its hallmarks—the inability to take risks. Such a trait could have dire consequences for the American economy and the governance of the country. "Innovation is the primary survival strategy in an increasingly complex global marketplace," observes Carolyn Woo, dean of the Mendoza College of Business at the University of Notre Dame. "And it hinges on the ability to explore, experiment, and take risks." The problems occurring in a connected world are going to need increasingly bold and creative solutions from citizens and leaders alike.

Risk is so shunned in academic settings that venturing an opinion in the classroom is now seen by college students as something dangerous, something to be avoided. Faculty all around the country have experienced what they themselves dub the "diminished-debate syndrome," and many are especially surprised that there is little discussion even in courses that traditionally spark lively discussion, such as ethics and philosophy. Students, they observe, now prefer the comfort of certainty and supplying the right answers, and are particularly willing to conform to the expectations of those on the rung of power above them. "Students are not assertive in the classroom," says the University of Virginia's John Portmann. "They are too willing to meet the expectation of teachers as well as parents. Conforming to expectations is harming them, because they are not thinking critically. It stunts intellectual development."

Portmann feels the effects are even more pernicious; they weaken the whole fabric of society. He sees young people becoming weaker right before his eyes, more responsive to the herd, too eager to fit in—not just less assertive in the classroom, but unwilling to disagree with their peers, afraid to question authority, more willing to conform to the expectations of those on the next rung of power above them. "Disagreement and criticism are really healthy, and stifling that is cause for concern." Learning how to debate and to argue on behalf of ideas and beliefs, and being forced to examine beliefs, are not only requirements for intellectual growth but core skills in maintaining democracy.

Over dinner one night, I asked a group of five or six undergraduates at a well-regarded midwestern university whether it was true that a new silence was falling over classrooms. I told them I had heard that students saw speaking up as too great a risk. They all shrugged, as if granting a unanimous "of course." Finally one looked me straight in the eye and said emphatically, "We didn't get here by rocking the boat." His classmates were nodding in agreement. It is a tragic day for American culture when the most vibrant feature of American democracy—speaking up to voice an opinion—is "rocking the boat." Keep in mind that these are the very students who are being trained as the future leaders of American business and society.

The Intolerability of Uncertainty

Having had no practice in taking risks, and having actually been *rewarded* for not doing so, with acceptance at selective colleges and M.B.A. programs, the very people who should be most willing to take calculated risks—the future leaders of America's business—are loath to do so, confides Joel Urbany, a professor of marketing and former associate dean of graduate programs at the Mendoza College of Business at the University of Notre Dame. "Many faculty members would like to teach at a higher level but get push back from students on structure and/or direction," he told me.

> We seem to have at least two segments of M.B.A. students—those sincerely interested in a rigorous learning experience and those who seek a more straightforward, streamlined education that simplifies the world for them. There is tremendous desire in the latter to reduce uncertainty in learning (i.e., to have things summarized and linearized for them). From all accounts, that segment appears to be growing; it used to be small and irrelevant, now it is large enough to

be having a real impact on learning experiences, norms, and student culture. Many students seek certainty, lists, and "clean" answers, and complain (at times en masse) about learning experiences that do not lay out precise enough expectations.

He is worried about at least four implications. "First, when we graduate students who seek and have been given no-risk learning and send them into a world in which ambiguity is the norm, they will have a long, painful entry into the marketplace. Second, such students deliver less value to their employers than they could. Third, no-risk learning defeats the most powerful principle of learning—that making mistakes (i.e., failing) provides the most compelling lessons and discrimination between right and wrong. Making mistakes is actually the less risky form of learning in the end. The lessons are large and tend to stick."

Last, he asks, how do you deal with this problem? "Do you challenge the behavior or accommodate it? Unfortunately, it seems that accommodation is the norm," and he cites student satisfaction surveys as the "driver" of accommodation to no-risk learning. With tuition at forty thousand dollars, administrators and faculty are themselves not willing to risk student disapproval. Urbany went on to praise a new required problem-solving course as stimulating a much-needed kind of thinking, but noted it did not reverse "the current systemic tale that has been building. And there seems to be little acknowledgment of this problem except in the trenches. At a minimum, I would expect that no-risk learning is one phenomenon we'll see with the upcoming generation, possibly with major implications for education."

"Corporations love these kids," notes Woo. "They're very compliant. They don't question anything." Anxiety has always been a recipe for conformity. But these are the kids who are being groomed to run the country. Woo and others fear that the current generation of M.B.A. students will compromise America's leadership, technological innovation, and competitiveness in a global marketplace just when we need such qualities most, by shrinking from innovation. "For them, all risk is unacceptable," says Woo. "Fear of failure underlies their fear of risk taking. They meet their need for risk in drugs, and they seek risk in extreme sports—because you can't fail at these."

In the silence falling over classrooms, democracy itself is at stake. Of the many things democracy is about, compliance isn't one of them.

Democracy demands dissent, the cultivation of rational argument, the expression of and respect for multiple viewpoints. The posing of critical questions. A pluralism of ideas. The welcoming of debate. It isn't possible to be fully informed on any issue without full discussion and open discourse. Dissent is both the exercise of democracy and its protector. In fact, whether evaluating our own government or those of others, we take dissent to be the most obvious indicator of democracy. The liberty to disagree is fundamental in democracy. And yet it is draining out of classrooms, along with the supporting skills of critical thinking.

Asking questions, valuing inquiry, do more than support democracy. They bolster the economic foundation of society, because they encourage people to see beyond convention, explore with their minds, and envision new possibilities. Remaining viable in the global marketplace demands inquiry and innovation, and innovation is the outgrowth of inquiry. By definition, innovation *is* rocking the boat.

Getting the Answers Right

So nonadaptive is the act of playing it safe that the felt need of the young to get all the answers right is producing a massive crisis in character and ethics. A 2006 survey of over five thousand students in thirty-two graduate schools in the United States found that 47 percent admitted to cheating at least once during the last academic year—and none more than students in graduate business programs. Fully 56 percent of "tomorrow's business leaders" confessed to cheating, a figure the authors felt vastly understates the true incidence of the problem. "Graduate business students are cheating at an alarming rate," said the report, linking it to a "me first" mentality spawned by competitiveness exacerbated by total immersion in an ideology of market efficiency that values the bottom line over social responsibility, as if shareholder interests were always aligned with society's best interests. The single biggest influence on cheating was the perception that everyone else would be doing it too.

The development of a culture of integrity in business schools would do more than restore fairness and ameliorate the competition for personal advantage, the authors commented. It would help create a vision of the world—and of *themselves*—that is inspiring in positive ways. It would, they point out, also impact mental health. Materialistic values are consistently associated with low rates of individual well-being—less happiness, less life satisfaction, less vitality, more anxiety and depression and drug use, more physical problems, poorer interpersonal relationships, and more antisocial behavior.

From her studies of the affluent, Columbia University's Suniya Luthar has her own perspective on the potential costs of "competitive lifestyles" and "the risks attached to wealth and status." The costs, she says, are paid not just by the children and their families but by everyone in society. "Many children of highly educated, affluent parents will likely come to assume positions of influence in society, and their own equanimity of spirit may have far-reaching ramifications. Depression vastly impairs productivity. And people who are unhappy, with a fragile, meager sense of self, can be more acquisitive than philanthropic, focused more on gaining more for themselves than on improving the lot of others."

Minds Matter More Now

Death-grip parenting is disabling the very kids who will be the leaders of the next generation. The pressures it places on kids are creating mental health problems that are unusually threatening to the future of the economy because we now live in a knowledge economy.

The industrial economy had little reason other than compassion to care about the mental health of workers. In the modern knowledge-based economy, psychological well-being is a critical factor in economic success. It is the mind and not the body that does the work. And a mind that is rigidified by perfectionism, constricted by anxiety, or paralyzed by depression can't meet the demands of the modern marketplace.

The modern knowledge economy needs workers who are autonomous, flexible, adaptive, and capable of handling changing circumstances, tasks, and knowledge. The world belongs to those who can experiment and explore in the face of uncertainty, who can draw on inner resources at times of confusion. It needs workers who have coping skills, are optimistic, and are willing to take risks. The knowledge economy requires a workforce that is especially unencumbered psychologically, emotionally resilient, and able to self-regulate emotions. More than at any time in history, mental health is essential for economic growth and productivity. And yet the hothouse environment kids are raised in robs them of resilience.

"I assist my Tae Kwon Do instructor at his school," a forty-year-old customs broker from South Carolina told me:

I come in contact with a wide cross section of children in the six- to eighteen-year-old range. Never in my life have I seen so many children seeming to live in an anesthetized, sanitized, and polarized cocoon of their parents' creation. So many of the boys seem, for lack of a better word, so "soft" and almost petrified of making any aggressive physical contact with another person, even during the sparring time, when they are being struck repeatedly by an opponent.

They seem to have no concept whatsoever that sometimes, for their own good and even safety, they may need to get their hands "dirty." I have witnessed these kinds of children repeatedly looking toward their parents during a sparring session, seeming to hope that one of their parents will come, touch them on the shoulder, and take their place, as if it were a tag-team match of some kind. The more they look at their parents, the more they get hit.

If they would just concentrate on what they are doing and defend themselves, instead of looking to their parents for some expected salvation, they would actually be very successful. However, their apparent parental dependence makes them more *vulnerable* rather than secure.

Sometimes, he notes, a parent has approached the instructor for "advice on how to help their precious little one 'have a little more confidence' during the sparring sessions, or asked for help with the 'discipline issue' they are having with the child. If our instructor dares to be honest by stating that the core issue is more than likely a result of the overprotectiveness of the parent, invariably the child will last one or two more classes and then the parent will pull them out of the TKD classes and search for another activity that will meet their child's 'special needs.' We're jeopardizing the future of the whole country if we do not take some corrective action soon."

Salvation from the Second Tier

A 2006 survey of 431 human resources officials, conducted by the Conference Board in association with three other organizations, found that "the future workforce is here and it is ill-prepared." Business leaders reported that while reading, writing, and arithmetic are fundamental to every employee's ability to do the job, applied skills—creativity, teamwork, critical thinking, communication—are essential for success in the new workplace. In fact, at all educational levels, the applied skills outrank in importance the basic knowledge skills. "The basics plus an array of applied and social skills—from critical thinking to collaboration to communications—defines workforce readiness in the twenty-first century," said the head of one of the survey's co-sponsoring organizations, the Partnership for 21st Century Skills. Nearly three-fourths of the survey respondents ranked creativity/innovation among the top-five applied skills needed—and projected to increase in importance for future graduates.

Is it possible that because the top-tier students are being bred to achieve in a constricting, risk-averse way, the problem-solving superstars, the people who will take the risks that underlie cultural innovation, and thus support the future of the economy, will come from the second tier? "It's not out of the question; that may come to pass," says Swarthmore's Barry Schwartz.

> Once you think you might actually fail, then all of a sudden you get a lot more nervous about risk taking. Risks have more consequences. The consequences are so high now that the fast-trackers don't want to fall off a cliff, and people who are largely operating outside the limelight probably have a lot more leeway. It's the second-tier kids in high school who become the interesting kids because people left them alone expecting not much from them, so they cultivate the things they are passionate about and before you know it they are first-tier.
>
> This competition for the handful of golden payoffs isn't a style you can discard. It just becomes the way you are in the world. It is too pervasive to be the thing you do for a while to get where you want to go and then you become your real self again. This becomes your real self. When does it stop? Not after you get into college, because then you're worried about not getting into medical school. Not after that, because you're worried about a residency. It doesn't ever stop.

Given the skyrocketing levels of depression among the young, are we breeding a population of people who are rotting from within, and in doing so are we handicapping ourselves as a culture? Schwartz didn't hesitate. "Absolutely and unequivocally we are."

In some ways, the children of immigrants are mentally healthier than their more privileged peers. "They seem both more mature and more grateful for the opportunity to be in college," says the University of Kentucky's Greg Moore. Because their parents lack knowledge of the college application process, they often have to organize and orchestrate operations that have come to dominate at least the last two years of high school, including campus visits, application strategies, financial documentation, SATs, application fees, essays and essays, and deadlines upon deadlines. They often have to hold down jobs as well. As a result, they develop inner resources for coping. They learn how to solve problems—because no one is available to do it for them.

A commercial real estate broker from a large firm in Southern California reports that his company is looking into ending its generous training program for new brokers. The current process is to hire recruits and train them well for a year—at full pay. The training includes that ever-challenging sales technique known as cold-calling. But the process is no longer working. In the past, the company could count on retaining 90 percent of its trainees. Now it is lucky to hold on to 30 percent of them. The novices are no longer willing to develop their sales skills on cold-calling. Dialing into uncertainty is more than they can handle, or want to. The experience has led the firm to rethink the whole idea of training. Rather than invest in the "entitlement generation," says the broker, the firm believes it can do better just by hiring people with some experience from other firms.

Recovery Is Possible

Although all the evidence suggests that we're well on our way to making kids more fragile and risk-averse, no one thinks that kids and young adults are *fundamentally* more flawed than in previous generations. Maybe many will "recover" from diagnoses too liberally slapped onto their experiences of distress.

In his own studies, the psychologist Robert Epstein has found that "although teens don't necessarily behave in a competent way, they have the *potential* to be every bit as competent—and incompetent—as adults," as measured on skills identified as essential for adulthood.

So is this the way things have to be?

There are signs of breakthrough. There are seeds of needed change. There are places where children are allowed to play on their own, allowed to develop responsibility, allowed to face the consequences of their own behavior. There are places where children are not infantilized by parents or their surrogates, the staff. There are renegade schools—not the politically alternative schools of the 1960s but pedagogically alternative schools for a new millennium—schools that foster the innate drive of children to become effective adults capable of innovative thinking, schools that recognize that their role must change. And some are thriving. It is probably unreasonable to expect to find the necessary adaptations along the conventional pathway. After all, the "best" and most competitive schools are part of the problem, even if they didn't create it.

And let's face it: some of the truest, most engaged, most meaningful learning is taking place outside of school, right in front of our faces—on the Internet, thanks to the widespread and constant availability of so much information in so many forms all the time, a mouse click away. Many adults fear the Internet as a new realm of child victimization. While there are some legitimate dangers, there is much more to the Internet than that. The Internet absorbs kids precisely because it opens worlds of possibilities, frees them to follow their own curiosity and expand their own identities.

Further, it seems entirely possible that young people can unlearn or muster the courage to disregard or reject the distorted concepts of success that have been force-fed to them until now. Parents, for their part, have to ease up on their visions of ever-present danger, give kids more credit—and allow them to take more risks. Release them, as one columnist puts it, from house arrest. Beginning on the playground. It's well within the realm of possibility. In late April 2007, I received this letter, reprinted in its entirety:

> In March 2007 I attended your workshop "A Nation of Wimps" at the —— High School. I found it very beneficial and thought you might like to hear something positive come out of it.
>
> My older daughter just turned 11. I didn't realize I was doing some helicopter parenting until I took your workshop. After that, I started to think about ways I could give her some of the freedom she's been dying for. One of the first things I did was to tell her to go ride her bike in our neighborhood. She was so totally taken aback, she said to me "Oh sure, now you're suddenly going to let me ride my bike by myself? What's wrong?" She also has gone on the bike

path with me on her bike while I walked our dog. (Although I'm having a more difficult time with that because I want to be accessible to her should she get hurt and I don't want her five miles ahead of me.)

I've stopped telling her when to take a shower or a bath. I told her I trusted her decision and I would let her decide when she needed one. This morning she got up and took one! She still gets upset because she wants to know if she smells or not, but I'm guessing the less I say, the better for her.

The other step I've taken—which is much harder for me—is to not tell her when her room needs to be cleaned. Let me tell you it is a total disaster. The only thing I've done is take away her allowance (no work, no money since she doesn't even try to keep it clean) and I have to admit I've back-pedaled a bit by telling her if she didn't clean her room soon I would clean it for her and she wouldn't have much stuff left.

I don't quite know how this will all play out, but I'm trying.

Again, thank you for a very informative workshop.

What does it take to prepare kids for the world they have to face? What will it take for them to develop capacities for abstract and strategic thinking? To unleash the ability to adapt to constantly changing conditions, to search for the information they will always need, and to innovate? To experiment and test hunches and hypotheses and novel approaches with zest even in the presence of imperfect data and to persevere despite failures or rejection? To identify meaningful information? To define problems articulately and communicate effectively? What will it take to produce a generation of society that is risk-tolerant and willing not merely to accept but to actually embrace and exploit the uncertainty of the future?

This is, of course, what we expect our schools to do—prepare students for the future that is now taking shape. Asking parents to be the hall monitors on kids' progress through school turns out to be an unfair burden on everyone. It's bad for the parent-child relationship, antithetical to the development of responsibility and autonomy in children. It's the means by which a parent's goals get entangled with, and become, a child's, and the child is unable to distinguish his or her own interests from those of the parent. Children who learn how to please their parents never learn how to please themselves or to find their own inner compass. Trapped by parental anxiety, they do not learn how to read the needs of their own environment or to respond to them. Many are plagued by a nagging sense of having failed their parents. They may come to believe they can never do anything special with their lives.

Such policies thwart the goals of child development by pitting the will of a conscientious parent against that of a child and can turn an otherwise reasonable parent into an angry nag if ever a child decides, for example, that talking to a friend is more important than homework. Ideally, schoolroom consequences or shaky performances by themselves would, over time, stimulate the child's sense of priority and responsibility. But instead the home becomes a tense battleground between anxious parent and perfectly ordinary child. A kid with an independent streak will wind up resisting, derailed from the critical task of practicing autonomy.

A Backlash Has Begun

It is bad enough that the hothouse approach to children's experience is consuming private life. But it is spilling into public life in various ways. The cultivation of preciousness of one's offspring seems to breed in parents the conviction that everyone else in the culture, or at least the neighborhood, is as interested in and delighted by children, specifically *their* children, as they are. This is a well-recognized psychological phenomenon known as the focusing fallacy; parents inflate the importance of their kids. That encourages them to cart the kiddies with them everywhere they themselves want to go—even to parties and restaurants, cafés, and other venues where grown-ups like to gather just to remind themselves that there is life beyond poop and Play-Doh, and where (at the risk of being judged uncaring by "nipple Nazis" and other extreme parents) they might actually enjoy a respite from the demands of their equally darling children.

But taking kids to adult playgrounds typically has an aggressive quality to it, because it tends to violate the primary purpose of such places and alter the atmosphere dramatically; it can turn a taproom into a playroom faster than you can say Guinness draft. The new parental aggressiveness is not going down everywhere as smoothly as Enfamil, and it could trigger the next great divide in political life.

Take the case of the Stroller Manifesto. The Patio Lounge is an arty, relaxed, couch-strewn bar in Park Slope, an upscale Bugaboo-infested neighborhood dotted with cafés and restaurants in brownstone Brooklyn. One Sunday night in the summer of 2005, a birthday party of ten new-comers filled the bar with double-wide strollers and rambunctious kids and drove out a few of the regulars, many of whom had come from afar for the Sunday night music program. The bartender, a thirty-six-year-old writer, was so angry he penned a screed and hung it at the bar's entrance.

His Stroller Manifesto declares the bar to be a child-free zone during his Sunday night shifts. "A bar is a place for adults to kick back and re-lax," it reads. "If you're a parent now, your child doesn't have to be the center of everyone else's universe too. Stop imposing your lifestyle on the rest of us in our sanctuary of choice." The episode spawned a Web site, strollerfree.com, dedicated to keeping bars kid- and stroller-free, so that patrons don't have "to curb their language or their behavior because there is a kid sitting next to them."

It's not yet clear whether the two events are the opening salvos in a widening culture war between the child-obsessed and everyone else, in-cluding garden-variety breeders, or a local skirmish of entertainment value only in New York. But mark the date; the backlash has begun against the culture of invasive parenting.

The pressures on kids to angle their way to a misguided vision of success reflect a culture of parents too entrenched in their fears to recognize how they are violating the developmental needs of their children. To a large degree their fears are fed by a system of schools that are increasingly out of step with the way kids learn—a fact parents seem to sense but not yet acknowledge. Instead of summoning their energy to make a public push for institutional change, parents prefer to define a public world of hazard, privatize their vision to their own kids, and shift the burden of achieve-ment wholly onto them. The more they privatize their fears and tighten their grip, the more fragile their kids become and the harder they make it for them to adapt to an ever-changing world. It's time for parents to back off. Safety is not a cure for uncertainty.

Conclusion: What Parents Can Do for Their Kids

Parents are so concerned about competitiveness they believe that they must do *everything* in their power to *not let their kids lose*. Not all kids, not the neighbor's kid, but *their* kid. So their solution is to give their own kids whatever advantages possible. It's now clear that's not good for kids at all, and it's not good for the parents. It is terrible for the teachers. And it's not good for the future of the country.

Although change is required at the systemic level, there are measures individual parents can take.

1. Let your children play. Allow them, starting when young, some totally unstructured time for exploration and free play. No schedule. No agenda. No adult coaches. No referees.

Play is neurobiologically constructive, helping to build the brain in ways that allow kids to control themselves and learn. There's evidence that conditions like ADHD may result *not* from faulty brain wiring but from restriction of the urge to play. Further, vigorous bouts of unstructured social play, especially in preschoolers—the kind of rambunctious play that adults often put a stop to—may be the best "therapy" for reducing the impulsive behaviors that characterize ADHD.

Abundant social play in animals activates genes for nerve growth in the executive portion of the brain. This is the raw material for development of the circuitry of self-regulation and attention. The evidence so far points to liberal amounts of rough-and-tumble play, for girls as well as boys, from ages three to six, to allow the nervous system to fully mature.

Play also helps with schoolwork in both the short and the long term. It maximizes attention, especially for boys, making kids *more* attentive after recess than before.

Play stimulates sophisticated language use, complex role-playing, and conceptual leaping. Even when little kids are playing make-believe, they are learning self-regulation. This is because it is so rich in collaborative dialogue. Kids come up with their own rules, then willingly make themselves stick to the rules they have invented.

Playing is so important that social behavior at recess in kindergarten predicts achievement at the end of first grade, as measured by class work and standardized tests of general knowledge, early reading, and math concepts. By a whopping 40 percent, peer play is significantly more predictive of academic success than standardized achievement tests. It is a gross mistake to think that play is time unproductively spent.

2. Eat dinner together at least five nights a week. From the earliest age. All around the same table. All eating the same meal. Nothing else on the table but conversation in which every family member gets to participate.

Even if young children have to be fed earlier by a caretaker, pull the high chair up to the table when you all sit down, so everyone comes to expect this time together. If you are not used to doing this, create some structure. Let each child have a chance to be in charge of the conversation for an evening. This is how love is communicated. This is where curiosity and intellect are nurtured. This is how the desire to be an effective adult is sustained. Miss Manners said it best: the dinner table is the boot camp of civilization.

But it does much more than all that. In a major longitudinal study of children growing up in suburban outposts of affluence and in inner cities, the factor that most correlates with achievement is kids having dinner with parents five or more times a week. Eating dinner with at least one parent on most nights predicted both adjustment *and* school performance—among both affluent and poor kids.

The simple little act of eating dinner together makes children feel valued, loved, and secure. It bolsters their sense of self. It's where they absorb values and information effortlessly, unaware, in the air they breathe. It's where they learn how to communicate effectively. In short, it's how kids become smart.

3. Learn how to criticize your kids.

The big element influencing perception of parental relationships is criticism. Criticism implying that affection or approval is conditional on good performance is lethal. What's destructive is the actual or threatened withdrawal of affection or approval, the expression of anger, when the child gets something wrong or disappoints you. That means no sighs or sounds of exasperation or irritation or annoyance.

That kind of criticism leads to perfectionism, and perfectionism leads to misery: It's a one-way ticket to anxiety about performance and to depression. It leads to enormous self-doubt. It wrecks self-esteem. It destroys resilience, and it kills passion and problem-solving ability—all the traits that will really carry kids to success.

Don't ever tell your kids second best is not good enough. That directly breeds perfectionism. If you feel disappointment in your child's performance, use it constructively. Regard it as a signal to have a fact-finding conversation with your child. Ask your child to evaluate his or her own performance. Ask, "Are you happy with it? Why? What did you get out of it?"

Ask your child, "What would you do differently next time?"

Ask your kid what he or she needs to do as well as what he or she wants. Don't raise your eyebrows. Maybe your child needs more sleep. Or to learn how to prioritize.

It's important to offer support verbally and nonverbally. Empathize with your kid. "This stuff is hard, isn't it?"

If your child left his homework for the last minute and consequently didn't do well on a test, don't put the knife in with "I told you so." Instead, capitalize on his own disappointment. "You're not happy with the way things turned out, are you?" And ask, "What can you do next time to make it come out the way you want?"

4. Go even further and take achievement pressure off kids. Let them find for themselves the rewards of doing well. Reconnect them with the ability to follow their own curiosity.

When kids are allowed to connect with their own internally driven curiosity, all you have to do for them to learn is to get out of their way. You can't stop them.

For the most part, achievement pressures are *internalized from parents* who push for perfection or are dissatisfied with second best. But achievement pressure confers no benefits in facilitating kids' academic success. And it is implicated in a range of disorders from anorexia to suicide.

There's a difference between excellence and perfection. Excellence involves enjoying what you're doing, feeling good about what you've learned, and developing confidence. Perfection involves feeling bad about a 98 and always finding mistakes no matter how good you are doing. And it's transmitted from parents to kids. A child makes all As and one B. All it takes is the raising of an eyebrow for the child to get the message.

Whatever else, perfectionism is a chronic source of stress and anxiety. But it loads yet a bigger stress on kids: it makes parental love feel way too conditional.

The biggest problem with pushing perfection may be that it conceals the real secret of success in life. Success hinges less on getting everything right than on how you handle getting things wrong. This is where creativity, passion, and perseverance come into play. In a flat world you make kids competitive not by pushing them to be perfect but by allowing them to become passionate about something that compels their interest.

The paradox of perfectionism is that the stress of trying to get everything right and not make mistakes undermines performance. It wrecks mental flexibility; it limits access to the full range of mental resources to solve problems.

5. Quit hovering over your kids. Let adulthood be fun again.

Children are not the only ones who are harmed by hyperconcern and micromanagement. Vigilance is enormously taxing—and it's taken a lot of the fun out of parenting. You may find it easier to give up some control if you recognize that you have exaggerated many of the dangers of childhood—and created many of the stresses and anxieties children are suffering from.

6. Keep your professional values at the office, where they belong. Stop turning parenthood into a profession.

It may be that people insert professional values in parenting because they are so rewarded for them at work. If they drop out of the workforce permanently or temporarily, they take all their professional expertise and efficiency and goal orientation and pour it into activities on behalf of their children, including school volunteering. But there's only a limited place at home for what they know so well—setting long-range goals, keeping complex schedules, managing things efficiently, and *controlling* outcomes. Professionalized parents turn everyday activities into high-stakes events and make competition part of the process.

There's no question that today's highly educated parents have formidable skills. If you need something else to do with them, put them at the service of *all* children. Volunteer to help kids who need help. Your own kids are going to grow up smart and motivated and passionate and happy if you let them make their own accommodations to life and let them find their own passions.

If you treat them well and make the home a comfortable place to be, your kids will automatically absorb your values. If you let them have progressive amounts of responsibility, they will learn how to problem-solve. That will automatically make them creative adults well prepared for the twenty-first century. Your kids are more competent than you realize, and they are dying for opportunities to demonstrate their competence.

7. Teach your kids how to tolerate discomfort. Teach frustration-tolerance skills and the ability to tolerate uncertainty.

Discomfort is the appropriate response to losing a game, to leaving one's homework at home, to getting a C in history. If kids aren't backed into a corner, the discomfort becomes aversive, and if they are allowed to experience it often enough, it becomes a stimulus to improving performance. Similarly, experiencing boredom motivates kids to poke around and find something to do that they like.

Making things easy for your kids now will make it hard for them later.

8. Learn how to praise your kids—and what for.

How you bestow praise on kids is important. Praise given the wrong way can reinforce the need to be perfect. Reward the process, the effort, not the talent or the product. Shifting focus to effort shows your kids the key to mastery.

When your kid gets a great grade on a paper, resist the urge to say "you're brilliant" or "you're really smart." Instead say, "You're a really good thinker." And specify what is good about the thinking: "It's great that you connected this to that." Or ask a question that focuses your child on the thinking: "What did you learn?" "What got you interested in this?"

Studies show that kids praised for their intelligence care more about their grades than about learning. And should they ever experience failure, they are less persistent than peers praised for their effort. If you praise kids' intelligence and then they fail, they think they're not smart anymore, and they lose interest in work. But kids praised for effort get energized in the face of difficulty.

Praising effort also gives your kids back the keys to their own mental health. The brain is built to generate positive mood states as it works toward a meaningful goal. Hard work toward a goal activates positive feelings and subdues negative ones.

Whatever else you do, do not supply material rewards for achievement. Do not give the kids a BMW—or even a Toyota. Instead, congratulate your kids. And offer praise—and the more specific it is to the challenge, the better off your kid will be. "That extra time in the library seems to have paid off." Ask your kid why things worked out so well and what he attributes his success to. You want your kid to understand exactly which efforts pay off in which situations.

Supplying external rewards destroys internal motivation. People stop wanting to participate in the activities *without* the rewards. And performance deteriorates as people start doing the minimum necessary to get the rewards. The prizes turn the activity into work, and that robs kids of their inspiration.

9. Encourage your children to problem-solve and take risks.

Go ahead and have high expectations for your kids. Communicate them clearly. Then support your kids in creating their own paths to those expectations.

What do you do if your kid makes a mistake, gets something wrong, or brings home a C? Take some time when you are not doing three other things or even one other thing and talk to your child very nonjudgmentally. Ask your child how she feels about her performance, how satisfied she is with it. Not how you feel about it, but how the child feels about it.

Teach and model brainstorming for new ideas and creative problem solving at the same time. Ask: "What's another way to look at that?" "What's another way you can get from here to there?"

Encourage your child to look at something from as many perspectives as possible. "How else might you have approached that?" You don't have to know the answer. "What else could you have said?" "What's another way to interpret that statement?" "How else could you have handled it?"

If your kid is stuck on a problem, don't get frustrated and take over the work. Ask questions. "Is this an addition or subtraction problem?" "What do you think is the best way to find the answer?" Feel free to give hints and suggestions: "Maybe you should try to add the whole numbers first." "Do you think you need to gather a little more information before you answer that question?"

Let your kids know that there is more than one right way to do almost everything.

Don't get chilly or critical toward your child because he or she doesn't see things the way you do. Innovation comes from seeing things differently.

10. Go all the way and help your kids fail. Allow your kids to mess up, to experience a little bit of failure, to experience discomfort, boredom.

Encourage your kids to try new things, do some hard things at which they are not good, and don't expect them to do everything perfectly. Try to get some fun out of such activities. A child who never experiences failure will view anything less than total success as a failure. A wholly sanitized childhood will only defer failure until later.

When your kids mess up, you can help them by letting them know you're not perfect and you weren't born knowing everything. No matter what they say to you, your kids see you as perfect; they see only your successes. So share with them your own mistakes, judiciously. Tell them what you learned from your mistakes. Giving yourself human dimensions plants in kids the idea that they can be like you and gives rise to the motivation to do so.

As you go through life, you should be sharing your own hard-won coping strategies, not as object lessons you ram down your kids' throats but as useful informational tidbits, which may or may not work for them, but it would be nice to put them on the buffet for sampling.

Don't protect your kids from the consequences of their mistakes. Let them connect cause and effect. Their errors generally are self-motivating if you don't make them feel disapproved or stupid or humiliated.

Failure teaches kids what doesn't work. When they are trying to figure something out, it is as important to know what doesn't work, and why, as it is to know what does work. Don't take over when they are not doing something well. Ask what *they* need to do it.

As a corollary, don't blame the system, the teachers, the test, or the referee when your kids make a mistake or foul out. And don't call in the lawyers.

11. Give your kids increasing responsibility for managing their own lives.

Stop managing their lives for them. If they leave a paper or a book at home, don't run it over to school. Let them feel what happens when they leave something behind. We're not dealing with life-or-death consequences here.

The childhood we've introduced to our children is very different from that in past eras. Children are far less integrated into adult society than they used to be. In changing the nature of childhood, we tend to assume that children can't handle difficult situations. So you rush in and do things for your kids, rather than let them flounder a bit and learn how to do something for themselves. I'm not suggesting you abandon them, but give them more credit for figuring things out.

Cease and desist being the timekeeper for your kids. Scheduling for your kids, and constantly reminding them where they have to be and when, puts them at a tremendous disadvantage when they get to college and have to manage their own time for the first time. They have trouble functioning. Their difficulties tackling life's petty routines loom large and undermine their ability to focus on schoolwork.

12. Take your own brains back. Get out of panic mode and switch to rational mode.

Just about everyone forty and over was caught off guard over societal changes and how fast and dynamic our switched-on, twenty-four-hour, hyperlinked, globalized lives now are. I think we reacted unthinkingly, automatically, by instinct—to protect our kids. We reacted not by trying to protect *all* kids but by trying to give *our own* kids an advantage.

It just so happens that the ways that we impulsively resorted to as protective turn out not to be. We now know kids are suffering from pressure and its early application, its intrusion into lives that are micromanaged by parents in person and via cell phone.

So how do parents get off the competitive treadmill they know they shouldn't be on? How do you get curiosity back into the curriculum? Just get together as a community and say, no more. We need to make education educate. We need to make sure that our kids are developing real mastery, which requires experimentation, not the fake mastery and plagiarism we know is going on. We need to make sure that our kids are becoming problem solvers, not robots who spit back only the right answers.

This can happen only if the adults make a decision as a whole community. You can refashion your kids' lives so that they can taste and enjoy real learning and have a shot at real success without compromising their mental health.

None of us knows what the world is going to look like in ten years. One way to prepare kids for the future is to relax and let them play now.

Acknowledgments

As isolating as writing is, no one writes a book alone. It takes an extraordinary environment to support the effort, focus, constant gathering and organizing of information, and thought—make that preoccupation—that a book requires. My environment was sustained by a few loyal souls.

This book would not exist at all were it not for Andrew Stuart, who saw my article "A Nation of Wimps" in the November/December 2004 issue of *Psychology Today* and gently suggested, and then just as gently persuaded me, there was a book in it, thus becoming my agent. Agent? More intellectual provocateur and troubleshooter as well as cheerleader and adviser.

Amy Hertz, thank you for recognizing the cultural moment and seizing it.

And thanks to Rebecca Cole, who applied exquisite care and sensitivity in editing the manuscript and offering suggestions to me.

For seeing me through the many months of isolation and hard mental labor—and the terrible loss that struck at the time of the book's birth—I owe more to John Portmann and to Dan and Hanna Greenberg than words can hold. My heart bursts with gratitude. From all over the world, even while working on their own books, they sent near-daily e-mails of friendship, encouragement, and mirth, sometimes their own observations, and often links to relevant reports or articles, and always, always they invited discussion and the thrashing out of ideas, by phone, by e-mail, and occasionally face-to-face. It didn't hurt that, in their different ways, they are on the front lines of the phenomenon I am describing— which is how I came to meet them in the first place.

If there is a midwife to this book, it is Kaja Perina, the talented editor in chief of *Psychology Today*, who encouraged me more than she knows and put up with far more than I had any right to expect. When I first had the idea for the article but already felt too burdened to tackle it, she cleared the way for me. And when the whisper of a book was first heard but I was deeply ambivalent, she said, matter-of-factly, "I always knew it was a book," as if that settled it. Then she made it a reality by granting me a part-time leave, and never failed to be gracious and accommodating when I was preoccupied with the writing or over deadline or both.

Deep thanks also to Jo Colman, CEO of *Psychology Today*, for giving me so much leeway, teasing the hell out of me all the way through but keeping me connected, and welcoming me back.

Every friend I have, and many family members, contributed something to this book. They told me true roll-the-eyeballs tales from their own lives, some of which enliven these pages. Or they were extra eyes and ears, and often an informal clipping service, making sure no article or program anywhere escaped my attention as I set about documenting the emerging culture of pernicious parenting.

Thanks, too, to my fellow members of the Bringing Theory to Practice Project, who assured me I was onto something. Many allowed me to interview them about their experiences in the educational trenches.

Philip Howard of Common Good, thank you for taking an interest in my ideas about play and inviting me to air them at a joint conference of the Brookings Institution and the American Enterprise Institute.

Thanks also to the schools, community groups, and parents around the country who invited me to speak to them. The opportunities, and the questions asked, helped me sharpen my ideas.

And for every person I encountered in the past two years who asked what I was working on, then nodded and smiled when I said, *"A Nation of Wimps,"* thank you. That was as energizing as all the triple espressos combined.

Notes

Introduction

p. 1 How about the recent survey: Hara Estroff Marano, "A Nation of Wimps," *Psychology Today,* Nov./Dec. 2004, pp. 58–70.

p. 1 Then there was the teacher: Ibid.; and author interview and personal communication with the teacher.

p. 2 It motivates us to change: Matthew Hutson, "The Doogie Howser Effect," *Psychology Today*, Jan./Feb. 2008, p. 21; Camille S. Johnson and Diederik A. Stapel, "When Different Is Better: Performance Following Upward Comparison," *European Journal of Social Psychology* 37, no. 2, pp. 258–75.

p. 2 And we seem to learn more: A. J. Wills et al., "Predictive Learning, Prediction Errors, and Attention: Evidence from Event-Related Potentials and Eye Tracking," *Journal of Cognitive Neuroscience* 19, no. 5 (May 2007), pp. 843–54; and A. J. Wills in EurekAlert, July 1, 2007.

p. 2 "Life is planned out for us": Marano, "Nation of Wimps"; and author interview with the Cornell University student.

p. 3 College, it seems: Hara Estroff Marano, "Crisis on the Campus," *Psychology Today's Blues Buster,* May 2002.

p. 3 Colleges are experiencing record demand: Marano, "Nation of Wimps"; Robert P. Gallagher, "National Survey of Counseling Center Directors, 2006," International Association of Counseling Services, Monograph Series No. 8P.

p. 3 mental state of students: Author interview with Steven Hyman, M.D.; also see Hara Estroff Marano, "Up Against the Ivy Wall 2004," *Psychology Today's Blues Buster,* March 2004.

p. 3 Parental efforts to protect: Lisa Belkin, "Parents Who Can't Resist Smoothing Life's Bumps," *New York Times,* Feb. 11, 2007; also see Chapter Nine.

p. 3 More than twenty-one million prescriptions: IMS Health, IMS Prescription Audit, March 2007.

p. 4 great deal of play: Marano, "Nation of Wimps."

p. 4 play is actually critical: Jaak Panksepp, "Attention Deficit Hyperactivity Disorders, Psychostimulants, and Intolerance of Childhood Playfulness: A Tragedy in the Making?" *Current Directions in Psychological Science* 7, no. 3 (June 1998), pp. 91–98.

p. 4 Dramatically fewer young people: Marano, "Nation of Wimps."

p. 4 Tremendous performance pressures: Ibid.

p. 4 really brightest kids underperform: Sian L. Beilock and Thomas H. Carr, "When High-Powered People Fail: Working Memory and 'Choking Under Pressure' in Math," *Psychological Science* 16, no. 2 (2005), pp. 101–5; also see Alexander J. Shackman et al., "Anxiety Selectively Disrupts Visuospatial Working Memory," *Emotion* 6, no. 1 (2006), pp. 40–61.

p. 4 Their lack of challenging: See Chapter Five.

p. 4 huge rise in self-harm: "National Survey of Counseling Center Directors, 2004."

p. 4 disproportionate investment: Barbara Dafoe Whitehead and David Popenoe, "The State of Our Unions: The Social Health of Marriage in America 2006."

p. 6 stepped way over the line: Author interview with Jeffrey Wood, Ph.D.

p. 6 parents co-opt developmental pathways: Hara Estroff Marano, "Parenting Style May Foster Anxiety," *Psychology Today,* Sept./Oct. 1994; Luc Goossens, "Parenting, Identity, and Adjustment in Adolescence" (invited address, Society for Research on Adolescence, March 24, 2006); and Koen Luyckx et al., "Parental Psychological Control and Dimensions of Identity Formation in Emerging Adulthood," *Journal of Family Psychology* (forthcoming).

ONE   *Welcome to the Hothouse*

p. 10 burgeoning belief that only she: Author interview with Daniel Greenberg, Ph.D.

p. 10 growing number of successful women: Eduardo Porter, "Stretched to Limit, Women Stall March to Work," *New York Times,* March 2, 2006, p. 1.

p. 10 elevate child rearing: Author interview with David Anderegg, Ph.D.

p. 10 Zangle is one such program: Author interview with Gigi Nichols.

p. 10 70 percent of the highly educated mothers: Discussion with over three hundred parents at the Community House, Birmingham, Mich.

p. 11 "feeding parental obsessiveness": Personal communications with parents of Birmingham, Mich.; also see Michael D. Clark, "Cyber Report Cards Keep Parents Posted on Grades," *Cincinnati Enquirer,* Sept. 28, 2005.

p. 11 "I noticed it immediately": Author interview with a Connecticut parent.

p. 12 wind up expelling: Jennifer Steinhauer, "Maybe Preschool Is the Problem: Only 4 Years Old and Expelled," *New York Times,* May 22, 2005.

p. 12 "The great effect of Head Start": Author interview with Steven Mintz, Ph.D.

p. 12 giant Citigroup company: Michael Powell, "Getting into Preschool: Top-Tier Clout Helps," *Washington Post,* Nov. 16, 2002.

p. 13 "My neighbor's boy": Author interview with the Connecticut parent.

p. 13 homeschooling, a phenomenon so appealing: "Homeschooling Grows Quickly in the United States," Reuters, March 2, 2006; and Doug Oplinger, "Approximately 1.1 Million Children in the United States Are Being Educated at Home," *Akron Beacon Journal,* Nov. 14, 2004.

p. 13 whatever parents choose to do: Doug Guthrie, "Kids Learn at Home, but No One's

Watching," *Detroit News,* Aug. 14, 2005; and Amanda Gefter, "Home-Schooling Special: Preach Your Children Well," *New Scientist,* Nov. 11, 2006.

p. 14 "Parents have told their kids": Author interview with John Portmann, Ph.D.; also see Hara Estroff Marano, "A Nation of Wimps," *Psychology Today,* Nov./Dec. 2004, pp. 58–70.

p. 14 "I wish my parents": Author interview with Anderegg.

p. 14 "I have found": Author interview with Alison Malmon.

p. 15 "One mother": Judith R. Shapiro, "Keeping Parents Off Campus," *New York Times,* Aug. 22, 2002; also see Marano, "Nation of Wimps."

p. 15 the California psychologist: Author interview with Robert Epstein, Ph.D.

p. 15 When he took over: Marano, "Nation of Wimps."

p. 15 17.6 percent of students: "CIRP Freshman Survey" (Higher Education Research Institute, UCLA, 2005).

p. 15 challenges of college: Robert J. Sternberg, "Finding Students Who Are Wise, Practical, and Creative," *Chronicle of Higher Education,* July 6, 2007; and Richard H. Hersh and John Merrow, *Declining by Degrees: Higher Education at Risk* (New York: Palgrave Macmillan, 2006).

p. 15 47 percent of high school students: "CIRP Freshman Survey" (2005).

p. 15 index of emotional overinvestment: Author interview with Peter Stearns, Ph.D.; also see Marano "Nation of Wimps."

p. 16 Parents who pay forty thousand dollars a year: Author interview with Arthur Levine, Ph.D.

p. 16 surveyed his faculty: Stephen C. Caulfield, "Ninth Leadership Forum: Student Health 2010: What Changes Will the Next Five Years Bring?" *Student Health Spectrum,* Feb. 2006, pp. 4–18.

p. 16 small eastern liberal arts college: Author interview with the administrator.

p. 17 hog administrative resources: Author interview with the vice president for student affairs.

p. 17 Officials at one well-known university: Author interview with the Reverend Mark L. Poorman, Notre Dame.

p. 17 "is equal to a thousand others": Author interview with the vice president of the university.

p. 18 Cedarcrest High School instituted: Robert Tomsho, "Senior Blues: When High Schools Try Getting Tough, Parents Fight Back," *Wall Street Journal,* Feb. 8, 2005.

p. 18 "We get painted as nitpicking asses": Perry Garrison in ibid.

p. 18 surprising prospective bosses: Sue Shellenbarger, "Helicopter Parents Go to Work: Moms and Dads Are Now Hovering at the Office," *Wall Street Journal,* March 16, 2006.

p. 18 manager of staffing services: Ibid.

p. 18 "It's unbelievable to me": Ibid.

p. 19 "We started referring to helicopter parents": Author interview with James Fay.

p. 19 "I expected them to cite school violence": Ibid.

p. 19 "snowplow parents": Glen Egelman, M.D., in Caulfield, "Student Health 2010," pp. 4–18.

p. 20 "Parents are our worst enemy": Personal communication from the soccer coach.

p. 20 "It's not something": Author interview with Marissa.

p. 21 lack a fierce internal struggle: Author interview with Richard Hersh, Ph.D.

p. 21 "the gray drizzle of horror": William Styron, *Darkness Visible: A Memoir of Madness* (New York: Random House, 1990).

p. 21 Disconnected from themselves: Author interview with Marissa.

p. 22 Adults with means: Ralph Gardner Jr., "Newly Desirable: Dormfront Property," *New York Times,* Feb. 3, 2005, p. F1.

p. 22 "We couldn't cope": Ibid.

p. 22 dropping out of the workforce: Porter, "Stretched to Limit."

p. 23 "spends all day talking about parenting": Personal communication from the mother.

p. 23 "I discovered that the other mothers": Author interview with the mother.

p. 24 Alpha Moms, or Moms to the Max: Randall Patterson, "Empire of the Alpha Mom," *New York,* June 20, 2005, pp. 18–23.

p. 24 "Maybe . . . there would be more": Maureen Dowd, "Mean, Nasty, and Missing," *New York Times,* Feb. 27, 2002.

p. 24 They hire specialists: Carla Rivera, "Tutors Prepare Them—for Preschool and Kindergarten," *Los Angeles Times,* Sept. 4, 2006; and Ralph Gardner Jr., "Tot Therapy," *New York,* April 19, 2004, pp. 34–39.

p. 24 shell out fifteen thousand dollars: College Confidential, IGAP Program, www.collegeconfidential.com/college_counseling/admission_guarantee.htm.

p. 25 fifteen applicants for every coveted slot: Powell, "Getting into Preschool."

p. 25 parents hire educational consultants: Rivera, "Tutors Prepare Them."

p. 25 "the search for distinction": Powell, "Getting into Preschool."

p. 25 "Birmingham and Bloomfield Hills are tops": Communication from a Birmingham, Mich., parent.

p. 26 "I have never seen": Jennifer Delahunty Britz in Alvin P. Sanoff, "Bribery Attempts, the Unbearable Pushiness of Parents, and Other Admissions Tales," *Chronicle of Higher Education,* July 7, 2006.

p. 26 dean of enrollment at Kalamazoo: Ibid.

p. 26 "harder to manage": Justin Pope, "Colleges Trying to Ground Moms, Dads Who Hover," *Seattle Times,* Aug. 29, 2005.

p. 26 Globalization . . . has done two things: Barry Schwartz, "Self-Determination: The Tyranny of Freedom," *American Psychologist,* Jan. 2000, pp. 79–88; and author interview with Barry Schwartz, Ph.D.

p. 28 widening gap between the rich and the rest of us: Panel Study of Income Dynamics (University of Michigan Institute of Social Research, Aug. 7, 2007).

p. 28 upper class now works harder: Louis Uchitelle and David Leonhardt, "Men Not Working, and Not Wanting Just Any Job," *New York Times,* July 31, 2006; and David Brooks, "Bye-Bye, Bootstraps," *New York Times,* Aug. 3, 2006.

p. 28 affluence that has overtaken: Author interview with Maurice Preter, M.D.

p. 28 Working harder than ever: David R. Francis, "Why High Earners Work Longer Hours," National Bureau of Economic Research, *NBER Digest,* July 2006, nber.org/digest/jul06/W11895; author interview with Preter; and Suniya S. Luthar, "The Culture of Affluence: Psychological Costs of Material Wealth," *Child Development* 74 (2003), pp. 1581–93.

p. 29 Americans' circle of friends: Miller McPherson et al., "Social Isolation in America: Changes in Core Discussion Networks over Two Decades," *American Sociological Review* 71

(June 2006), pp. 353–75; and Henry Fountain, "The Lonely American Just Got a Bit Lonelier," *New York Times,* July 2, 2006.

p. 29 "ideological affluence": Interview with Preter.

p. 29 "Because the adult workplace": Communication from a Michigan woman.

p. 30 "It's easy to get sucked in": Author interview with a Connecticut woman.

p. 31 "The emphasis on performance": Author interview with Edward Spencer, Ph.D.

p. 31 children, unlike their parents, are digital natives: Marc Prensky, "Digital Natives, Digital Immigrants," *On the Horizon* 9, no. 5 (Oct. 2001).

p. 32 "I see the interactions": Author interview with the teacher.

p. 32 skyrocketing rates of overuse injuries: Bill Pennington, "Doctors See a Big Rise in Injuries for Young Athletes," *New York Times,* Feb. 22, 2005; and Howard P. Chudacoff, *Children at Play: An American History* (New York: New York University Press, 2007).

p. 32 Dr. Sally Harris is one of them: Kendra Marr, "No Vacation from Mishaps: Doctors See Rise in Overuse Injuries in Teen Athletes," *San Jose Mercury News,* Aug. 22, 2006.

p. 33 "You get a kid": Pennington, "Doctors See a Big Rise in Injuries for Young Athletes."

p. 33 nature of her child's injury: Marr, "No Vacation from Mishaps."

p. 33 "It's amazing": Interview with a suburban Michigan mother.

p. 33 openly reward superspecialization: Bob Hohler, "Are You Kidding? Shoe Companies Set Their Sights on Players as Young as 12," *Boston Globe,* July 25, 2006.

p. 34 "We're going to find them": Sonny Vaccaro in ibid.

p. 34 Nike recently made its own bid: Hohler, "Are You Kidding?"

p. 34 never hears parents complain: Ibid.

p. 34 According to Dr. Lyle Micheli: Pennington, "Old Before Their Time: Overuse Injuries Afflict the Young," *New York Times,* Feb. 23, 2005.

p. 34 "some kind of shot": Angela Smith, M.D., in ibid.

T W O   *Rocking the Cradle of Class*

p. 35 far more flaunted: Author interview with Steven Mintz, Ph.D.

p. 36 no longer just *buy* a stroller: Hara Estroff Marano, "Rocking the Cradle of Class," *Psychology Today,* Oct. 2005, pp. 52–56.

p. 36 "A stroller is part of the parents' image": Ibid.; also see Dan Berrett, "These Days, It Has to Do a Lot More Than Roll," *New York Times,* July 3, 2005.

p. 37 "It is what inspires": www.grumblemagazine.com/articles/crack/harvard/index.html

p. 37 proof of the accessorization of children: Author interview with David Anderegg, Ph.D.; also see Marano, "Rocking the Cradle of Class."

p. 37 Jim Conroy . . . tells the story of a father: Alvin P. Sanoff, "Bribery Attempts, the Unbearable Pushiness of Parents, and Other Admissions Tales," *Chronicle of Higher Education,* July 7, 2006.

p. 37 "More than in the past": Steven Mintz in Marano, "Rocking the Cradle of Class"; and author interview with Mintz.

p. 37 "This is my second chance": Author interview with attendees.

p. 38 "Nervousness about globalization": Mintz in Marano, "Rocking the Cradle of Class."

p. 38 "Even the food": Ibid.

p. 38 Today 13 percent of white children: Marano, "Rocking the Cradle of Class."

p. 38 "Our society seems": Author interview with Mintz.

p. 38 driving the status engines: Marano, "Rocking the Cradle of Class."

p. 38 One new mini trend: Ibid.

p. 39 market for costly kiddie couture fashion: Chelsea Emery, "Boomer Parents Buy Cashmere for Infants and Toddlers," Reuters, Aug. 13, 2006.

p. 39 ninety-dollar cashmere rompers: Ibid.

p. 39 "digital immigrants": Marc Prensky, "Digital Natives, Digital Immigrants," *On the Horizon* 9, no. 5 (Oct. 2001), with credit to John Perry Barlow.

p. 39 shrinkage of free time: Marano, "Rocking the Cradle of Class."

p. 39 Approximately 20 percent of American families: Ibid.

p. 40 marital dissatisfaction: Bart Soenens et al., "Maladaptive Perfectionistic Self-Representations: The Mediational Link Between Psychological Control and Adjustment," *Personality and Individual Differences* 38 (2005), pp. 487–98; and Koen Luyckx et al., "Parental Psychological Control and Dimensions of Identity Formation in Emerging Adulthood," *Journal of Family Psychology* (forthcoming).

p. 40 "critical turning point": Lynda Lytle Holmstrom, David A. Karp, and Paul S. Gray, "Getting In: Family Dynamics and the College Application Process Project" (Boston College Sociology Department), 2004.

p. 40 "identities and aspirations": David A. Karp, Lynda Lytle Holmstrom, and Paul S. Gray, "Of Roots and Wings: Letting Go of the College-Bound Child," *Symbolic Interaction* 27, no. 3 (2004), pp. 357–82; also see Marano, "Rocking the Cradle of Class."

p. 40 "More and more, parents have come": Author interview with Lynda Lytle Holmstrom; also see Marano, "Rocking the Cradle of Class."

p. 41 "It's clear to upper-middle-class parents": Lynda Lytle Holmstrom in Marano, "Rocking the Cradle of Class."

p. 41 stick close enough to home: Lynda Lytle Holmstrom, David A. Karp, and Paul S. Gray, "Leaving Home for College: Expectations for Selective Reconstruction of Self," *Symbolic Interaction* 21 (1998), pp. 253–76.

p. 41 They're terrified of doing laundry: Lynda Lytle Holmstrom, David A. Karp, and Paul S. Gray, "Why Laundry, Not Hegel? Social Class, Transition to College, and Pathways to Adulthood," *Symbolic Interaction* 25, no. 4 (2002), pp. 437–62.

p. 41 "They've never had to manage": Author interview with Holmstrom.

p. 41 The word "scary": Holmstrom, Karp, and Gray, "Why Laundry, Not Hegel?"

p. 42 "identity capital": Marano, "Rocking the Cradle of Class."

p. 42 "Upper-middle-class family life": Holmstrom, Karp, and Gray, "Why Laundry, Not Hegel?"

p. 42 colleges are being forced: Sue Shellenbarger, "Tucking the Kids In—in the Dorm: Colleges Ward Off Overinvolved Parents," *Wall Street Journal,* July 28, 2005, p. D1.

p. 43 emerging generation of professionally educated women: Marano, "Rocking the Cradle of Class."

p. 43 "Seeing children as a well-designed product": Author interview with Anderegg.

p. 43 mothers are more highly educated: Marano, "Rocking the Cradle of Class."

p. 44 Anderegg cites a mom: Ibid.

p. 44 Mothering is a difficult job: Author interview with Suniya S. Luthar, Ph.D.

p. 44 women of peak working age: Rita Giordano and Lini Kadaba, "New Career Path: Pro Mom," *Philadelphia Inquirer,* May 14, 2006.

p. 44 "Parents are generally aware": Author interview with Luthar.

p. 44 "They are successful": Ibid.

p. 44 It underwrites perfectionistic strivings: Marano, "Rocking the Cradle of Class."

THREE   *Parenting to Perfection*

p. 45 "My sister in the U.S.": Personal communication from an American mother now living in Germany.

p. 45 "I find parents less willing": Author interview with Peter Stearns, Ph.D.

p. 46 "Parents treat children as projects": Steven Mintz in Hara Estroff Marano, "Rocking the Cradle of Class," *Psychology Today,* Oct. 2005, pp. 52–56.

p. 46 "The fewer kids you have": David Anderegg in ibid.

p. 46 parents are spending more time: Author interview with Stearns.

p. 46 "well-organized, regimented childhoods": Ibid.

p. 47 "Not only do people expect": Barry Schwartz, "Self-Determination: The Tyranny of Freedom," *American Psychologist,* Jan. 2000, pp. 79–88.

p. 47 while people do indeed exert: Ibid.; and Sheena S. Iyengar, Rachel E. Wells, and Barry Schwartz, "Doing Better but Feeling Worse: The Paradox of Choice," *Psychological Science* 17, no. 2 (2006), pp. 143–50.

p. 47 "The more we are allowed": Schwartz, "Self-Determination."

p. 47 "officially acceptable style": Ibid.

p. 48 "If someone does a task": Multidimensional Perfectionism Scale (MPS), in Randy O. Frost et al., "The Dimensions of Perfectionism," *Cognitive Therapy and Research* 14 (1990), pp. 449–68.

p. 48 "Most people who are successful": Author interview with Randy O. Frost, Ph.D.

p. 48 Concern with mistakes: Ibid.

p. 49 "Overly demanding": Ibid.

p. 49 Demanding and harsh parents: Randy O. Frost et al., "The Development of Perfectionism: A Study of Daughters and Their Parents," *Cognitive Therapy and Research* 15, no. 6 (1991), pp. 469–89.

p. 49 most associated with psychopathology: Randy O. Frost and Patricia A. Marten, "Perfectionism and Evaluative Threat," *Cognitive Therapy and Research* 14, no. 6 (Dec. 1990), pp. 559–72.

p. 49 The conditionality of love: Marano, "Rocking the Cradle of Class."

p. 49 "There's a difference": Miriam Adderholdt, Ph.D., in ibid.

p. 50 Once perfectionism seeps: Marano, "Rocking the Cradle of Class."

p. 50 hyperattuned to signs of possible failure: Author interview with Frost.

p. 50 truly subversive aspect: Ibid.

p. 50 an outcome Frost sees in athletes: Ibid.

p. 50 writing ability and perfectionism: Ibid.

p. 51 incessant worry about mistakes: Gordon L. Flett and Paul L. Hewitt, "The Perils of Perfectionism in Sports and Exercise," *Current Directions in Psychological Science* 14, no. 1 (2005), pp. 14–18.

p. 51 cognitively based academic skills: Sian L. Beilock and Thomas H. Carr, "When High-Powered People Fail: Working Memory and 'Choking Under Pressure' in Math,"

Psychological Science 16, no. 2 (2005), pp. 101–5; and Sian L. Beilock et al., "When Paying Attention Becomes Counterproductive: Impact of Divided Versus Skill-Focused Attention on Novice and Experienced Performance of Sensorimotor Skills," *Journal of Experimental Psychology: Applied* 8, no. 1 (2002), pp. 6–16.

p. 52 It's more effective: Author interview with Angela Duckworth, Ph.D.; also see Elizabeth Hartley-Brewer, "Future Imperfect? Resisting the Lure of Perfectionism," *Young Minds Magazine: Education Policy* (Sept./Oct. 2002), pp. 31–33.

p. 53 two distinct sources: Luc Goossens, "Parenting, Identity, and Adjustment in Adolescence" (invited address, Society for Research on Adolescence, March 24, 2006). Also see Bart Soenens et al., "Maladaptive Perfectionistic Self-Representations: The Mediational Link Between Psychological Control and Adjustment," *Personality and Individual Differences* 38 (2005), pp. 487–98; and Koen Luyckx et al., "Parental Psychological Control and Dimensions of Identity Formation in Emerging Adulthood," *Journal of Family Psychology* (forthcoming).

p. 53 increasing autonomy of their children: Goossens, "Parenting, Identity, and Adjustment in Adolescence"; Soenens et al., "Maladaptive Perfectionistic Self-Representations"; and Luyckx et al., "Parental Psychological Control."

p. 53 Parents are most apt to resort: Bart Soenens et al., "In Search of the Sources of Psychologically Controlling Parenting: The Role of Parental Separation Anxiety and Parental Maladaptive Perfectionism," *Journal of Research on Adolescence* 16, no. 4 (Dec. 2006), pp. 539–59; and Luyckx et al., "Parental Psychological Control."

p. 54 "lack an appropriate sense of empathy": Goossens, "Parenting, Identity, and Adjustment in Adolescence."

p. 54 controlling parenting style: Ibid.

p. 54 ongoing dynamic process: Ibid.

p. 54 "Children of upper-class": Suniya S. Luthar and Shawn J. Latendresse, "Children of the Affluent: Challenges to Well-Being," *Current Directions in Psychological Science* 14, no. 1 (2005), pp. 49–53.

p. 55 *high pressure for achievement*: Suniya S. Luthar and Bronwyn E. Becker, "Privileged but Pressured? A Study of Affluent Youth," *Child Development* 73 (2002), pp. 1593–1610; and author interview with Suniya S. Luthar, Ph.D.

p. 55 kids' self-reported adjustment: Luthar and Latendresse, "Children of the Affluent"; and Suniya S. Luthar, "The Culture of Affluence: Psychological Costs of Material Wealth," *Child Development* 74 (2004), pp. 1581–93.

p. 55 overscheduling by itself: Suniya S. Luthar, Karen A. Shoum, and Pamela J. Brown, "Extracurricular Involvement Among Affluent Youth: A Scapegoat for 'Ubiquitous Achievement Pressures'?" *Developmental Psychology* 42, no. 3 (May 2006), pp. 583–97.

p. 55 sensitive as they are to perceived criticism: Luthar and Latendresse, "Children of the Affluent."

p. 55 "It takes away our old notion": Author interview with Steven Mintz.

p. 55 "a lot of underlying worries": Author interview with David Elkind, Ph.D.

p. 56 "Parenting is not an engineering task": Anderegg in Marano, "Rocking the Cradle of Class."

p. 56 "Seeing kids as a well-designed product": Ibid.

p. 57 become a religion: Marano, "Rocking the Cradle of Class."

p. 57 "If being a parent": Author interview with David Anderegg.

p. 57 "Everything students do is calculated": Barry Schwartz, "Top Colleges Should Select Randomly from a Pool of 'Good Enough,'" *Chronicle of Higher Education,* Feb. 25, 2005.

p. 58 "They become adults": Author interview with Anderegg.

p. 58 "When in the pursuit of perfection": Ibid.

p. 58 fusion of passion and perseverance: Peter Doskoch, "The Winning Edge," *Psychology Today,* Nov./Dec. 2005; and Angela Duckworth et al., "Grit: Perseverance and Passion for Long-Term Goals," *Journal of Personality and Social Psychology* 92, no. 6 (2007), pp. 1087–1101.

p. 58 those with grit are more likely: Doskoch, "Winning Edge"; and Duckworth et al., "Grit."

p. 59 25 percent of the differences: Doskoch, "Winning Edge."

p. 59 single best yardstick: Author interview with Duckworth.

p. 59 What fuels grit is probably passion: Duckworth et al., "Grit"; and Doskoch, "Winning Edge."

p. 59 need for grit is generally hidden: Doskoch, "Winning Edge."

p. 59 students of Asian background: Ibid.

p. 59 "Even a quarter century ago": Author interview with Elkind.

p. 60 "It's hard to know": David Elkind in Hara Estroff Marano, "A Nation of Wimps," *Psychology Today,* Nov./Dec. 2004, pp. 58–70.

p. 60 "They wouldn't ever dream": Author interview with Anderegg.

p. 60 children of working-class immigrants: Vivian Tseng, "Unpacking Immigration in Youths' Academic and Occupational Pathways," *Child Development* 77, no. 5 (Sept./Oct. 2006), pp. 1434–45.

p. 61 According to a recent study: Ibid.

FOUR   *We're All Jewish Mothers Now*

p. 63 "The mother-child relationship": Myrna Hant, "TV Jewish Mothers: The Creation of a Multiethnic Heroine" (eScholarship Repository, University of California, 2003).

p. 63 "intense and insatiable": Ibid.

p. 64 If they hit a minor speed bump: Author interview with Ellen McGrath, Ph.D.

p. 64 emotional attachment of parent to child: John Bowlby, *Attachment* (New York: Basic Books, 1969); John Bowlby, *A Secure Base: Parent-Child Attachment and Healthy Human Development* (New York: Basic Books, 1988); and Ronit Roth-Hanania and Maayan Davidov, "Attachment," in *Encyclopedia of Applied Psychology* (Boston: Elsevier, 2004), vol. 1, pp. 191–202.

p. 66 "Human connections create": Daniel J. Siegel, *The Developing Mind: Toward a Neurobiology of Interpersonal Experience* (New York: Guilford, 1999). Also see Daniel J. Siegel, "Toward an Interpersonal Neurobiology of the Developing Mind: Attachment Relationships, 'Mindsight,' and Neural Integration," *Infant Mental Health Journal* 22 (2001), pp. 67–94; and B. J. Casey, *Developmental Psychobiology* (Washington, D.C.: American Psychiatric Publishing, 2004).

p. 67 "The signals sent by each member": Siegel, "Toward an Interpersonal Neurobiology of the Developing Mind."

p. 68 "safe haven": Mary D. Salter Ainsworth et al., *Patterns of Attachment: A Psychological Study of the Strange Situation* (Hillsdale, N.J.: Lawrence Erlbaum Associates, 1978).

p. 69 Observers discern three basic patterns: Ibid.; and Mary Main, "The Organized

Categories of Infant, Child, and Adult Attachment," *Journal of the American Psychoanalytic Association* 48 (2000), pp. 1055–95.

p. 69 Studies show that securely attached infants: Siegel, *Developing Mind;* Eric I. Knudsen et al., "Economic, Neurobiological, and Behavioral Perspectives on Building America's Future Workforce," *Proceedings of the National Academy of Sciences* 103, no. 27 (2006); and Amie Ashley Hume and Nathan A. Fox, "Ordinary Variations in Maternal Caregiving Influence Human Infants' Stress Reactivity," *Psychological Science* 17, no. 6 (2006), pp. 550–56.

p. 69 Inwardly, however, the biological picture: Siegel, *Developing Mind;* and Siegel, "Toward an Interpersonal Neurobiology of the Developing Mind."

p. 69 Other infants display: Ainsworth et al., *Patterns of Attachment.*

p. 70 psychological vulnerability: Christine Heim and Charles B. Nemeroff, "Neurobiology of Early Life Stress: Clinical Studies," *Seminars in Clinical Neuropsychiatry* 7, no. 2 (April 2002), pp. 147–59; and Allan N. Schore, *Affect Dysregulation and Disorders of the Self* (New York: Norton, 2003).

p. 70 about 65 percent of children: Ainsworth et al., *Patterns of Attachment.*

p. 71 internal working model: John Bowlby, *Separation* (New York: Basic Books, 1973); Susan Johnson et al., "Evidence for Infants' Internal Working Models of Attachment," *Psychological Science* 18 (June 2007), pp. 501–2; and Mario Mikulciner, "Attachment Working Models and the Sense of Trust: An Exploration of Interaction Goals and Affect Regulation," *Journal of Personality and Social Psychology* 74 (1998), pp. 1209–24.

p. 72 separation is absolutely necessary: Bowlby, *Attachment;* Bowlby, *Secure Base;* and Ainsworth et al., *Patterns of Attachment.*

p. 73 what psychologists call mentalizing: Siegel, *Developing Mind.*

p. 74 "Separation is necessary for internalizing": Author interview with David Anderegg, Ph.D.

p. 74 optimal level of caregiver sensitivity: Siegel, *Developing Mind;* and Maura Sheehy, "Attachment Anxiety: Can You Be Too Close to Your Baby? Some Say Yes," *Child,* Feb. 2004.

p. 74 "Minor separations prepare children": Mark Solms, "Sigmund Freud Today," lecture presented at the New York Neuropsychoanalysis Society, May 6, 2006.

p. 75 any expression of autonomous functioning: Luc Goossens, "Parenting, Identity, and Adjustment in Adolescence" (invited address, Society for Research on Adolescence, March 24, 2006); and Bart Soenens et al., "Maladaptive Perfectionistic Self-Representations: The Mediational Link Between Psychological Control and Adjustment," *Personality and Individual Differences* 38 (2005), pp. 487–98; and Koen Luyckx et al., "Parental Psychological Control and Dimensions of Identity Formation in Emerging Adulthood," *Journal of Family Psychology* (forthcoming).

p. 75 resulting attachment panic: Siegel, *Developing Mind;* and Schore, *Affect Dysregulation and Disorders of the Self.*

p. 75 Clean Shopper looks harmless: www.cleanshopper.com.

p. 76 "maximum protection": Ibid.

p. 76 safety concerns have eclipsed: Richard Louv, "America's Dangerous Aversion to Risk," *San Diego Union-Tribune,* Dec. 6, 2005.

p. 77 "cozy liner": www.cleanshopper.com.

p. 77 Sexual crimes against children: David Finkelhor and Lisa Jones, "Why Have Child

Maltreatment and Child Victimization Declined?" *Journal of Social Issues* 62, no. 4 (2006), pp. 685–716; David Finkelhor et al., "The Victimization of Children and Youth: A Comprehensive National Survey," *Child Maltreatment* 10, no. 1 (Feb. 2005), pp. 5–25; David Finkelhor and Lisa M. Jones, "Explanation for the Decline in Child Sexual Abuse Cases," *Juvenile Justice Bulletin* (U.S. Department of Justice Office of Juvenile Justice and Delinquency Prevention, Jan. 2004), pp. 1–12; Lisa Jones and David Finkelhor, "The Decline in Child Sexual Abuse Cases," *Juvenile Justice Bulletin* (U.S. Department of Justice Office of Juvenile Justice and Delinquency Prevention, Jan. 2001), pp. 1–12; Lisa M. Jones et al., "Why Is Sexual Abuse Declining? A Survey of State Child Protection Administrators," *Child Abuse & Neglect* 25 (2001), pp. 1139–58; Crimes Against Children Research Center, University of New Hampshire, "The Decline of Sexual Abuse Cases," www.unh.edu/ccrc/the_decline_sexual_abuse.html; and Emily M. Douglas and David Finkelhor, Crimes Against Children Research Center, University of New Hampshire, "Childhood Sexual Abuse Fact Sheet," www.unh.edu/ccrc/factsheet/index.html.

p. 77 greatest threat of child physical and sexual harm: Douglas and Finkelhor, "Childhood Sexual Abuse Fact Sheet"; and Editorial, "Sex Offenders in Exile," *New York Times*, Dec. 30, 2006.

p. 78 Cinderella Effect: Martin Daly and Margo Wilson, "The 'Cinderella Effect': Elevated Mistreatment of Stepchildren in Comparison to Those Living with Genetic Parents," *Trends in Cognitive Sciences* 9 (2005), pp. 507–8. Also see Martin Daly and Margo Wilson, "Violence Against Stepchildren," *Current Directions in Psychological Science* (1996), pp. 77–81; Martin Daly and Margo Wilson, "Child Abuse and Other Risks of Not Living with Both Parents," *Ethology & Sociobiology* 6 (1985), pp. 197–210; and Martin Daly and Margo Wilson, *The Truth About Cinderella: A Darwinian View of Parental Love* (London: Weidenfeld & Nicolson, 1998).

p. 78 forty to one hundred times the chance: Benjamin Radford, "Predator Panic: A Closer Look," *Skeptical Inquirer*, Sept. 1, 2006, pp. 20–23.

p. 78 "Ninety percent of sexual offenses": Richard B. Krueger, "The New American Witch Hunt," *Los Angeles Times*, March 11, 2007. Also see Douglas and Finkelhor, "Childhood Sexual Abuse Fact Sheet"; and Lori Robertson, "States Aim to Stop Sex Offenders: Will New Laws Keep Children Safe?" *Children's Beat* (Fall–Winter 2006), pp. 6–8.

p. 78 a review of studies: David Finkelhor, "Prevention of Sexual Abuse Through Educational Programs Directed Toward Children," *Pediatrics* 120, Sept. 2007, pp. 1–6; Linda Lisanti, "Educators Teach Kids to Protect Themselves from Sexual Abuse," *Express-Times*, Feb. 29, 2004.

p. 78 recent Ohio law: Sharon Coolidge, "Sex-Abuse List Grows: No Trial Necessary, No Statute of Limitations," *Cincinnati Enquirer*, Sept. 25, 2006.

p. 78 registry is a fearmongering attempt: Ibid.; and Laurence Hammack and Lindsey Nair, "Epidemic or Easy Target?" *Roanoke Times*, Nov. 19, 2006.

p. 79 "Imagine teaching preschool": Personal communication from the board member.

p. 79 According to the U.S. Department of Justice: David Finkelhor and Richard Ormrod, "Kidnaping of Juvenile: Patterns from NIBRS [National Incident Based Reporting System]," *Juvenile Justice Bulletin* (U.S. Department of Justice Office of Juvenile Justice and Delinquency Prevention, June 2000), pp. 1–12.

p. 80 predictable errors in evaluating risk: Elke U. Weber, "Psychology of Decision-Making" (Center for Research on Environmental Decisions, Columbia University), 2006.

p. 80 oversensitive to negative input: Tiffany A. Ito et al., "Negative Information Weighs More Heavily on the Brain: The Negativity Bias in Evaluative Categorizations," *Journal of Personality and Social Psychology* 75, no. 4 (1998), pp. 887–900.

p. 80 We wind up overconfident: Weber, "Psychology of Decision-Making."

p. 80 At least 40 percent of all kids: National Institute of Mental Health, "Preventive Sessions After Divorce Protect Children into Teens," Oct. 15, 2002.

p. 80 knocks kids for a loop: E. Mavis Hetherington et al., "Long-Term Effects of Divorce and Remarriage on the Adjustment of Children," *Journal of the American Academy of Child Psychiatry* 24, no. 5 (Sept. 1985), pp. 518–30; Karen S. Peterson, "Divorce Need Not End in Disaster," *USA Today*, Jan. 13, 2002; and Richard Corliss and Lisa McLaughlin, *Time*, "Does Divorce Hurt Kids?" Jan. 28, 2002, p. 44.

p. 81 long-term effects are truly insidious: Judith Wallerstein et al., *The Unexpected Legacy of Divorce* (New York: Hyperion, 2000).

p. 81 rampant sexualization of their daughters: Ruth La Ferla, "Fashion Aims Young," *New York Times*, Aug. 24, 2006; Rosa Brooks, "No Escaping Sexualization of Young Girls," *Los Angeles Times*, Aug. 25, 2006; and Karen MacPherson, "Is Childhood Becoming Oversexed?" *Pittsburgh Post-Gazette*, May 8, 2005.

p. 81 fate of JonBenet Ramsey: Brooks, "No Escaping Sexualization of Young Girls"; also see Steven Parker, "JonBenet Ramsey: Are There Lessons to Be Learned from Her Tragic Story?" Healthy Children, WebMDblog, Aug. 16, 2006, blogs.webmd.com/healthy-children/2006/08/jonbenet-ramsey-are-there-lessons-to.html.

p. 82 flirtatious little Bratz dolls: MacPherson, "Is Childhood Becoming Oversexed?"

p. 82 similarly deep denial: National Center on Addiction and Substance Abuse at Columbia University, 11th Annual Survey of Teenagers and Parents (Aug. 2006).

p. 82 50 percent of teens find alcohol: Ibid.

p. 82 "These parents don't understand": Joseph A. Califano in Lois Romano, "Survey Finds Parents in 'Denial' on Teens' Risks," *Washington Post*, Aug. 18, 2006.

p. 83 risk is actually very necessary: Gregory Berns, *Satisfaction: The Science of Finding True Fulfillment* (New York: Henry Holt, 2005).

p. 84 mother in Birmingham, Michigan: Personal communication.

p. 84 organic cotton T-shirt: Cara Schrock, "Allergy Safe-Tee," www.alphamom.com, July 7, 2006.

F I V E   *Cheating Childhood*

p. 85 Suspended between reality and unreality: Brian Sutton-Smith, *The Ambiguity of Play* (Cambridge, Mass.: Harvard University Press, 1998).

p. 85 Like teasing, its psychological sibling: Hara Estroff Marano, "The Art of Teasing," *Psychology Today*, Nov./Dec. 1999.

p. 86 Yet in the animal kingdom: Hara Estroff Marano, "The Power of Play," *Psychology Today*, Nov./Dec. 1999.

p. 86 "We need play": Jaak Panksepp, "The Archaeology of Mind: Sources of Joy and Sadness Within the Brain" (International Neuropsychoanalysis Society, New York, June 4, 2005); also see Eric I. Knudsen et al., "Economic, Neurobiological, and Behavioral

Perspectives on Building America's Future Workforce," *Proceedings of the National Academy of Sciences* 103, no. 27 (2006).

p. 87 "a primary place": Sutton-Smith, *Ambiguity of Play.*

p. 87 play prompts us to see: Robert Root-Bernstein in Kaja Perina, "The Genius of Play," *Psychology Today,* Sept./Oct. 2003.

p. 87 In a study he conducted: Ibid.

p. 87 "Civilization arises": Johan Huizinga, *Homo Ludens: A Study of the Play-Element in Culture,* trans. R. F. C. Hull (London: Routledge and K. Paul, 1949).

p. 88 "does not just allow you": Simon Baron-Cohen, "The Biology of the Imagination," *Entelechy,* no. 9 (Summer/Fall 2007).

p. 88 going the way of the hula hoop: Howard P. Chudacoff, *Children at Play: An American History* (New York: New York University Press, 2007); also see Hara Estroff Marano, "A Nation of Wimps," *Psychology Today,* Nov./Dec. 2004, pp. 58–70.

p. 88 doing away with recess: Marano, "Nation of Wimps."

p. 88 play is under assault: Kathy Hirsh-Pasek, opening remarks, Play=Learning Conference (New Haven, Conn., June 10–11, 2005).

p. 88 percentage of time: Ibid.

p. 88 four-billion-dollar tutoring industry: Ibid.; also see Carla Rivera, "Tutors Prepare Them—for Preschool and Kindergarten," *Los Angeles Times,* Sept. 4, 2006.

p. 88 In 1998, children were spending: Hirsh-Pasek, opening remarks, Play=Learning Conference.

p. 88 Free time decreased: Ibid.

p. 89 play is equipment intensive: Chudacoff, *Children at Play.*

p. 89 Americans spent $25 billion on toys: Ibid.

p. 89 "It's normal for children": David Anderegg in Marano, "Nation of Wimps."

p. 89 sex play is universal: Jaak Panksepp, "Long-Term Psychobiological Consequences of Infant Emotions: Prescriptions for the Twenty-first Century," *Infant Mental Health Journal* 22, no. 1 (2001), pp. 132–73.

p. 89 Active play often gets stopped: Panksepp, "Archaeology of Mind."

p. 89 "They've been told by their coaches": Barbara Carlson in Marano, "Nation of Wimps."

p. 89 "Children aren't getting any benefits": Author interview with David Elkind.

p. 90 it's in play that the cognitive skills: Hara Estroff Marano, *Why Doesn't Anybody Like Me? A Guide to Raising Socially Confident Kids* (New York: William Morrow, 1998).

p. 91 wired deep into our brains: Panksepp, "Archaeology of Mind."

p. 91 take away play: Author interview with Jaak Panksepp, Ph.D.

p. 91 rough-and-tumble play: Panksepp, "Archaeology of Mind."

p. 91 turns on hundreds of genes: Nakia S. Gordon et al., "Socially Induced Brain 'Fertilization': Play Promotes Brain-Derived Neurotrophic Factor Transcription in the Amygdala and Dorsolateral Frontal Cortex in Juvenile Rats," *Neuroscience Letters* 341 (2003), pp. 17–20.

p. 92 What play does, by stimulating neurogenesis: Ibid.; and Nakia S. Gordon et al., "Expression of c-fos Gene Activation During Rough and Tumble Play in Juvenile Rats," *Brain Research Bulletin* 57, no. 5 (2002), pp. 651–59.

p. 92 "helps program higher brain areas": Jaak Panksepp, "Attention Deficit Hyperactivity

Disorders, Psychostimulants, and Intolerance of Childhood Playfulness: A Tragedy in the Making?" *Current Directions in Psychological Science* 7, no. 3 (June 1998), pp. 91–98.

p. 92 not from faulty brain wiring: Ibid.; Jaak Panksepp et al., "Modeling ADHD-Type Arousal with Unilateral Frontal Cortex Damage in Rats and Beneficial Effects of Play Therapy," *Brain and Cognition* 52 (2003), pp. 97–105; Jaak Panksepp, "ADHD and the Neural Consequences of Play and Joy: A Framing Essay," *Consciousness & Emotion* 3, no. 1 (Aug. 2002), pp. 1–6; and Jaak Panksepp et al., "Treatment of ADHD with Methylphenidate May Sensitize Brain Substrates of Desire: Implications for Changes in Drug Abuse Potential from an Animal Model," *Consciousness & Emotion* 3, no. 1 (Aug. 2002), pp. 7–19; Kenneth R. Ginsburg and the Committee on Communications and Committee on Psychosocial Aspects of Child and Family Health, "The Importance of Play in Promoting Healthy Child Development and Maintaining Strong Parent-Child Bonds," American Academy of Pediatrics, Oct. 9, 2006.

p. 93 "rambunctious shenanigans": Jaak Panksepp, "Beyond a Joke: From Animal Laughter to Human Joy?" *Science,* April 1, 2005, pp. 62–63.

p. 93 6 to 16 percent of American children: Panksepp, "Attention Deficit Hyperactivity Disorders."

p. 93 "We need to worry": Panksepp, "Archaeology of Mind."

p. 93 when they were given one hour per day: Ibid.

p. 94 "Most psychiatric problems": Ibid.

p. 94 recent neuroscience conference: Ibid.

p. 94 deep dopamine reward circuits: Ibid.

p. 94 "Play is a tool of nature": Ibid.

p. 94 drugs commonly used to treat ADHD: Panksepp, "Attention Deficit Hyperactivity Disorders."

p. 95 psychostimulants can sensitize: Panksepp et al., "Treatment of ADHD."

p. 95 "they make our animals more urgently materialistic": Ibid.

p. 95 "What we have in play": Author interview with Brian Sutton-Smith, Marano, "Power of Play."

p. 96 "Play confers resistance": Panksepp, "Archaeology of Mind"; "The Genesis of Play: The Biological Sources of Joy and Social Bonding, International Neuropsychoanalysis Society, New York, June 3, 2006.

p. 96 animals at play: Ibid.

p. 96 "Play is the most powerful source": Panksepp, "Archaeology of Mind."

p. 96 "There are no data": Anthony Pellegrini, "Outdoor Play" (paper presented at the Play=Learning Conference).

p. 97 periodic recess breaks: Ibid.

p. 97 People learn tasks better: Anthony Pellegrini and Catherine Bohn, "The Role of Recess in Children's Cognitive Performance and School Adjustment," *Educational Researcher* 34, Jan.–Feb. 2005, pp. 13–19.

p. 97 kids and adults are more attentive: Pellegrini, "Outdoor Play."

p. 97 "Parents and teachers should be aware": Ibid.

p. 97 peer interaction on the playground: Marano, *Why Doesn't Anybody Like Me?*

p. 97 only positive associations with school: Pellegrini, "Outdoor Play."

p. 97 sophisticated and rich language use: Laura E. Berk, "Play and Self-Regulation" (paper presented at the Play=Learning Conference).

p. 97 the minute teachers or other adults: Ibid.

p. 98 social behavior at recess: Anthony Pellegrini, "Kindergarten Children's Social Cognitive Status as a Predictor of First Grade Success," *Early Childhood Research Quarterly* 7 (1992), pp. 565–77.

p. 98 play actively stimulates development: Cynthia L. Elias and Laura E. Berk, "Self-Regulation in Young Children: Is There a Role for Sociodramatic Play?" *Early Childhood Research Quarterly* 17, no. 2 (Summer 2002), pp. 216–38.

p. 98 pretend play has such powerful effects: Ibid.

p. 98 come up with their own rules: Ibid.

p. 98 "The paradox": Ibid.

p. 99 "It's important to let children": Pellegrini, "Outdoor Play."

p. 99 "Adults tend to stop": Panksepp, "Archaeology of Mind."

p. 99 Rough-and-tumble social play: Eric Scott and Jaak Panksepp, "Rough-and-Tumble Play in Human Children," *Aggressive Behavior* 29 (2003), pp. 539–51.

p. 99 "The big thing about play": Author interview with Sutton-Smith.

p. 99 kids who got the chance to play: Scott and Panksepp, "Rough-and-Tumble Play."

p. 99 study done in the United States: Marano, "Power of Play."

p. 99 "The opposite of play": Brian Sutton-Smith in ibid.

p. 99 emotionally disturbed children: Marano, "Power of Play."

p. 99 "One of the only things": Author interview with Brian Sutton-Smith.

p. 99 if traumatized children are not given: Marano, "Power of Play."

p. 100 Mice deprived of play: Author interview with Sutton-Smith.

p. 100 Animals that do not play at mothering: Ibid.

p. 100 survey of 1,106 mothers: Shelly Glick Gryfe, "The Power of Play: How to Change the Conversation: A Custom Study Conducted for Fisher-Price by Yankelovich" (paper presented at the Play=Learning Conference).

p. 100 "I think that we are all anxious": Hirsh-Pasek, opening remarks, Play=Learning Conference.

p. 101 "In fifty years": Edward Zigler, closing remarks, Play=Learning Conference.

p. 101 "The movement toward": Ibid.

SIX   *Meet Mom and Dad, the New Hall Monitors*

p. 102 Parents are asked to invest hours: Author interview with Judith Sills, Ph.D.; also see Tracy Jan, "Websites Let Parents Look over Children's Shoulders at Schools," *Boston Globe,* Aug. 14, 2005.

p. 103 school day is extended: Nancy Zuckerbrod and Melissa Trujillo, "Massachusetts Leading National Effort for Longer School Days," Associated Press, Feb. 25, 2007.

p. 103 Start dates for the school year: Ibid. Also see Peter Whoriskey, "Parents Campaign to Take Back Kids' Summers," *Washington Post,* Jan. 22, 2006; and Maria Glod, "Parents, Teenagers Think More Zzzz's May Yield Some A's," *Washington Post,* Jan. 29, 2006.

p. 103 considerable evidence that Advanced Placement: Andrew Mollison, "Surviving a Midlife Crisis: Advanced Placement Turns Fifty," *Education Next,* no. 1 (Winter 2006).

p. 103 only one of every twenty: Diane Ravitch, "The Fall of the Standard-Bearers," *Chronicle of Higher Education,* March 10, 2006.

p. 103 "Do we want widgets": Kathy Hirsh-Pasek, opening remarks, Play=Learning Conference (New Haven, Conn., June 10–11, 2005).

p. 104 "educators think the only way": Ibid.

p. 104 Barely a third of American students: Jay P. Greene and Marcus A. Winters, "Public High School Graduation and College-Readiness Rates: 1991–2002" (Education Working Paper No. 8, Manhattan Institute for Policy Research, Feb. 2005).

p. 104 only 1.4 million students: Greg Forster, "The Embarrassing Good News on College Access," *Chronicle of Higher Education,* March 10, 2006.

p. 104 over ninety thousand dollars a year: Richard D. Kahlenberg, "Cost Remains a Key Obstacle to College Access," *Chronicle of Higher Education,* March 10, 2006.

p. 104 According to a 2004 report: Ibid.

p. 104 "wandering around one of the nation's": Ibid.

p. 105 According to a 2006 Harris poll: "The Harris Poll No. 45, Few U.S. Adults Give High Marks to the Nation's Public Schools for Quality of Education," HarrisInteractive, June 2, 2006, www.harrisinteractive.com/harris_poll/index.asp?PID-672.

p. 106 thicket of tests: Michael Winerip, "Bitter Lesson: A Good School Gets an 'F,'" *New York Times,* Jan. 11, 2006.

p. 106 test is growing increasingly unfair: Mark Franek, "Time to Think," *New York Times,* March 29, 2006.

p. 106 In 2005, forty thousand, or 2 percent: Ibid.

p. 107 "It is clear": Ibid.

p. 107 Colleges had begun dropping SATs: Tamar Lewin, "Students' Path to Small Colleges Can Bypass SAT," *New York Times,* Aug. 31, 2006.

p. 107 test scores of students, not measures of student learning: Ibid.; and JoAnne Viviano, "Education: What $110,064 Buys," *Psychology Today,* Jan./Feb. 2005.

p. 107 testing can truly be helpful: Richard Higgins et al., "The Conscientious Consumer: Reconsidering the Role of Assessment Feedback in Student Learning," *Studies in Higher Education* 27, no. 1 (Feb. 2002), pp. 53–64.

p. 107 Where's the High in Higher Education?: Richard Hersh, address to the Bringing Theory to Practice Conference (May 2004).

p. 107 It's a mistake: Richard H. Hersh and John Merrow, *Declining by Degrees: Higher Education at Risk* (New York: Palgrave Macmillan, 2005).

p. 107 "the minimum price of admission": Editorial, *New York Times,* Feb. 26, 2006.

p. 108 most recent findings: "A First Look at the Literacy of America's Adults in the 21st Century" (2003 National Assessment of Adult Literacy, National Center for Education Statistics, Dec. 2005).

p. 108 "What's disturbing": Mark S. Schneider, commissioner of education statistics, in Lois Romano, "Literacy of College Graduates Is on Decline," *Washington Post,* Dec. 25, 2005.

p. 108 But scores actually *fell:* "First Look at the Literacy of America's Adults in the 21st Century."

p. 108 "You have the possibility": Doug Lederman, "Graduated but Not Literate," www.insidehighered.com, Dec. 16, 2005.

p. 109 "It is hard not to be embarrassed": Ross Miller in ibid.

p. 109 high school dropouts will earn: U.S. Bureau of the Census, 2005; John Bridgeland et al., "The Silent Epidemic," Bill and Melinda Gates Foundation, March 2006.

p. 109 In a 2006 study: Greg Toppo, "Dropouts Say Their Schools Expected Too Little of Them," *USA Today*, March 5, 2006.

p. 109 no less intelligent: Hara Estroff Marano, *Why Doesn't Anybody Like Me? A Guide to Raising Socially Confident Kids* (New York: William Morrow, 1998).

p. 109 fully half the would-be dropouts: Michael Crow, president of Arizona State University, remarks about Access ASU, Science Coalition Media Dinner (March 22, 2006).

p. 110 Boys are especially likely to be casualties: Peg Tyre, "The Trouble with Boys," *Newsweek,* Jan. 30, 2006; and Lawrence Diller, "Don't Drug Them: Parents' Obsession with Their Children's Self-Esteem Plus Profit-Driven Diagnoses Create a Dangerous Prescription," *San Francisco Chronicle,* Nov. 19, 2006.

p. 110 diagnoses of learning disabilities: Diller, "Don't Drug Them."

p. 110 boys who say they don't like school: Tyre, "Trouble with Boys."

p. 110 44 percent of the student body: Jennifer Delahunty Britz, "To All the Girls I've Rejected," *New York Times,* March 23, 2006.

p. 110 Learning disabilities: Morbidity and Mortality Weekly, Report 54, Centers for Disease Control and Prevention, Nov. 4, 2005, p. 1107.

p. 111 stimulant drugs used to treat ADHD: Jaak Panksepp, "Attention Deficit Hyperactivity Disorders, Psychostimulants, and Intolerance of Childhood Playfulness: A Tragedy in the Making?" *Current Directions in Psychological Science* 7, no. 3 (June 1998), pp. 91–98.

p. 111 more appropriate solution: Diller, "Don't Drug Them."

p. 112 "the tedium of school": Paul Steinberg, "Attention Surplus? Re-examining a Disorder," *New York Times,* March 7, 2006.

p. 113 "multiple intelligences": Howard Gardner, *Frames of Mind: The Theory of Multiple Intelligences* (New York: Basic Books, 1983).

p. 113 Take physical movement: Susan Wagner Cook et al., "Gesturing Makes Learning Last," *Cognition* in press, published online June 11, 2007; Susan Goldin-Meadow et al., "Explaining Math: Gesturing Lightens the Load," *Psychological Science* 12, no. 6 (2001), pp. 516–22; and Karen J. Pine et al., "Hand Tied and Tongue Tied: The Effects of Prohibiting Gestures on Children's Lexical Retrieval Ability" (paper presented at the Society for Research in Child Development, 2005).

p. 114 It develops analytical skills: Nell O'Malley, "Kids' Leisure Time Becoming More Solitary, Artwork Shows," OSU News & Communications Services, Feb. 16, 2006.

p. 114 "Infants are motivated": Roberta Michnick Golinkoff and Kathy Hirsh-Pasek, "Baby Wordsmith: From Associationist to Social Sophisticate," *Current Directions in Psychological Science* 15 (2006), pp. 30–33.

p. 114 We learn more from our mistakes: A. J. Wills et al., "Predictive Learning, Prediction Errors, and Attention: Evidence from Event-Related Potentials and Eye Tracking," *Journal of Cognitive Neuroscience* 19, no. 5 (May 2007), pp. 843–54; and A. J. Wills in EurekAlert, July 1, 2007.

p. 115 At best, it breeds only a desire: Author interview with David Anderegg, Ph.D.

SEVEN   *From Scrutiny to Fragility*

p. 117 what creates anxious children: Hara Estroff Marano, "A Nation of Wimps," *Psychology Today,* Nov./Dec. 2004, pp. 58–70.

p. 117 About 20 percent of babies: Hara Estroff Marano, "Overprotective Parenting: The Age of Anxiety," *Psychology Today,* Sept./Oct. 1994, pp. 18–19; and Jerrold F. Rosenbaum et al., "Behavioral Inhibition in Childhood: A Risk Factor for Anxiety Disorders," *Harvard Review of Psychiatry* 1, no. 1 (May/June 1993), pp. 2–16.

p. 118 key factor lay in the degree: Marano, "Parenting Style May Foster Anxiety"; and Marano, "Nation of Wimps."

p. 118 "Overprotectiveness brings out the worst": Michael Liebowitz, in Marano, "Nation of Wimps."

p. 118 unusually high proportion: Author interview with Michael Liebowitz, M.D.

p. 119 ongoing studies: Frances A. Champagne and Michael J. Meaney, "Stress During Gestation Alters Postpartum Maternal Care and the Development of the Offspring in a Rodent Model," *Biological Psychiatry* 59, no. 12 (2006), pp. 1227–35; and Christian Caldji et al., "Variations in Maternal Care in Infancy Regulate the Development of Stress Reactivity," *Biological Psychiatry* 48, no. 12 (2000), pp. 1164–74.

p. 119 how mothers touch and fondle: Amie Ashley Hane and Nathan A. Fox, "Ordinary Variations in Maternal Caregiving Influence Human Infants' Stress Reactivity," *Psychological Science* 17, no. 6 (2006), pp. 550–56; and Eric I. Knudsen et al., "Economic, Neuro-biological, and Behavioral Perspectives on Building America's Future Workforce," *Proceedings of the National Academy of Sciences* 103, no. 27 (2006).

p. 119 Early handling creates: Dong Liu et al., "Maternal Care, Hippocampal Synapto-genesis, and Cognitive Development in Rats," *Nature Neuroscience* 3 (2000), pp. 799–806; and Dong Liu et al., "Maternal Care, Hippocampal Glucocorticoid Receptors, and Hypothalamic-Pituitary-Adrenal Response to Stress," *Science,* Sept. 12, 1997, pp. 1659–62.

p. 120 "handling effect": Liu et al., "Response to Stress."

p. 120 ability to consolidate memory: Liu et al., "Cognitive Development in Rats."

p. 120 ability to pay attention: Champagne and Meaney, "Stress During Gestation."

p. 120 affection transmitted through touch: Knudsen et al., "Economic, Neurobiological, and Behavioral Perspectives."

p. 121 Kagan's studies at Harvard: Marano, "Nation of Wimps"; Marano, "Parenting Style May Foster Anxiety"; and Joseph Biederman et al., "Further Evidence of Association Be-tween Behavioral Inhibition and Social Anxiety in Children," *American Journal of Psychiatry* 158 (Oct. 2001), pp. 1671–79.

p. 121 "Children need to be gently encouraged": Liebowitz in Marano, "Nation of Wimps."

p. 121 Studies of children with disorders: Benedict Carey, "Parenting as Therapy for Child's Mental Disorders," *New York Times,* Dec. 22, 2006; M. Mazurowa and A. Popielarska, "Effect of Parent Attitudes on the Development of Psychomotor Disorders in Epileptic Children," *Polish Journal of Neurology and Neurosurgery* 10, no. 2 (March–April 1976), pp. 219–23; and Arthur Lubow, "A Transcendent Voice," *New York Times Magazine,* Oct. 1, 2006.

p. 122 parents who are oversolicitous: Nathan A. Fox et al., "Behavioral Inhibition: Linking Biology and Behavior Within a Developmental Framework," *Annual Review of Psychology* 56 (2005), pp. 235–62.

p. 122 pattern of negative reactivity: Ibid.

p. 122 behaviorally inhibited children: Author interview with Liebowitz.

p. 123 adjustable belt: Jeffrey J. Wood, "Parental Intrusiveness and Children's Separation

Anxiety in a Clinical Sample," *Child Psychiatry and Human Development* 37 (2006), pp. 73–87.

p. 123 intrusive and distracting: Ibid.; and author interview with Jeffrey J. Wood, Ph.D.

p. 123 amount of intrusive help: Wood, "Parental Intrusiveness."

p. 124 "Parents who act intrusively": Jeffrey J. Wood, et al. (under review), "An Experimental Test of Intrusive Parenting as an Intervening Variable in Child Anxiety Trajectories over the Course of One Year."

p. 124 "When we look at the linkage": Author interview with Wood.

p. 125 Wood pauses to remember: Ibid.

p. 126 critical factor in emotional adjustment: Albert Bandura, *Self-Efficacy: The Exercise of Control* (New York: Worth, 1997).

p. 126 opportunity for rising: Ibid.; and Jeffrey J. Wood et al., "Parenting and Childhood Anxiety: Theory, Empirical Findings, and Future Directions," *Journal of Child Psychology and Psychiatry* 44, no. 1 (2003), pp. 134–51.

p. 127 resulting sense of accomplishment: Bandura, *Self-Efficacy*; and Wood et al., "Parenting and Childhood Anxiety."

p. 127 "have no self-confidence": Author interview with Wood.

p. 127 study of middle-class elementary school children: Ibid.

p. 127 "They generally provide": Ibid.

p. 127 "Self-confidence . . . is an important": Ibid.

p. 128 "One key aspect": Ibid.

p. 128 overregulation of children's activities: Ibid.

p. 128 highly regimented childhoods: Author interview with Peter Stearns, Ph.D.

p. 129 In a recent professional article: Wood, "Parental Intrusiveness."

p. 129 "When children with anxiety": Ibid.

p. 130 less able to cope with pain: Carmen R. Green et al., "The Unequal Burden of Pain: Disparities and Differences," *Pain Medicine* 6, no. 1 (Jan. 2005).

p. 130 generation gap in chronic pain: Ibid.

p. 130 "A hovering parent": Author interview with Jerome Kagan, Ph.D.

p. 130 concern, by itself, can be crippling: Liat Feingold, "Self-Awareness of Reading Disability—a Motivating or Hindering Factor?" (abstract of unpublished work furnished by the researcher).

p. 131 lost its productivity: Ibid.

p. 131 "When a child": Personal communication from Liat Feingold.

p. 131 contradict the currently accepted wisdom: Ibid.

p. 132 Such efforts transform: Feingold, "Self-Awareness of Reading Disability."

p. 132 "It's important that children": Personal communication with Feingold.

p. 132 "There is a high level": Author interview with Wood.

p. 133 "There's an internal motivation": Ibid.

p. 133 one bad grade: Ibid.

p. 134 "Many parents have some strong": Author interview with Lynne Siqueland, Ph.D.; also see Lynne Siqueland and Guy Diamond, "Engaging Parents in Cognitive-Behavioral Treatment for Children with Anxiety Disorders," *Cognitive and Behavioral Practice* 5, Summer 1998, pp. 81–102.

p. 134 "But when kids": Author interview with Siqueland.

p. 134 "They feel 'It's so painful for me' ": Siqueland and Diamond, "Engaging Parents."

p. 135 "Parents' tendency": Author interview with Siqueland. Also see Lynne Siqueland et al., "Anxiety in Children: Perceived Family Environments and Observed Family Interaction," *Journal of Clinical Child Psychology* 25, no. 2 (1996), pp. 225–37; and Siqueland and Diamond, "Engaging Parents."

p. 136 "It's not that the parents": Author interview with Wood.

p. 136 "But it's as if": Ibid.

p. 136 "We have developed": Author interview with Stearns.

p. 137 "Often parents think": Mark A. Sperling, M.D., in Stephen S. Hall, "The Short of It," *New York Times Magazine,* Oct. 16, 2005.

p. 137 stunningly disappointing average: Hall, "Short of It."

p. 137 "The biggest side effect": Alan D. Rogol, M.D., in ibid.

p. 137 Behaviorally inhibited children: Fox et al., "Behavioral Inhibition."

p. 138 Children who go to day care: Ibid.

p. 138 "It smacks of a parent": Author interview with Wood.

p. 138 "attachment parenting": www.askdrsears.com.

p. 138 prescription for natural childbirth: Ibid.

p. 139 "Kids tell us all the time": Author interview with Daniel Greenberg, Ph.D.

p. 139 summer camp has been transformed: Lisa Gubernick, "Under Pressure from Parents, Camps Add No-Fun Options," *Wall Street Journal,* Feb. 21, 2003.

p. 139 "with separation anxiety": Judith Warner, "Loosen the Apron Strings," *New York Times,* July 20, 2006.

p. 139 Parents scour them: Kim Hart, "Camp E-Mailaway," *Washington Post,* July 8, 2006.

p. 140 Being looked at all the time: Marano, "Nation of Wimps."

p. 140 "If every drawing": David Anderegg in ibid.; also see Heather Pick, "Online Language Leaves Parents in the Dark," WBNS-TV-DT, Channel 10, Columbus, Ohio, April 28, 2006.

p. 141 Danish psychologist Bent Hougaard: Maria Carling, "The High Price of a Friction-Free Childhood," *Svenska Dagbladet,* Dec. 1, 2004.

EIGHT *Crisis on the Campus*

p. 142 psychological distress is rampant: Hara Estroff Marano, "Crisis on the Campus," *Psychology Today's Blues Buster,* May 2002; and Stephen C. Caulfield, "Ninth Leadership Forum: Student Health 2010: What Changes Will the Next Five Years Bring?" *Student Health Spectrum,* Feb. 2006, pp. 4–18.

p. 142 Through their doors: Hara Estroff Marano, "Up Against the Ivy Wall in 2004," *Psychology Today's Blues Buster,* March 2004.

p. 142 9 percent of all college students: Robert P. Gallagher, "National Survey of Counseling Center Directors, 2005," International Association of Counseling Services, Monograph Series No. 80.

p. 142 severity of student mental health problems: Author interview with Robert Gallagher, Ph.D.; and Hara Estroff Marano, "A Nation of Wimps," *Psychology Today,* Nov./Dec. 2004, pp. 58–70.

p. 142 15 percent of college students: Marano, "Nation of Wimps"; John F. Greden, M.D., introductory remarks, Depression on College Campuses Conference (Ann Arbor, Mich., March 6–7, 2003); and Richard Kadison and Theresa Foy DiGeronimo, "College of the Overwhelmed: The Campus Mental Health Crisis and What to Do About It," Jossey-Bass, 2004.

p. 142 In a 2005 survey: American College Health Association, "National College Health Assessment" (Spring 2005).

p. 143 collective forms of distress: Gallagher, "National Survey of Counseling Center Directors, 2005."

p. 143 self-reported depression: Kadison, "College of the Overwhelmed."

p. 143 obsessive pursuit: Marano, "Up Against the Ivy Wall in 2004."

p. 143 sexual assaults have quadrupled: Gallagher, "National Survey of Counseling Center Directors, 2005."

p. 143 375 cases: Ibid.

p. 143 Anorexia or bulimia: Marano, "Nation of Wimps."

p. 143 eating disorders are on the rapid rise: Author interview with Armando Favazza, M.D.

p. 143 disparaging one's body: Lauren E. Britton et al., "Fat Talk and Self-Presentation of Body Image: Is There a Social Norm for Women to Self-Degrade?" *Body Image: An International Journal of Research* 3, no. 3 (Sept. 2006), pp. 247–54.

p. 143 "I have a friend": Author interview with the college official.

p. 143 mental state of students: Author interview with Steven Hyman, M.D.; and Steven Hyman, M.D., in Marano, "Nation of Wimps."

p. 143 increasingly complex psychological problems: Marano, "Crisis on the Campus."

p. 144 There isn't a meeting: Author interview with Hyman; also see Marano, "Up Against the Ivy Wall in 2004."

p. 144 "It's an important, nationwide problem": Author interview with Hyman.

p. 144 "By the tenth or eleventh week": Author interview with Russ Federman; also see Marano, "Up Against the Ivy Wall in 2004."

p. 144 colleges are also reluctant: Marano, "Up Against the Ivy Wall in 2004."

p. 144 10 percent of students report problems: Marano, "Crisis on the Campus."

p. 144 ten-thousand-student campus: Richard Boyum, "Suicidal Behavior in College Students" (University of Wisconsin–Eau Claire Counseling Services), SelfCounseling.com.

p. 144 Ninety-one percent of counseling centers: Gallagher, "National Survey of Counseling Center Directors, 2005."

p. 145 In 2001, 85 percent of North America's: Marano, "Crisis on the Campus."

p. 145 By 2005, 96 percent of counseling centers: Gallagher, "National Survey of Counseling Center Directors, 2005."

p. 145 counseling center directors reported increases: Ibid.

p. 145 "Every director": Richard Kadison, M.D., in Marano, "Crisis on the Campus."

p. 145 four million college students: "School Enrollment in the United States: Current Population Reports" (United States Census Bureau, Oct. 2005); also see John Luciew, "Peer Pressure, Society Erode Boundaries," *Patriot-News* (Pa.), Aug. 25, 2004.

p. 145 not as much surveillance: Author interview with Morton Silverman, M.D.

p. 145 over-relying on medications: Marano, "Up Against the Ivy Wall in 2004."

p. 145 "Counseling centers are struggling": Author interview with Federman.

p. 146 "Universities feel the need": Author interview with Joseph Behan, Ph.D.

p. 146 40 percent of seniors: Sherry A. Benton et al., "Changes in Counseling Center

Client Problems Across 13 Years," *Professional Psychology: Research and Practice* 34, no. 1 (2003), pp. 66–72.

p. 146 Colleges are reeling: Marano, "Crisis on the Campus."

p. 146 attending the nation's elite institutions: Kadison in ibid.

p. 146 about 5 percent of American children: American Academy of Child and Adolescent Psychiatry, "Facts for Families: The Depressed Child," July 2004.

p. 147 antidepressant prescriptions doubled: Maggie Fox, "Antidepressant Use Way Up in U.S. Kids—Study," Reuters, April 2, 2004.

p. 147 "Many who wouldn't have gotten": Kadison in Marano, "Crisis on the Campus."

p. 147 significant proportion: Hara Estroff Marano, "Mending Minds: Lessons for College," *Psychology Today's Blues Buster,* May 2002.

p. 147 "They think college": Author interview with Rosemarie Rothmeier, Ph.D.; also see Marano, "Mending Minds."

p. 147 "biggest concern": Marano, "Mending Minds."

p. 147 "Many students stop taking": Author interview with Rothmeier; also see Marano, "Mending Minds."

p. 147 14 percent of college students: Marano, "Up Against the Ivy Wall in 2004."

p. 147 number-one prescribed drug: Hara Estroff Marano, "What's in a Pill?" *Psychology Today's Blues Buster,* May 2002.

p. 148 Of two thousand students: Author interview with Richard Kadison, M.D.

p. 148 over 25 percent of campus counseling: Gallagher, "National Survey of Counseling Center Directors, 2005."

p. 148 "It's an indirect indicator": Author interview with Silverman.

p. 148 "They're going back": Marano, "Crisis on the Campus."

p. 148 "They say, 'My son or daughter' ": Author interview with Mark H. Reed; also see Marano, "Crisis on the Campus."

p. 149 "There are increases": Author interview with Silverman; also see Marano, "Crisis on the Campus."

p. 149 "We're seeing more depression": Author interview with Silverman; also see Marano, "Crisis on the Campus."

p. 149 counseling directors confess: Marano, "Crisis on the Campus."

p. 149 366 campus counseling centers: Gallagher, "National Survey of Counseling Center Directors, 2005."

p. 150 "It's difficult to tell": Author interview with Reed; also see Marano, "Crisis on the Campus."

p. 150 in one typical week: Robert P. Gallagher, "National Survey of Counseling Center Directors, 2001" (International Association of Counseling Services, Monograph Series No. 80).

p. 150 "Every fall": Author interview with John Portmann; also see Marano, "Nation of Wimps."

p. 151 "The number is way up": Author interview with a university vice president for student affairs.

p. 151 Tied directly to the increase: Isabel Goldenberg, M.D., in Caulfield, "Student Health 2010"; also see Estelle Maartmann-Moe, A.P.R.N., in Caulfield.

p. 151 more than 40 percent of collegians: American College Health Association, "National College Health Assessment"; and Kadison, "College of the Overwhelmed."

p. 151 Binge drinking is rising fastest: "Underage Drinking in the United States: A Status Report, 2005" (Center on Alcohol Marketing and Youth at Georgetown University, March 2006).

p. 153 more than seventy thousand: Ibid.

p. 153 51 percent of those who drank: Aaron M. White, "Prevalence and Correlates of Alcohol-Induced Blackouts Among College Students: Results of an E-Mail Survey," *Journal of American College Health* (Nov. 2002), p. 117; and Katy Butler, "The Grim Neurology of Teenage Drinking," *New York Times,* July 4, 2006.

p. 153 prior to full brain maturation: Michael D. DeBellis et al., "Prefrontal Cortex, Thalamus, and Cerebellar Volumes in Adolescents and Young Adults with Adolescent-Onset Alcohol Use Disorders and Co-morbid Mental Disorders," *Alcoholism: Clinical and Experimental Research* 29, no. 9 (Sept. 2005), pp. 1590–1600; Anna E. Goudriaan et al., "Decision-Making and Binge Drinking: A Longitudinal Study," *Alcoholism: Clinical and Experimental Research* 31 (June 2007), pp. 928–38; and Butler, "Grim Neurology of Teenage Drinking."

p. 153 increases the risk of later alcoholism: Butler, "Grim Neurology of Teenage Drinking."

p. 154 reduces the perception of impairment: Sionaldo Eduardo Ferreira et al., "Effects of Energy Drink Ingestion on Alcohol Intoxication," *Alcoholism: Clinical and Experimental Research* 30, no. 4 (April 2006), pp. 598–606.

p. 154 changing nature of social life: Author interview with Bernardo Carducci, Ph.D.

p. 154 "everyone binges": Author interview with professional observer.

p. 154 "In college": Greg Moore, M.D., in Caulfield, "Student Health 2010."

p. 155 "It's the fragility": Author interview with Joyce Bylander, Ph.D.

p. 155 "Only a few years ago": Goldenberg in Caulfield, "Student Health 2010."

p. 155 The shocker is: Ibid.

p. 155 put meaning in their lives: Author interview with Paul Joffe, Ph.D.

p. 156 MySpace phenomenon: Author interview with Edward Spencer, Ph.D.

p. 156 "pharming": Caulfield, "Student Health 2010"; also see Rogette Esteve, "Extra (Mental) Credit: The Use of Psychostimulants on College Campuses," *Triple Helix* (Fall 2005).

p. 157 perceptible drop in interaction: "CIRP Freshman Survey" (Higher Education Research Institute, UCLA, Feb. 2005).

p. 158 care about promoting ethnic understanding: Ibid.

p. 158 "I loved poetry": Author interview with Marissa.

p. 159 I have talked to counselors: Marano, "Crisis on the Campus"; and Marano, "Up Against the Ivy Wall in 2004."

p. 160 "I encounter this a lot": Author interview with Marie van Tubbergen, Ph.D.; also see Hara Estroff Marano, "Holding It Together," *Psychology Today's Blues Buster,* May 2002.

p. 161 But that is not the case: Marano, "Crisis on the Campus."

p. 161 "Suicide is not a good marker": Morton D. Silverman in ibid.; and author interview with Silverman.

p. 161 "We're no longer": Kadison in Marano, "Crisis on the Campus"; and author interview with Kadison.

p. 161 Where Harvard's mental health service: Marano, "Crisis on the Campus."

p. 161 MIT is still reeling: Ibid.

p. 161 ultimately settled in 2006: Eric Hoover, "In a Surprise Move, MIT Settles Closely Watched Student-Suicide Case," *Chronicle of Higher Education,* April 14, 2006.

p. 161 "We can't do that": Kadison in Marano, "Crisis on the Campus."

p. 162 366 campus counseling centers: Robert P. Gallagher, "National Survey of Counseling Center Directors, 2004" (International Association of Counseling Services, Monograph Series No. 80).

p. 162 mandatory leave policies: Jason Feirman, "The New College Dropout," *Psychology Today,* May/June 2005.

p. 162 "fun czar": "Harvard Hires 'Fun Czar' to Spice Up Student Life," Reuters, Jan. 13, 2005.

p. 162 recognized as prime time: Marano, "Mending Minds."

p. 163 "It's more stressful": Mark H. Reed in ibid.

p. 163 damaging to centers of learning: Robert M. Sapolsky et al., "Hippocampal Damage Associated with Prolonged Glucocorticoid Exposure in Primates," *Journal of Neuroscience* 10 (1990), pp. 2897–2902.

p. 163 "They really suffer": Michael Doyle, Ph.D., in Marano, "Mending Minds."

p. 164 "Now we're seeing the opposite": Rosemarie Rothmeier, Ph.D., in ibid.

p. 164 "More students have a family history": Silverman in Marano, "Crisis on the Campus."

p. 164 "You have to have an internalized": Linda K. Hellmich, Ph.D., in Marano, "Mending Minds."

p. 164 "It's confusing": Pamela L. Graesser, M.Ed., in ibid.

p. 166 This is a generation: Hans Geser, "Towards a Sociological Theory of the Mobile Phone" (Release 3.0, May 2004); and Elena Kennedy and Barbara K. Hofer, "The Electronic Tether: The Influence of Frequent Parental Contact on the Development of Autonomy and Self-Regulation in Emerging Adulthood" (abstract, March 2006).

p. 167 "Kids need more connection": Author interview with Behan.

p. 167 "Many students lack": Jacqueline Pistorello, Ph.D., in Marano, "Mending Minds."

p. 168 "Diversity is a big challenge": Author interview with the administrator.

p. 168 Yes, it's exciting: Author interview with Christine M.; and Hara Estroff Marano, "The Sources of Their Discontent," *Psychology Today's Blues Buster,* March 2004.

p. 168 "In the atmosphere": Author interview with Sarah C.; and Sarah C. in Marano, "Up Against the Ivy Wall in 2004."

p. 169 But athletes are now: Nanci Hellmich, "Athlete's Hunger to Win Fuels Eating Disorders," *USA Today,* Feb. 6, 2006.

p. 169 self-injury is making dramatic marks: Marano, "Mending Minds"; Janis Whitlock et al., "Self-Injurious Behaviors in a College Population," *Pediatrics* 117, no. 6 (June 2006), pp. 1939–48; author interview with Federman; and Joan Jacobs Brumberg, "Are We Facing an Epidemic of Self-Injury?" *Chronicle of Higher Education,* Dec. 8, 2006.

p. 170 "It has now reached": Hara Estroff Marano, "Driven to Distraction," *Psychology Today's Blues Buster,* March 2004; author interview with Federman; and Janis Whitlock et al., "The Virtual Cutting Edge: The Internet and Adolescent Self-Injury," *Developmental Psychology* 42, no. 3 (2006), pp. 407–17.

p. 170 nearly 70 percent of college counseling: Marano, "Driven to Distraction"; and Robert P. Gallagher, "National Survey of Counseling Center Directors, 2003," International Association of Counseling Services, Monograph Series No. 80.

p. 170 polar opposite of suicide: Marano, "Driven to Distraction"; Jennifer Harris, "Self-Harm: Cutting the Bad Out of Me," *Qualitative Health Research* 10, no. 2 (March 2000), pp. 164–73; and author interviews with Federman and Favazza.

p. 170 "These students go about cutting": Author interview with Pamela L. Graesser, M.Ed., director of counseling at Rivier College, N.H.

p. 170 random sampling: Whitlock et al., "Self-Injurious Behaviors in a College Population."

p. 171 "How do I know I exist?": Whitlock et al., "Virtual Cutting Edge."

p. 171 Self-harm is a serious symptom: Marano, "Driven to Distraction"; and author interview with Federman.

p. 171 "The primary reason": Author interview with Pistorello.

p. 171 searching for authenticity: Harris, "Self-Harm"; Josie Appleton, "Self-Harm: Cut It Out," *Spiked-Central,* Aug. 5, 2004; and Gregory T. Eels, "Mobilizing the Campuses Against Self-Mutilation," *Chronicle of Higher Education,* Dec. 8, 2006.

p. 171 "to some sort of reality": Keith Ablow, "Speaking in the Third Person, Removed from Reality," *New York Times,* Nov. 1, 2005, p. F5.

p. 171 positive ramifications: Author interview with Portmann; and John Portmann, *Bad for Us: The Lure of Self-Harm* (Boston: Beacon, 2004).

p. 172 "When there is no feeling": Harris, "Self-Harm."

p. 172 "There's a euphoric element to it:": Author interview with Favazza.

p. 172 "It's basically a home remedy": Author interview with Arthur Nielsen, M.D. Also see Hara Estroff Marano, "Cutting: A Form of Protest," *Psychology Today,* Nov./Dec. 2004; Armando Favazza, "Self-Injurious Behavior in College Students," *Pediatrics* 117, no. 6 (June 2006), pp. 2283–84; and Marilee Strong, *A Bright Red Scream: Self-Mutilation and the Language of Pain* (New York: Viking, 1998).

p. 172 average U.S. children: Jean Twenge, "The Age of Anxiety? Birth Cohort Changes in Anxiety and Neuroticism, 1952–1993," *Journal of Personality and Social Psychology* 79 (2000), pp. 1007–21.

p. 172 cultural component to self-harm: Harris, "Self-Harm"; and Armando Favazza, *Bodies Under Siege: Self-Mutilation in Culture and Psychiatry* (Baltimore: Johns Hopkins University Press, 1996).

p. 173 Physical pain helps people disconnect: Author interview with Federman; and Harris, "Self-Harm."

p. 173 "Forty years ago": Author interview with Federman.

p. 174 "There is such a passivity": Author interview with Joseph Behan.

p. 174 lack of cultural outlets: Author interviews with Federman and Behan.

p. 174 most effective treatment: Marsha M. Linehan et al., "Two-Year Randomized Controlled Trial and Follow-Up of Dialectical Behavior Therapy vs. Therapy by Experts for Suicidal Behaviors and Borderline Personality Disorder," *Archives of General Psychiatry* 63 (July 2006), pp. 757–66.

NINE   *Arrested Development*

p. 176 By every measure of adulthood: Frank F. Furstenberg Jr. et al., "Growing Up Is Harder to Do," *Contexts* 3, no. 3 (Summer 2004), pp. 33–41.

p. 176 According to a recent report: Frank F. Furstenberg Jr. et al., "Between Adolescence and Adulthood: Expectations About the Timing of Adulthood" (Research Network Working Paper No. 1, Network on Transitions to Adulthood, July 29, 2003).

p. 177 Nearly two-thirds: Ibid.

p. 177 dismantling the hierarchical relationship: Hara Estroff Marano, "When to Fire Your Parents," *Psychology Today,* March/April 1992.

p. 177 "It's hard to know": Author interview with David Elkind, Ph.D.

p. 177 "They often need a period": Author interview with Peter Stearns, Ph.D.

p. 178 "The precursor to marriage": Author interview with Bernardo Carducci, Ph.D.

p. 178 It takes them longer: Author interview with Elkind. Also see Hans Geser, "Sociology of the Mobile Phone: Pre-teen Cell Phone Adoption: Consequences for Later Patterns of Phone Usage and Involvement" (Sociology in Switzerland Online Publications, Sociologic Institute of the University of Zurich, April 2006).

p. 178 "Kids are constantly": Author interview with the Cornell student.

p. 179 "The number of students": Author interview with the counseling staff member.

p. 179 Today kids move away: Leysia Palen and Amanda Hughes, "When Home Base Is Not a Place: Parents' Use of Mobile Telephones," *Personal and Ubiquitous Computing* 11, no. 5 (June 2007), pp. 339–48, published online Aug. 31, 2006; Ralph Gardner Jr., "In College, You Can Go Home Again and Again," *New York Times,* Dec. 14, 2006; and Geser, "Sociology of the Mobile Phone."

p. 180 In 2000 only 38 percent: www.studentmonitor.com.

p. 180 "the larger tendency": Hans Geser, "Towards a Sociological Theory of the Mobile Phone" (Release 3.0, May 2004).

p. 180 average age of cell phone adoption: Geser, "Sociology of the Mobile Phone"; and Yuki Noguchi, "Connecting with Kids, Wirelessly," *Washington Post,* July 7, 2005, p. 1.

p. 180 researchers have found: Geser, "Sociology of the Mobile Phone."

p. 181 overweight negative experience: Robert William Blum, "Depression and Debilitating Expressions of Depression Within Student Populations" (Bringing Theory to Practice Project Meeting, April 2004); and Geser, "Towards a Sociological Theory of the Mobile Phone."

p. 181 Just that morning: Author interview with the vice president for student affairs of a well-regarded eastern university.

p. 182 when Mom and Dad are on speed dial: Author interview with David Anderegg, Ph.D.; also see Geser, "Towards a Sociological Theory of the Mobile Phone."

p. 182 "shocked year by year": Author interview with Barbara K. Hofer, Ph.D.

p. 182 she posted a Web-based survey: Personal communication with Barbara K. Hofer.

p. 183 research findings were presented: Elena Kennedy and Barbara K. Hofer, "The Electronic Tether: The Influence of Frequent Parental Contact on the Development of Autonomy and Self-Regulation in Emerging Adulthood" (abstract, March 2006).

p. 183 "particularly surprised": Personal communication from Hofer.

p. 183 "Our study implicates": Ibid.; also see Kennedy and Hofer, "Electronic Tether."

p. 184 "If there's a daily phone call": Author interview with Hofer.

p. 184 "I was pretty shocked": Ibid.

p. 184 Fully 30 percent of first-year students: Kennedy and Hofer, "Electronic Tether."

p. 185 best kind of support: Personal communication with Hofer.

p. 185 permanent present: Hara Estroff Marano, "A Nation of Wimps," *Psychology Today,* Nov./Dec. 2004, pp. 58–70; Geser, "Towards a Sociological Theory of the Mobile Phone"; and Betsy Israel, "The Overconnecteds," *New York Times,* Nov. 5, 2006, pp. 20–23.

p. 185 "The first thing students do": Author interview with Carducci.

p. 186 "The cell phone effects": Geser, "Towards a Sociological Theory of the Mobile Phone."

p. 186 same neural circuits: Marano, "Nation of Wimps"; Jacqueline N. Wood and Jordan Grafman, "Human Prefrontal Cortex: Processing and Representation Perspectives," *Nature Reviews/Neuroscience* 4 (Feb. 2003), pp. 139–47; and Heather L. Urry et al., "Making a Life Worth Living: Neural Correlates of Well-Being," *Psychological Science* 15, no. 6 (2004), pp. 367–72.

p. 186 cumulative burden of psychological stress: Geser, "Towards a Sociological Theory of the Mobile Phone."

p. 186 "You get used to things": Author interview with Carducci; also see Geser, "Towards a Sociological Theory of the Mobile Phone."

p. 187 promote a kind of tribalism: Geser, "Towards a Sociological Theory of the Mobile Phone."

p. 187 "regressive social insulation": Ibid.; also see Gardner, "In College, You Can Go Home Again and Again."

p. 187 "public space is no longer": Geser, "Towards a Sociological Theory of the Mobile Phone."

p. 187 cell phone "emancipates" people: Ibid.

p. 188 "Students don't talk": Barry Checkoway, Demonstration Project Report, Bringing Theory to Practice Project Recognition Conference (Washington, D.C., June 7, 2006).

p. 188 "psychologically regressive": Geser, "Towards a Sociological Theory of the Mobile Phone."

p. 188 "pacifiers for adults": Carlin Flora, "Hi-Tech Tethers: The Perils of Being in Touch Too Much," *Psychology Today,* Jan./Feb. 2007, pp. 53–54.

p. 188 "You're always able": Author interview with the psychologist in training.

p. 189 "grooming calls": Geser, "Towards a Sociological Theory of the Mobile Phone."

p. 189 71 percent of parents: Personal communication with Hofer.

p. 190 weaken the power: Geser, "Towards a Sociological Theory of the Mobile Phone."

p. 190 newest generation: Steven Barrie Anthony, "Cellphones: Just a Leash for Children?" *Los Angeles Times,* June 21, 2006.

p. 190 device of pure control: Eric Benderoff and Mike Hughlett, "Cellular Leash Lets Parents Track Kids," *Chicago Tribune,* April 13, 2006; Anthony, "Cellphones"; and Janet Zimmerman, "Prying Parents: High-Tech Spying Breaks Teens' Trust, Experts Say," *Press-Enterprise,* Sept. 4, 2006.

p. 192 Harvard College Handbook for Parents: www.fdo.fas.harvard.edu.

p. 192 Colleges spend days: Joan Raymond et al., "The Fine Art of Letting Go," *Newsweek,* May 16, 2006; and Tim Christie, "At UO Teaching Moms and Dads to Let Go," Eugene (Ore.) *Register-Guard,* July 30, 2005.

p. 192 "a stream of encouraging": Mark Thompson, "How to Cope with Sending a Child Off to College," Newswise, July 26, 2005.

p. 192 University of Vermont: Sue Shellenbarger, "Tucking the Kids In—in the Dorm: Colleges Ward Off Overinvolved Parents," *Wall Street Journal,* July 28, 2005, p. D1.

p. 193 parents have shown up: Ibid.

p. 193 "For parents who are really struggling": Thompson, "How to Cope with Sending a Child Off to College."

p. 193 College Parents of America: Shellenbarger, "Tucking the Kids In—in the Dorm."

p. 193 "college parent experiences": Amy Rainey, "Survey Provides Further Evidence of

High Parental Involvement with College Students," *Chronicle of Higher Education,* March 31, 2006; also see www.collegeparents.org.

p. 194 permaparents are only too happy: Pamela Paul, "The PermaParent Trap," *Psychology Today,* Sept./Oct. 2003, pp. 40–53.

p. 194 "No one gets married": Author interview with the college student.

p. 194 in-house adulthood: Katherine Newman and Sofya Aptekar, "Sticking Around: Delayed Departure from the Parental Nest in Western Europe" (Research Working Paper, Network on Transitions to Adulthood, May 2006).

p. 194 "start-up adults": Mel Levine, "College Graduates Aren't Ready for the Real World," *Chronicle of Higher Education,* Feb. 18, 2005.

p. 195 Dwelling almost exclusively: Robert Epstein, "Trashing Teens," *Psychology Today,* March–April 2007; Robert Epstein, *The Case Against Adolescence: Rediscovering the Adult in Every Teen* (Sanger, Calif.: Quill Driver Books, 2007); and author interview with Robert Epstein, Ph.D.

p. 195 Peer culture might even be: Kaja Perina, "Love's Loopy Logic," *Psychology Today,* Jan./Feb. 2007, pp. 68–77.

p. 195 "Middle-class adults": Author interview with Stearns.

p. 196 scale of infantilization: Author interview with Epstein.

p. 197 raise the driving age: Thomas M. Keane Jr., "Time to Let Go," *Boston Globe Magazine,* April 30, 2006, p. 16.

p. 197 Insurance Institute for Highway Safety: Ibid.

p. 197 proposed driving-age curb: *Boston Globe Magazine,* May 7, 2006, p. 16.

p. 197 61 percent of Americans: Keane, "Time to Let Go."

p. 197 measured fourteen competencies: Epstein, *Case Against Adolescence.*

TEN   *Born to Be Stressed*

p. 198 As we visualize our goals: Jacqueline N. Wood and Jordan Grafman, "Human Prefrontal Cortex: Processing and Representation Perspectives," *Nature Reviews/Neuroscience* 4 (Feb. 2003), pp. 139–47; and Heather L. Urry et al., "Making a Life Worth Living: Neural Correlates of Well-Being," *Psychological Science* 15, no. 6 (2004), pp. 367–72.

p. 199 deeper dopamine reward system: Gregory Berns, *Satisfaction: The Science of Finding True Fulfillment* (New York: Henry Holt, 2005); and author interview with Gregory Berns.

p. 199 feeling bad is sometimes good: Author interview with Berns.

p. 199 "The housing office": Personal communication with the teaching assistant.

p. 199 "because each household": Personal communication with the stepmother.

p. 200 two brands of happiness: Urry et al., "Making a Life Worth Living"; and Caryl D. Ryff et al., "Positive Health: Connecting Well-Being with Biology," *Philosophical Transactions of the Royal Society of London* 359 (2004), pp. 1383–94.

p. 200 How the brain establishes: Hara Estroff Marano, "Depression: Beyond Serotonin," *Psychology Today,* March/April 1999, pp. 30–36, 72–76; Richard J. Davidson, "Anxiety and Affective Style: Role of Prefrontal Cortex and Amygdala," *Biological Psychiatry* 51 (2002), pp. 68–80; Steven K. Sutton and Richard J. Davidson, "Prefrontal Brain Asymmetry: A Biological Substrate of the Behavioral Approach and Inhibition Systems," *Psychological Science* 8, no. 3 (May 1997), pp. 204–10; Diego A. Pizzagalli et al., "Frontal Brain Asymmetry and Reward

Responsiveness," *Psychological Science* 16, no. 10 (2005), pp. 805–13; Eddie Harmon-Jones et al., "The Effect of Personal Relevance and Approach-Related Action Expectation of Relative Left Frontal Cortical Activity," *Psychological Science* 17, no. 5 (2006), pp. 434–40; and author interviews with Richard J. Davidson.

p. 201 they differ in affective style: Richard J. Davidson, "What Does the Prefrontal Cortex 'Do' in Affect: Perspectives on Frontal EEG Asymmetry Research," *Biological Psychiatry* 67 (2004), pp. 219–33; and Davidson, "Anxiety and Affective Style."

p. 202 "In ten-month-old infants": Author interview with Davidson.

p. 203 Buddhist meditation: Marano, "Depression"; Hara Estroff Marano, "Buddhism and the Blues," *Psychology Today's Blues Buster,* Oct. 2003; Katherine Ellison, "Mastering Your Own Mind," *Psychology Today,* Sept./Oct. 2006; and author interviews with Davidson.

p. 203 "Satisfying experiences are *difficult*": Berns, *Satisfaction.*

p. 203 fundamental division: Author interview with Berns.

p. 204 "Dopamine activation": Ibid.

p. 205 "That is generally the case": Ibid.

p. 205 What he's really talking about: Ibid.

p. 205 understanding that the brain: Marano, "Depression"; and author interview with Bruce McEwan, Ph.D.

p. 206 "Living a life": Author interview with Berns.

p. 206 What challenge does: Ibid.

p. 206 "Damage Model": Hara Estroff Marano, "How to Survive Practically Anything: An Author Interview with Steven Wolin and Sybil Wolin," *Psychology Today,* Jan./Feb. 1992, pp. 36–39.

p. 207 "There is an increased risk": Ibid.

p. 208 preferentially notice and weight: Tiffany A. Ito et al., "Negative Information Weighs More Heavily on the Brain: The Negativity Bias in Evaluative Categorizations," *Journal of Personality and Social Psychology* 75, no. 4 (1998), pp. 887–900; and N. Kyle Smith, "Being Bad Isn't Always Good: Affective Context Moderates Attention Bias Toward Negative Information," *Journal of Personality and Social Psychology* 90, no. 2 (2006), pp. 210–20.

p. 208 Boredom is a lot like hunger: Michael W. Otto, "Stress, Distress Intolerance, and Drug Dependence" (National Institute on Drug Abuse, Grant No. 3R01DA017904–02S1).

p. 209 susceptibility to boredom: Hope M. Seib and Stephen J. Vodanovich, "Cognitive Correlates of Boredom Proneness: The Role of Private Self-Consciousness and Absorption," *Journal of Psychology* 132, no. 6 (Nov. 1998), pp. 642–52; and Stephen J. Vodanovich and John D. Watt, "Boredom Proneness and Psychosocial Development," *Journal of Psychology* 133, no. 3 (1999), pp. 303–14.

p. 210 cardinal feature of ADHD: American Psychiatric Association, *Diagnostic and Statistical Manual of Mental Disorders:* Fourth Edition, American Psychiatric Publishing, 2000.

p. 210 Perhaps ADHD is powered by anxiety: Frances H. Gabbay, "Inhibitory Control: Toward a Vulnerability Phenotype" (National Institute on Drug Abuse, Grant No. 5R01DA018674–03).

p. 211 born to be stressed: Berns, *Satisfaction;* and author interview with Berns.

p. 213 breeds a sense of purpose: Urry et al., "Making a Life Worth Living."

p. 213 mental health professional who founded: Personal communication with the mental health professional.

ELEVEN   *Whose Shark Tank Is It, Anyway?*

p. 215 "Parents perceive the world": David Anderegg in Hara Estroff Marano, "A Nation of Wimps," *Psychology Today,* Nov./Dec. 2004, pp. 58–70.

p. 215 "We have a competitive frenzy": Peter Stearns in ibid.; and author interview with Peter Stearns, Ph.D.

p. 217 "I had a woman": Elizabeth J. Roberts, "A Rush to Medicate Young Minds," *Washington Post,* Oct. 8, 2006.

p. 218 "Parents and teachers today": Ibid.

p. 218 "Parents are not forced": Ibid.

p. 218 "entry drug": Gardiner Harris, "Proof Is Scant on Psychiatric Drug Mix for Young," *New York Times,* Nov. 23, 2006.

p. 218 1.6 million American children and teenagers: Ibid.

p. 219 "After you get them": Ranga Krishnan in ibid.

p. 220 "On the most rudimentary level": John Perry Barlow, "The Economy of Ideas," *Wired,* March 1994.

p. 220 "you are terrified": John Perry Barlow, "A Declaration of the Independence of Cyberspace," Electronic Frontier Foundation, www.eff.org, Feb. 8, 1996.

p. 221 "Today's students are no longer": Marc Prensky, "Digital Natives, Digital Immigrants," *On the Horizon* 9, no. 5 (Oct. 2001).

p. 221 version of childhood: Hara Estroff Marano, "Rocking the Cradle of Class," *Psychology Today,* Sept./Oct. 2005, pp. 52–56.

p. 222 "Parents feel like": Author interview with David Anderegg, Ph.D.

p. 223 "Exams are a fact of life": Author interview with the teacher.

p. 224 "I spend so much time": Laine Keslin Ettinger, "A Passion for the Movies? Yes, Yes . . . Yes!" *New York Times,* Jan. 8, 2006.

p. 224 growing percentage of women: Barbara Dafoe Whitehead and David Popenoe, "The State of Our Unions: The Social Health of Marriage in America 2006."

p. 225 "Life with children": Ibid.

p. 225 estimated $237,000: Ibid.

p. 225 percentage of households: Ibid.

p. 226 parents who base their own self-worth: Missa Murry Eaton and Eva M. Pomerantz, "When Parents' Self-Worth Is Contingent on Children's Performance: Implications for Parents' Mental Health" (paper presented at the Society for Research in Child Development, April 9, 2005).

p. 227 "All parents feel bad": Author interview with Missa Murry Eaton, Ph.D.

p. 227 separate series of studies: Ibid.

p. 228 "What I notice": Author interview with Amy Sohn.

p. 228 confront their own mediocrity: John Portmann in Marano, "Nation of Wimps."

p. 229 "There is a huge": Author interview with Anderegg.

p. 229 "You understand": Ibid.

p. 229 "We focus so much": David Elkind, Ph.D., in Marano, "Nation of Wimps."

TWELVE *Class Dismissed*

p. 230 worst nightmare: Hara Estroff Marano, "Class Dismissed," *Psychology Today,* May/June 2006, pp. 94–99.

p. 230 "I've learned a lot": Ben in ibid.; and Ben, senior thesis (April 8, 2005).

p. 231 "Ben was a kinesthetic learner": Marano, "Class Dismissed"; and author interview with Pam.

p. 231 When Jeffrey H. and his wife: Marano, "Class Dismissed."

p. 232 "They stand, they totter": Ibid.; and author interview with Daniel Greenberg, Ph.D.

p. 232 Ben accepted the bribe: Marano, "Class Dismissed."

p. 232 "Ben has had a great year": Author interview with Pam.

p. 233 "I didn't come away": Kirsten Olsen, May 30, 1987, Sudbury Valley Thesis Presentations, 1970–2004 (Sudbury Valley School Press, 2005).

p. 233 Stephanie was sinking: Marano, "Class Dismissed."

p. 233 "shared my indifference": Ibid.

p. 234 Current educational theory: Ibid.

p. 234 "Students govern the school": Personal communication with Jason, a graduate.

p. 235 "They structure their own education": Marano, "Class Dismissed."

p. 236 "I'm not thrilled": Ibid.

p. 236 longitudinal study: Daniel Greenberg et al., *The Pursuit of Happiness: The Lives of Sudbury Valley Alumni* (Framingham, Mass.: Sudbury Valley School Press, 2005).

p. 237 "They don't want kids to suffer": Author interview with Greenberg.

p. 237 "It's an issue of control": Ibid.

p. 237 "We must learn to live": Ibid.

p. 237 "Had I gone through": In Mimsy Sadofsky, afterword to the new Japanese edition of *Free at Last,* reprinted in *Sudbury Valley School Journal* 35, no. 3 (Jan. 2006), pp. 5–27.

p. 240 "stealth" or "accidental" learning: " 'Stealth' Learning Engages Students at International Manufacturing Technology Show 2004 Student Summit, IMTS 2004," PRNewswire, Sept. 13, 2004.

p. 240 act of playing is fundamentally different: John Seely Brown, "Learning, Working, and Playing in the Digital Age: Creating Learning Ecologies" (paper presented at the Conference on Higher Education of the American Association for Higher Education, March 23, 1999).

p. 240 "Unlike education acquired through textbooks": John Seely Brown, "You Play World of Warcraft? You're Hired: Why Multiplayer Games May Be the Best Kind of Job Training," *Wired,* April 2006.

THIRTEEN *"We Didn't Get Here by Rocking the Boat"*

p. 243 not so obsessively monitored: Howard P. Chudacoff, *Children at Play: An American History* (New York: New York University Press, 2007).

p. 244 "Innovation is the primary": Author interview with Carolyn Woo, Ph.D.

p. 244 "diminished-debate syndrome": Michiko Kakutani, "Critic's Notebook: Debate? Dissent? Discussion? Oh, Don't Go There!" *New York Times,* March 23, 2002.

p. 244 "Students are not assertive": Author interview with John Portmann, Ph.D.

p. 245 Having had no practice: Personal communication from Joel Urbany, Ph.D.

p. 245 "Many faculty members": Ibid.

p. 246 "Corporations love these kids": Author interview with Woo.

p. 247 2006 survey: Donald L. McCabe et al., "Academic Dishonesty in Graduate Business Programs: Prevalence, Causes, and Proposed Action," *Academy of Management Learning & Education* 5, no. 3 (Sept. 2006); and Katherine Mangan, "Survey Finds Widespread Cheating in M.B.A. Programs," *Chronicle of Higher Education,* Sept. 18, 2006.

p. 248 "Many children of highly educated": Suniya S. Luthar and Shawn J. Latendresse, "Children of the Affluent: Challenges to Well-Being," *Current Directions in Psychological Science* 14, no. 1 (2005), pp. 49–53.

p. 248 creating mental health problems: Rifka Weehuizen, "Mental Capital: A Preliminary Study into the Psychological Dimension of Economic Development" (Dutch Council for Health Research, Nov. 2006).

p. 248 knowledge economy requires a workforce: Ibid.; and Eric I. Knudsen et al., "Economic, Neurobiological, and Behavioral Perspectives on Building America's Future Workforce," *Proceedings of the National Academy of Sciences* 103, no. 27 (2006).

p. 248 "I assist my Tae Kwon Do instructor": Personal communication from the customs broker.

p. 249 2006 survey: Jill Casner-Lotto and Linda Barrington, "Are They Really Ready to Work? Employers' Perspectives on the Basic Knowledge and Applied Skills of New Entrants to the 21st Century Workforce" (Conference Board, Oct. 2006); and Robert J. Sternberg, "Finding Students Who Are Wise, Practical, and Creative," *Chronicle of Higher Education,* July 6, 2007.

p. 250 "It's not out of the question": Author interview with Barry Schwartz, Ph.D.

p. 251 "They seem both more mature": Greg Moore, M.D., in Stephen C. Caulfield, "Ninth Leadership Forum: Student Health 2010: What Changes Will the Next Five Years Bring?" *Student Health Spectrum,* Feb. 2006, pp. 4–18.

p. 251 commercial real estate broker: Personal communication from the broker.

p. 251 "although teens don't necessarily": Author interview with Robert Epstein, Ph.D.; also see Robert Epstein, *The Case Against Adolescence: Rediscovering the Adult in Every Teen* (Sanger, Calif.: Quill Driver Books, 2007).

p. 252 Release them . . . from house arrest: Richard Louv, "America's Dangerous Aversion to Risk," *San Diego Union-Tribune,* Dec. 6, 2005.

p. 252 "In March 2007 I attended": Personal communication from a parent. Reprinted with permission from the parent.

p. 254 Many are plagued: Author interview with David Anderegg, Ph.D.

p. 254 instead the home becomes: Author interview with Daniel Greenberg, Ph.D.

p. 254 Stroller Manifesto: Lynn Harris, "Apple Juice, Straight Up?" salon.com, Dec. 7, 2005, and Amy Sohn, "A Glass of Wine and a Pacifier, Please," *New York,* July 31, 2006.

Index

About the Author

Hara Estroff Marano is an award-winning writer and editor-at-large for *Psychology Today*. Her articles have appeared in many other publications, including the *New York Times*, the *Los Angeles Times*, *New York* magazine, *Wilson Quarterly*, *USA Today*, *Smithsonian*, and *Ladies' Home Journal*. She writes a regular advice column for *Psychology Today* called "Unconventional Wisdom" and is a columnist for msn.com and an international edition of *Marie Claire*. She is also the author of *Why Doesn't Anybody Like Me?: A Guide to Raising Socially Confident Kids*. Marano sits on the board of the Bringing Theory to Practice Project. The mother of two adult sons, she lives in Brooklyn, New York.